SCENES OF MADNESS

SCENES OF MADNESS

A psychiatrist at the theatre

Derek Russell Davis

Tavistock/Routledge
London and New York

First published in 1992
by Routledge
11 New Fetter Lane, London EC4P 4EE

Simultaneously published in the USA and Canada
by Routledge
a division of Routledge, Chapman and Hall Inc.
29 West 35th Street, New York, NY 10001

© 1992 Derek Russell Davis

Typeset in Linotron Palatino by
J&L Composition Ltd, Filey, North Yorkshire
Printed and bound in Great Britain by
Biddles Ltd, Guildford and King's Lynn

British Library Cataloguing in Publication Data
Davis, Derek Russell 1914–
Scenes of madness.
1. Man. Mental disorders
I. Title
616.89

Library of Congress Cataloging in Publication Data
Davis, Derek Russell.
Scenes of madness/Derek Russell Davis.
p. cm.
Includes bibliographical references (p.) and index.
1. Mental illness—Case studies. 2. Mental illness in
literature—Case Studies. I. Title.
RC509.8.D38 1991
616.89–dc20
90–24258
CIP

ISBN 0–415–05678–0

CONTENTS

ACKNOWLEDGEMENTS

I have had the good fortune to have spent much of my working life in a university post, first in Cambridge and then in Bristol, where I have had opportunities to learn from friendly conversations with colleagues, not only in the medical school, but also in other faculties. I do not doubt that they will forgive me that I name no names. That I do not does not mean that I am ungrateful. To Dr Harold Maxwell, with whom I have enjoyed desultory conversations for more than twenty years, I owe the push that led me to approach a publisher. One special acknowledgement – this is of the help I have had from Marit, with whom I have shared the pleasures of innumerable visits to the theatre over many years in several countries.

1

INTRODUCTION

What can we learn from plays about madness? Plays when they portray madness put it into the context of the events and circumstances that have afflicted the person. Also, they identify the significant others in the system of relationships of which he or she is or has been a member. Thus Hamlet's madness is presented as a consequence of such events as his father's murder, his uncle's assumption of the throne, his mother's remarriage, and what he sees as his rebuff by Ophelia. Among the significant others are his dead father, uncle, mother, Ophelia, Laertes, Polonius and Horatio. The crises in his relationships with them make up the context in which his madness appears. The play, in telling how his madness, feigned or otherwise, develops and recovers, provides a model of madness that is of interest to all those who meet madness in their professional work or their daily lives.

The understanding plays give of madness is all the more vivid because the events are presented dramatically, feelings being evoked as well as intellectual curiosity. For this and other reasons the playgoer may learn as much about madness at the theatre as from any book about psychiatry. But what is learnt is different.

Plays describe scenarios of madness. With few exceptions, they say little or nothing about either the mental mechanisms or the biological factors. Psychoanalysis concerns itself, amongst other things, with mental mechanisms, such as repression, projection and displacement. Psychiatry, at least that in Britain, is dominated by ideas that the essential causes of mental illness lie in disorders in biochemical or metabolic functions, for which a predisposition has been inherited. As a general rule, the explanations it offers reduce the symptoms of illness to what is seen as the essential underlying disorder.

Reductionism has been the prevailing approach in the medicine of the twentieth century, with immense successes to its credit, such as the insulin treatment of diabetes that arose from the discovery of the part played in the symptoms by disorder in the metabolism of carbohydrates. As a consequence of these and other successes, not least those in the control of infections, claims have been made that reductionist explanations are scientific whereas those defining the context are not truly so. Yet to distinguish between what is science and what is not on the basis of the form of the explanation is foolish. What matters is adherence to the rules of science as a discipline, with its three essentials: fidelity to the evidence, rigour in logical formulation and scepticism.

Essays, whether in psychiatry, psychoanalysis or literary criticism, are to be judged without prejudice by the quality of the discipline. Each hypothesis has to be tested by asking such questions as: Does it accommodate the behaviours to be explained? Is it belied by other behaviours? Is there an alternative hypothesis that fits better? The testing may be no more elaborate than that applied in doing a crossword puzzle: do the down words and the across words corroborate one another?

A proper and useful approach towards explaining behaviour, whether mad or sane, is to define its context or, especially, the part it plays in exchanges between one person and another or others within a system of relationships. The context and associated behaviours show whether reddening of the face is the blush of modesty or the flush of anger. Any differences in the underlying biochemistry may have little or no relevance. Again, that the person in Stevie Smith's poem is 'not waving but drowning' is shown by the context that he is 'much too far out'.[1]

Reddening of the face illustrates another point in the development of medicine at the turn of the century and in the approach adopted in this book. This is that behaviour, bodily changes and mental activity tend to be adaptive in that they are components of the organism's repertoire of response to changes in the environment, the response being the means by which the 'fixity' of 'its interior milieu' (to use Claude Bernard's terms[2]) is maintained. The response is adaptive even if in the particular circumstances it proves to be inappropriate. The common practice of opening a window when the room is too warm may be mal-adaptive on a summer's day when it is warmer outside. Getting angry when frustrated may embarrass attempts to remove the source of the anger.

The principle has been stated in the more general form: 'The living body is an agency of such sort that each disturbing influence induces by itself the calling forth of compensatory activity to neutralize or repair the disturbance.'[3] Increasing the blood flow through the face is thus part of the means by which body temperature is kept constant. The parts played in adaptation by blushing and flushing are less certain.

It is a useful assumption that behaviour is always an attempt at adaptation, however inappropriate it may be in the particular circumstances. Freud made the point in these terms: 'Any given process originates in an unpleasant state of tension.' 'Its ultimate issue coincides with the relaxation of this tension, i.e. with avoidance of pain or with the production of pleasure.'[4] If that were true, Freud continued, then 'the vast majority of our psychic processes would necessarily be accompanied by pleasure, or would conduce to it, while the most ordinary experience emphatically contradicts any such conclusion.' This is the 'neurotic paradox' that pervades all discussion of madness.

The madness portrayed in plays is to be seen as attempts to resolve interpersonal problems. Behaviour persisted in although it causes pain and destruction challenges any such theory. Biological theories suppose that madness reflects a morbid process, something that has gone wrong, psychological theories that it reflects a process that is potentially adaptive although ill-suited to the particular circumstances. It is as well to remember that a painful inflammation, such as a boil or an abscess, testifies to the efforts being made by the organism to deal with the invasion of disease-producing micro-organisms.

FIRST STEPS

This book has had a long incubation period. One reason why I chose, just before the start of the Second World War, to embark on a career in psychiatry was the keen expectation, heightened by the recent discovery of phenylketonuria as a cause of one form of mental handicap, that the breakthroughs in medicine just over the horizon would lie in the discovery of the errors of metabolism underlying mental illness. As a junior member of the medical staff of a mental hospital I was put each morning to supervise patients while they recovered from comas induced by large doses of insulin, then seen as a promising treatment for schizophrenia. I had the job too of injecting a drug into depressed patients in order to induce epileptic fits; this was the precursor of the electroconvulsive treatment (ECT) still in occasional use.

Listening to patients and hearing about what had happened to them in their lives soon led me to have second thoughts about what breakthroughs were to be worked for. I remember one 18-year-old youth who was receiving the coma treatment. He had been admitted urgently a few days after his father had been taken into another hospital dangerously ill with a coronary thrombosis. He had burst into his mother's bedroom after she had gone to bed and declared, 'Le roi est mort! Vive le roi!'. He had then smashed up a cabinet containing his father's prized collection of china. Alarmed, she had seen his behaviour as having sexual significance. He had probably seen it more as dethroning a tyrannous father. 'When the king dies', he said to me, 'the son takes the throne.'

Having read some of Freud's work, I knew about 'displacement' as a 'primary process' by which 'psychical energy' is transferred from an intensely charged object or idea to a weakly charged one, in this case from the father to the china cabinet.[5] Recognising too the relevance of the story of Oedipus, I began to look for manifestations of oedipal conflicts in the other schizophrenic patients passing through our beds, and soon found, as others had done, that incestuous, patricidal and matricidal impulses are rather common. They had often arisen after a critical change in the patient's relationship with his mother or father, as a result of, for instance, the illness or death of a parent or other member of the family, or the return home of the father after a period of absence; this last was relativly common at the end of the war. In several cases the mother's remarriage or taking of a lover appeared to play an important part in the development of the illness, as it does in the cases of Orestes and Hamlet.

The descriptions of mental illness then to be found in the textbooks did not satisfy me. Mostly they presented the symptoms, without putting them into a context, as if they were soft neurological signs or as reflecting 'derailment' of brain processes – appropriate descriptions when the causes are sought

4

in disorder in brain functions. Defining the part played by the symptoms in the interaction of one person with another leads to another form of explanation: the two forms are complementary and not mutually exclusive.

Then I began to recognise the similarities of the patients I was treating to such characters as Oswald and Helene Alving (in *Ghosts*), Ellida and Dr Wangel (in *The Lady from the Sea*), Blanche Dubois (in *A Streetcar Named Desire*), King Lear and Orestes. In these my early days in psychiatry I made plans to assemble, one day when I had had time to do the work, a collection of the models of illness to be found in plays.

Sophocles' *King Oedipus* provides one model, as Freud has shown, but there are many others. I was later given some encouragement by the reception given to my case-reports of Oswald as a young man suffering from a serious mental illness,[6] Ellida as depressed and treated suitably by 'conjoint therapy',[7] and Macbeth as caught up in a vicious circle of ambition and despair.[8] This book implements plans I have had in mind for many years.

THE OEDIPUS LEGEND AS A MODEL

Freud, attaching great importance to the oedipal conflicts in the dynamics of psychoneurosis, although not in major mental illness, of which he had had little experience, pointed out[9] that 'psychoneurotics are only distinguished by exhibiting on a magnified scale feelings of love and hatred for their parents which occur less obviously and less intensely in the minds of most children'. 'The profound and universal power to move of the legend of King Oedipus' can only be understood if this statement has 'an equally universal validity'.

In his study of such plays as *Hamlet* and *Rosmersholm* he reduced the manifestations of illness to the Oedipus complex. Thus he said of Rebecca West:[10] 'Everything that happened to her at Rosmersholm was from the very first a consequence of the Oedipus complex – an inevitable replica of her relations with her mother and Dr West.' Bernard Shaw's summary of the plot of *Rosmersholm*, in contrast, written in 1891, does not mention Dr West at all or the incest theme.[11]

In focusing on Oedipus' killing of Laius and marriage of Jocasta, Freud's viewpoint, which is that of the son, leaves out other essentials in the dynamics of the family. He was of course well aware of the fear commonly felt by an older man that he will be dethroned by a younger man or by his son.[12] Had he stood back from the psychoanalyst's usual position and brought the whole family into his field of vision, his account of the legend would have included Laius' fear of his son as well as other ingredients of the legend.[13]

He made the discovery of the Oedipus complex through the analysis of his own dreams. Its main importance was that it showed that the roots of unconscious wishes lie in experience in early childhood. It was of lesser importance that it cast a spotlight on just one aspect of Sophocles' play, leaving others in darkness.

Cursed by Pelops for his kidnapping and homosexual rape of Chrysippus, Laius had been warned by the oracle that he would perish at the hands of his son, and in consequence had refrained from sexual intercourse with Jocasta, except on the one occasion when she had inveigled him into her arms when he was intoxicated, and Oedipus had been conceived. He had instructed Jocasta to destroy the new-born Oedipus. Not obeying him in full, she had him abandoned and exposed on the mountainside, where he was found by a shepherd. Later, on the road to Thebes, Laius had started the fight with Oedipus that had ended in his death. Oedipus too had been warned that he was fated to kill his father, but had not known that Laius was his father. In marrying Jocasta he gained, not only her love, but also his father's position of power.

The scenario makes a different impression when Oedipus' killing of Laius is put into the context of these other ingredients. The Oedipus complex is then too simple a formula. An impartial observer would see Laius' death as the result of the interaction between him and Oedipus in the context of the expectations fostered in each of them by others.

To put this point in other terms, the behaviour of each is explained by reference to the interpersonal as well as the intrapsychic processes affecting them. Some plays, it is true, induce the spectator to identify with a particular character, and to see the events through that character's eyes.[14] Most plays, in showing how characters interact with one another, are as much concerned with the interpersonal processes as the intrapsychic. How the interpersonal processes reveal the intrapsychic is to be discussed in later chapters.

6

FAMILY PROCESSES

Breakthroughs in the definition of the metabolic and biochemical errors underlying mental disorder have been achieved, although not quite in the decisive form that was expected fifty years ago, and have led to major advances in treatment. Biological theories have dominated psychiatry therefore during the last two or three decades, and have led to treatments that have done much to alleviate suffering.

One of the reasons why the biological theories have prevailed has lain in the poor development of the psychological theories, and especially those that put the madness into the context of interpersonal, or especially family, processes. There have been some successes, notably those achieved by Theodore Lidz and his colleagues in the Yale Department of Psychiatry in their studies in the 1960s of the 'intrafamilial environment' in which schizophrenic patients have grown up.[15] R. D. Laing, amongst others, opened up at about the same time the discussion of the part played by family processes in determining the onset and the symptoms of schizophrenic illnesses.[16]

Crucial to the approach in this book is the theory of 'systems', introduced into psychotherapy in the 1950s and 1960s, notably by Gregory Bateson and his colleagues at Palo Alto.[17] This theory, derived from cybernetics (a theory based on analogies between the behaviour of man and machine), is concerned with the regulation through communication by two or more persons of each other's behaviour. Its essence lies in the recognition that when two or more persons are related to – that is, interact with – each other in a system or organisation, the behaviour of one changes only when there are corresponding changes in the behaviour of the other or others.

The studies by the pioneers of the family processes in mental illness have been vigorously stoned by those, living themselves in glass houses, who insist on the biological causes of mental illness, on the grounds of their weaknesses in method and concept. The weaknesses can hardly be denied. Certainly, they warrant scepticism and caution in accepting the findings, but do not justify dismissing the findings as not deserving further consideration. The findings have received less attention, I think, than they deserve, and still have less influence than they should do in the investigation and, especially, the treatment of the mentally ill.

The claims made for the the efficacy of the neuroleptic drugs in the treatment of mental illness have detracted from the importance given to family processes. However, the pendulum has been swinging, and there is now more scepticism about the part drugs should play, and as a consequence some revival of interest in studies of family processes, not as a rival but as a complementary approach. My hope is that this book will do something to fan the flames of interest by showing that there are lessons to be learnt at the theatre about the circumstances in which mental illnesses arise, change in character, and recover. There are no simple formulas.

THIS BOOK'S APPROACH

Many psychotherapists share this interest, and have turned to plays for illumination of the family processes they observe in their patients. However, most of the papers they have contributed have started with the question: What light do the discoveries made in the consulting room throw on the meanings of plays?

The question I start with goes the other way round: What light do the discoveries of playwrights throw on the madness observed in family, friends, neighbours and acquaintances as well as patients, not only in the consulting room, but also in their everyday lives? I try to do for plays something of what Lillian Feder has done for literature.[18] She has made 'a study of representative literary explorations of the deranged mind' in order to 'reveal some of the discoveries regarding mental functioning and aberration that imaginative writers have made in their very depictions of madness'. I cover a wider range of plays but at less depth than does Bennett Simon in his study of the plays of ancient Greece in *Mind and Madness in Ancient Greece*.[19]

My approach has been to assemble, from plays written at various times in history, many and diverse instances of behaviour deemed by one or more characters in the play to reflect madness or something like it. I have not started out with any definition of madness or mental illness. I have first defined the context of the mad behaviour, after studying what part the playwright has shown the behaviour to play within a system of relationships, and then identified the interpersonal processes in the development of the madness and also in its recovery in those cases in which there is recovery. They are relatively few because many plays end in tragedy. In the final chapter I formulate conclusions on what the common processes are, and how they are affected by the interventions of others.

2

LESSONS AT THE THEATRE

The highest moral purpose aimed at in the highest species of the drama, is the teaching of the human heart, through its sympathies and antipathies, the knowledge of itself; in proportion to the possession of which knowledge, every human being is wise, just, sincere, tolerant and kind.

(P. B. Shelley[1])

The audience in the theatre achieve an intuitive understanding of the madness afflicting one or more of the characters on the stage. Hamlet's madness is enigmatic, but they understand it when Claudius does not, because the text as presented by the actors gives them information not available to Claudius, such as that given to Hamlet at the start of the play by the ghost of his father.

In other plays the information that makes the madness understandable is revealed gradually. Shakespeare in most of his plays takes the audience into his confidence and puts them into possession of the relevant facts, often through a revealing soliloquy or the comments of another character. Also, the audience feel sympathy for Hamlet whereas Claudius does not, as indeed they do for Ophelia. Hamlet and Ophelia, like other tragic heroes, evoke pity. The plays that survive in the repertoire tend to make the madness they depict understandable, and the understanding illuminates the playgoer's own experience and enlarges sensibility.

There are two obvious lessons. One is that behaviour that appears strange or extravagant while information is lacking may appear less so or more reasonable when additional information has been given. A step in psychotherapy to be taken at an early stage is thus to find out more about the events and circumstances that have affected the patient. The second lesson is that sympathy with the patient assists understanding.

THE CHALLENGE TO ATTITUDES

The purpose of the playwright, as of other artists, is, as Ibsen puts it, 'to depict human beings, their humours and their destinies, against a background of certain operative social conditions and attitudes'. The problems posed by human behaviour are brought to life as they are played out on the stage. Presented in a fresh way they are elucidated. The playwright's obligation is not to solve them, but to present them authentically. 'My job', Ibsen said, 'is to ask, not to find solutions.' Chekhov asserted likewise that it is obligatory for the artist to present the problem correctly, not to solve it.

In doing so the playwright tends to challenge commonly held attitudes and assumptions, and incurs the risk of being attacked for subverting morals or other established principles. Plays are sometimes so attacked and occasionally banned, and theatres have been closed. Performance of Ibsen's *Ghosts* was banned by the police in Germany for two years or so. In England the play, described by newspaper critics after its first performance as 'this disgusting representation', 'candid foulness', 'scandalous', 'novel and perilous nuisance' and 'gross, almost putrid indecorum',[2] was not licensed by the Lord Chamberlain for public performance until 1913, more than thirty years after it was written, when there was some relaxation in the censorship. If the play had not caused alarm, Ibsen remarked, 'there would have been no necessity for me to write it.'

Spring Awakening, written in 1891 by Frank Wedekind, whom the young Brecht described as one of the great educators of the new Europe (like Tolstoy and Strindberg), had to wait fifteen years before it was performed, because its presentation of the sexual urges and hang-ups of adolescents was regarded as obscene. It was banned from public performance in England until 1963. *The Round Dance* by Arthur Schnitzler had to wait twenty years. There are many examples of the dismissive condemnation of plays. A critic described Ibsen's *Rosmersholm* on its first production in London as 'studies of insanity best fitted for the lecture room in Bedlam'.[3] Similar comments have

11

been made about many other plays, Strindberg's *The Dance of Death* among them.

A play does not usually get into the repertoire of public theatres if it deals with forms of behaviour that the theatre-going public regard as unsavoury or disagreeable. For this reason the issues arising from homosexual relationships and incest have been explored as a general rule less often and less openly in the theatre than in novels or films.[4] Open reference to them was hardly possible at all until there was some relaxation in the 1950s in what was permissible. Even in 1956 Arthur Miller's *A View from the Bridge* was banned from showing in a public theatre, but was shown in a club theatre, because of one scene in which two men kiss. A playwright may also be subjected to pressures from producers and sponsors to modify the text to make it more acceptable to them.[5]

The range of behaviours explored in the theatre is wider now than it used to be, despite occasional attempts to reintroduce censorship, and plays about homosexuality are being staged. A notable example is Martin Sherman's *Bent*,[6] staged recently at the National Theatre, which throws light on homosexual relationships and gives them dignity in the extreme conditions of a Nazi concentration camp, a setting that distances the events for a contemporary English audience just sufficiently to keep the distress within bounds.

It is commonplace for a play when first produced, perhaps in a small theatre or theatre club, to arouse puzzlement or bewilderment about what motivates the characters when it explores and exposes to discussion aspects of human behaviour that are unfamiliar or not often observed in everyday life, and that might otherwise remain hidden. Behaviour is made sense of and illuminated that may not be amenable to study by the methods of either experimental or clinical psychology.

Little is to be found in textbooks of psychology or psychiatry about the conditions in which murderous impulses arise, for instance, or the effects on the murderer of having murdered. Such impulses are difficult topics for systematic study, but are themes in several of the plays of ancient Greece – for example, *The Oresteia*, *Ajax* and *Heracles* – and of Shakespeare's plays – such as *Julius Caesar* and *Macbeth*.[7]

The murderers of Banquo in *Macbeth* (3.1) explain why they are capable of murder, one being 'so weary with disasters,

12

tugged with fortune, that I would set my life on any chance to mend or be rid on't', and the other 'so incensed' by 'the vile blows and buffets of the world . . . that I am reckless what I do'. The murderers of Clarence in *Richard III* (1.4) show themselves to be keenly aware of the consequences for them, which are 'to be damned for killing him, from the which no warrant can defend me'.

Plays may provide illustrations too of the state of mind of a person preparing to kill. Lady Macbeth cannot carry out her 'fell purpose'. She had done it, 'had he not resembled my father as he slept' (2.2.12–13). For Macbeth, reality and fantasy become blurred. Is the dagger he sees 'in form as palpable as that which now I draw' (2.1.40–1), 'a dagger of the mind, a false creation, proceeding from the heat-oppressed brain' (38–9)? It 'marshall'st me the way that I was going' (41). He enters into a 'half-world' in which 'nature seems dead', and he is subject to 'wicked dreams'. Moving 'like a ghost' and as if watching himself in a dream in which 'the sure and firm-set earth hear not my steps', he goes to murder Duncan (33–64). He does so while in a dream-like state in which he is largely dissociated from reality.

These and other plays enlarge understanding in areas other-wise little explored. The general public, as well as psychologists, often refer to the Greek plays when trying to explain how destructive or murderous impulses arise in the course of family feuds. Throughout history they have looked to plays for some understanding of the many other forms of disturbing behaviour they encounter in their lives.

THE QUESTIONS TO BE ADDRESSED

What light do the discoveries of playwrights as expressed in what their characters say throw on the nature of madness, the contexts in which it occurs, how it changes in relation to other events and how recovery comes about? Most of the plays I examine are established in the repertoire in Britain and are generally well known. I have occasionally included a less well-known play when there has been a particular reason for doing so. My purpose is to show the potentiality of plays as a source of understanding about madness, and there are many other plays that would have served equally well. I have had to make choices. The few chosen have been an arbitrary sampling of the many. They are the ones that have seized my interest or been drawn to my attention. The many references to plays by Ibsen reflect my special interests, at least in part. His plays, unrivalled in the precision and depth of the descriptions they give of behaviour, and a rich source of examples of madness, serve my purpose especially well.

I have restricted myself to plays performed in the live theatre. It may be that there is as much to be learnt about madness at the cinema or on the television, but plays for the theatre have the advantages that more lies in the written text, which is readily available, and that conversations between characters can be observed more directly. At the cinema and on television, attention tends to be more focused and more selective.

There is much to learn about madness from fairy tales or myths, as Jung has shown, or novels, painting or other art forms. A novelist has a privileged access to the thoughts of characters, which psychotherapists do not have, and a novel, like Virginia Woolf's *Mrs Dalloway*, has much to say about the thoughts and feelings of the mad, and how they perceive the world around them.[8]

Plays have the further advantage that the playwright's thoughts and feelings are shared with the audience by being externalised and made manifest by the actors as interactions between persons. The audience, like the psychotherapist, have to make do with what is expressed and communicated, verbally and non-verbally, in speech, gesture, or body-language.

Patterns of behaviour have changed during the nearly two and a half thousand years covering the writing of the plays I refer to, from ancient Greece to the present time. However, what a play describes is seldom to be regarded as peculiar to the time at which it was written; the themes in it have a degree of generality. It is remarkable how durable has been the popular interest in plays from previous centuries, such as the plays of ancient Greece, which are still regularly performed on the stages of many countries. Many new versions are provided by modern playwrights. Consider the many plays based on the story of Antigone.[9]

THE EDUCATIVE PURPOSE

The purpose of plays is to entertain as well as to educate. If it does not entertain, if it is not interesting, a play does not attract an audience, other than perhaps of scholars. A play may perhaps be entertaining without being educative, but there are few plays that do not have an educative effect on the attitudes of the audience towards the ordinary problems of living. They spread ideas and comment on them, provide models of behaviour and affect values. The devices of the theatre are aids to thinking critically and constructively about the world. A few plays have had a profound effect, such as Ibsen's *A Doll's House*, which made an important contribution to the debate at the end of the last century, as it still does, on the rights and responsibilities of men and women in marriage.

Many comments made in plays have been incorporated into popular thinking as often-quoted capsules of understanding – for example, 'Whom God wishes to destroy, he first makes mad',[10] 'Though this be madness, yet there is method in't',[11] 'Give sorrow words',[12] and 'The course of true love never did run smooth'.[13]

What is portrayed in the theatre is, like memory, an imaginative – that is, a creative – reconstruction of reality, not as it has been, but as it might be or might have been. It is not a copy of life although it is rooted in it. The playwright is a poet, even if he does not write in verse, and not a historian or scientist or philosopher. It is for science, not drama, to describe how madness generally is and to explain it in the terms of a theory. It is for history to tell how it was manifest in particular individuals or cultures, and for philosophy to enquire into the basis of knowledge about it. The playwright gives meaning to the madness by putting it into a context of relationships between people. He creates dreams, it has been said.[14] A scientist expounds or interprets them,[15] not in popular terms but in the terms of a scientific theory.

There are characters in plays who are historians, scientists or philosophers, and what they have to say may be of interest as a commentary on the state of knowledge in their field. But this commentary is to be regarded, not as a source of information, not even as exploring ideas, but as revealing aspects of the characters and the contexts in which they are living. Brecht's *The Life of Galileo* is about Galileo and the context in which he was living and researching, and is not an essay in the history of science in the seventeenth century. Stoppard's *Jumpers* is not a discourse on the existence of a moral absolute, but is about the relationships of the philosopher George, his beautiful wife Dotty, his colleague Archie and Inspector Bones.

The versions of events given by so-called historical plays are highly misleading if they are accepted as accounts of what has actually happened. Those reported in *Macbeth* and *Hamlet* have obviously no more than a remote basis in reality. *Richard III* gives a version of historical events that was likely to please the audience at the time it was written, but Shakespeare greatly modified their sequence and timing to serve his dramatic purpose. Also, quasi-historical plays – for instance, Brian Friel's *Making History* – provide opportunities for exploring the myths that underlie contemporary political attitudes, in this case those in Northern Ireland that are derived from the myth of Hugh O'Neill, Earl of Tyrone, as a heroic champion of the Catholic cause.

In *Mary Stuart* Schiller made both Elizabeth Queen of England and Mary Queen of Scots twenty years or so younger than they were at the time of Mary's execution, and portrayed a confrontation between them although it is unlikely that they ever met face to face. His purpose was to contrast the experience, styles and expectations of the fictive characters and explore the effects on them of the signing by Elizabeth of the warrant for Mary's execution. Her signing, presented as a half-hearted response to political pressures, adds to the constraints on her. Certainly it does nothing to free her from the threat to political safety Mary is said to represent. Mary on the other hand feels freed as she faces with composure the 'everlasting liberty' of death.

MODELS FROM PLAYS

The accounts of madness given by historians and scientists tend to be based on encounters between patients and doctors[16] in a clinical setting. Plays explore the experience of madness, not necessarily labelled as such and largely outside encounters with doctors, as well as being outside asylums, hospitals or other medical institutions. They put the madness into the context of a crisis in the afflicted character's relationships with others, the misunderstandings, quarrels, rivalries and feuds he is engaged in being presented on the stage or being told of. For these and other reasons the pictures they give of madness are different.

They provide simplified, schematic representations of complex processes – not proofs of theories, but models, which are but the first steps in developing theory and preparing for scientific study. Models from plays are holistic in that they show how words and actions are interconnected parts of a whole, and how the madness of one person forms part of a pattern of interactions between people. 'Patients are only pieces of a total situation which I have to explore' is how the doctor in T. S. Eliot's *The Cocktail Party*[17] makes the point.

Opinions differ on the value of the models derived from plays. Some regard them as too simple, and suppose that there must be more to madness than they suggest there is, for there is a general tendency to suppose that madness is mysterious and defies explanation. Perhaps there is more to it, and all that plays do is to provide caricatures in outline of what people have experienced, some features being enhanced for dramatic purposes, some diminished, others omitted. Some are brought closer together in time, place or situation so as to give coherence or unity and so enhance the dramatic effect.

At best a play presents what the playwright has himself learnt about human behaviour. At least it provides new ways of thinking about madness. The point is put satirically by Karl Kraus:[18] 'Science should feel flattered, and reassured that its efforts are not wasted, if its results are confirmed by the conclusions of the artistic imagination.'

OTHELLO

The contrast between a playwright's and a psychiatrist's presentation of madness is illustrated by what Shakespeare, speaking through his characters, says and what some modern psychiatrists say about Othello's madness. Othello is taken in by Iago's deceptions, when others are not, because he is vulnerable, psychiatrists have argued,[19] by reason of internal factors. Iago merely fans the flame of jealousy already embedded in Othello's personality, there being signs of jealousy, the 'central symptom of his psychosis', before he does so.

Shakespeare puts Othello's jealousy into its context, and allows the supposition that others of like experience in a like situation would behave similarly. Othello's madness is then to be understood without going beyond the text. Few would deny that the text itself gives enough information to make the madness understandable.

The psychiatric approach and Shakespeare's are not in conflict, but are different ways of looking at the issues. The play is educative because it shows, without resort to any hidden factors inherent in the person's constitution, how envy, betrayal, jealousy and murder can arise out of relationships between men and women. Who is not vulnerable as Othello proves to be? Who would not have been deceived in the circumstances?

Othello is a treatise about jealousy, although a less thorough treatise than *The Winter's Tale*, his jealousy being seen as an example of how people react in particular circumstances as a typical, generic or universal pattern, not as an exceptional or abnormal pattern by reason of specific individual pathology. To see the play as merely a case-history detracts from its interest to a theatre audience. Iago succeeds in deceiving Othello because he has gone to great trouble to plant doubts in him about Desdemona's fidelity. Jealousy arises out of what is feared as much as out of what is known to have happened. That Desdemona has not been unfaithful does not mean that the jealousy is morbid. The coincidences convince Othello, a stranger as well as black, and without 'those soft parts of conversation that chamberers have', who is already insecure because of his precarious position as a former slave in Venetian society. He is sensitive to any suggestion that she might deceive him, for this and the other reasons the play tells us of, not least her father's warning to him: 'She has deceived her father, and may thee' (1.3.290).

Like Cordelia she perceives 'a divided duty':

> I am hitherto your daughter. But here's my husband;
> And so much duty as my mother show'd
> To you, preferring you before her father,
> So much I challenge that I may profess
> Due to the Moor, my lord.

> (1.3.183)

There is no other mention in the play of her mother, who is presumably dead. Her father has been possessive of her and has been hostile to Othello, accusing him of having 'practised on her with foul charms, abused her delicate youth with drugs or minerals that weakens motion' (1.2.73–5). This is an example of the preference for a biological explanation before what would be an uncomfortable explanation in terms of change in the relationship between father and daughter. It is not uncommon in the contemporary world for a father to accuse his daughter's boyfriend of similar practices, especially if he comes from a different culture. The audience are unlikely to think that Desdemona is under the influence of drugs.

Several things combine to predispose Othello to doubts about her faithfulness. To make a sound marriage requires that a daughter, and equally so a son, emancipates herself from her parents, more so than Desdemona appears to have done. If emancipation is incomplete, rivalries and conflicts may persist between the generations and serve as a nucleus for the growth of jealousy in the husband, as in the case of Othello, or anger in the father, as in the case of Brabantio and also King Lear.

Their marriage is the more vulnerable because they are an ill-assorted pair, mismatched in age, religion, race and manners. He may well entertain doubts about her motives for making what for her is an unconventional marriage. Also, his attitudes have been coloured by what he has learnt about women during his career as a soldier.

She is of crucial importance to him: 'But I do love thee! And when I love thee not, chaos is come again' (3.3.91–2), he says. But he is aware of the limits on his possessiveness: 'O, curse of marriage! That we can call these delicate creatures ours and not their appetites!' (265–7). His anger and suspicion growing, he does not stop to reflect, this volatility arising from his social insecurity. Her denial that she has offended him convinces him only that she is guilty of perjury as well. But is it necessary to suppose that his conviction reflects a morbid tendency?

Emilia sees it differently. She makes a general, although partisan, statement about men and women: Men 'are all but stomachs, and we are all but food; They eat us hungrily, and when they are full, they belch us' (3.4.100–2). She enlarges later on in the play about the circumstances in which 'wives do fall': 'Have we not . . . frailty, as men have? Then let them use us well; else let them know,/The ills we do, their ills instruct us so' (4.3.84–99).

19

CASE-HISTORIES, MEMORIES AND DREAMS

The information the playwright gives the audience about what a fictive character has experienced makes up a case-history, although it is more than that – a case-history similar in many respects to one worked up by a psychotherapist. Much of it is derived from the anamnesis; that is, the recollection of what has happened. In many plays the past is gradually revealed – for example, *King Oedipus* and *Ghosts* – as each character tells about his previous experiences in much the same way as characters do in short stories or patients in the consulting room. The case-history in a play, because it leaves out details of lesser relevance, may convey a more vivid understanding of madness than is achieved in the consulting room. For one thing, the playwright selects the information so as to give shape or meaning to the madness.

Plays are like memories when what happens is presented as if recalled. 'The scene is memory and is therefore non-realistic,' Tennessee Williams writes in his introduction to *The Glass Menagerie*. Laura in this play is a transformation of his sister Rose, to whom he remained very close, and whose fate as revealed in the play was to haunt him;[20] she developed a schizophrenic illness. He gives his own name, 'Tom', to the male narrator. New meanings are found as the past is imaginatively reconstructed through recall.

Plays, memories, day-dreams and dreams are alike in being imaginative reconstructions. 'Find out all about dreams, and you will have found out all about insanity.' This remark by the distinguished neurologist Hughlings Jackson was quoted with approval by Freud[21] as a justification for the effort he put into the study of dreams. Dreams are played out in the theatre of sleep, it has been said. Although Jackson's remark has proved to be too optimistic, there is no doubt that the study of dreams has contributed greatly to the understanding of madness. Much can be learned from plays too which widens and deepens that understanding.

Whatever disadvantages they have, plays have the advantage over dreams and case-histories as material for study that the data lie in what is written and only what is written in the text, which is available for study equally to anyone who wishes to undertake it. The data, though circumscribed, may be lavish. Consider how much we are told about Hamlet's madness. A play may be as rich in relevant detail as any case-history, even if it leaves out some of what the psychotherapist might wish to know. What he finds out about a patient's history is often as incomplete.

Dreams take place on a different plane of psychic reality, and the records made of them tend to be incomplete, selective and unreliable. Also, the account a person gives of a dream tends to be improved in the telling, being dramatised to become a more coherent mini-play. Similarly, case-histories, recorded by psychotherapists who participate themselves in the processes of recollection, are inevitably selective and tend to have a greater degree of coherence than is warranted by the patient's stumbling utterances.

What plays have to say about common patterns of behaviour can be critically discussed. Sometimes interpretations can be tested out in performance. Also, a critical reception for new studies of plays is ensured by a body of interested scholars, many of whom work in the humanities. Psychiatrists have much to learn if they engage in cooperative studies with scholars from other disciplines.

EXCHANGES WITH THE HUMANITIES[22]

Psychiatrists, who in their treatment of patients apply theories, concepts and methods from many branches of knowledge, biological and social, have shown as a profession remarkably little interest in the humanities, though this may be changing. One reason has been that the humanities, which belong to the arts faculties of universities, are seen as distinct from the natural and social sciences, this view reflecting the nineteenth-century distinctions between *Geistes-* and *Naturwissenschaft* and the belief that the moral and the natural have to be studied by different methods.

Their lack of interest contrasts with the keen interest shown in many arts departments, from which flow a stream of publications, in the psychopathology of the famous, writers and artists, and the characters they have created. Many scholars in the arts have come under the influence of psychoanalysis. The physical separation of most psychiatric centres (and some medical schools) from the universities has hampered collaboration.

Scholars on both sides have shown a particular interest in the mental processes of the famous and of geniuses, the latter often being thought prone to be degenerate. One pioneer was Möbius,[23] who introduced the term 'pathography' to describe his studies of Rousseau, Goethe and Nietzsche, which were published in the first decade of this century; another, Karl Jaspers, who wrote on Nietzsche, Strindberg and Van Gogh.[24] Freud, who admitted to 'a particular fascination in studying the laws of the human mind as exemplified in outstanding individuals',[25] wrote not only about artists, such as Leonardo da Vinci and Dostoevsky, but also about such fictive characters as Hamlet, Lady Macbeth and Rebecca West.[26] In doing so he applied the methods he had developed in the analysis of dreams. Many other scholars have discussed what the literary critic can learn from psychoanalysis.[27]

One reason for the emphasis on the exceptional, the creative and the abnormal has been curiosity about the relationship of abnormality or degeneracy to achievement.[28] Another is that in the biographies of such people we may see, as Jaspers put it, 'what can never be observed for the average patient or institutional inmate, and what will add depth to our knowledge'.[29] Strindberg, Van Gogh and Dostoevsky are of special interest because in their work they were concerned less with representing the outer world they shared with others, and more with expressing their inner reality.

A partnership with other scholars asks more of psychiatrists than to provide 'specialist reports for the use of professional biographers or historians'[30] or advise on such questions of nosology as: Did Flaubert suffer from epilepsy?[31] Did Strindberg suffer from schizophrenia?[32] They have more to offer. In their work with patients they become familiar with manifestations of crises in systems of relationships as wonderful as anything that happens in plays, and not any different in their essence. The phenomena are similar although traditions of description and interpretation are different.

There is a tradition that has led psychiatrists to turn to literature and plays, firstly for models, and then for illustrations of their theories. Victorian psychiatrists turned to Shakespeare for models of the madness they saw in their patients. For J. C. Bucknill, a distinguished physician superintendent of an asylum in the middle of the last century, Ophelia was 'the very type of a class of cases' of deranged women 'by no means uncommon'.[33]

It has become common for a director or actor to interpret a character by reference to a model derived from clinical studies. In the eighteenth century Garrick's innovative interpretation of King Lear owed much to George Cheyne's *The English Malady*,[34] with its optimism that sanity could be restored. In the second quarter of the twentieth century interpretations tended to be influenced by the psychoanalytic ideas then being widely discussed. Interest in them reached a peak before the Second World War.

Not all the models have been well taken. Thus Ophelia's self-disgust has recently been said to be a part of bulimia, a clinical syndrome related to anorexia nervosa, in which refusal of food alternates with a tendency to overeat and then vomit.[35] These symptoms are not reported by Shakespeare. Such resort to clinical studies is extraordinary and hardly to be recommended – far better to stay within the bounds of the text.

THE THERAPEUTIC EFFECTS

There is a distinction to be made between education and therapy, although they overlap. Education shows people how to search for general truths, whereas therapy helps them to find a formula for living in the particular circumstances affecting them. Plays serve the first purpose; they often happen to serve the latter as well.

Those who in the Platonic tradition prefer the search for truth tend to criticise the formulae developed in novels and plays as offering easy solutions. Thus Iris Murdoch[36] describes the good novel as 'therapy which resists the all-too-easy life of consolation and fantasy'; bad novels merely 'work out an author's personal conflicts, with no respect for things as they are rather than as the author might wish them to be'. Chekhov puts a different value on consolation and fantasy when through Treplev, the aspiring playwright in *The Seagull*, he says: 'We don't have to depict life as it is, or as it ought to be, but as we see it in our dreams.'[37]

Aristotle, who is quoted with approval by Freud,[38] said that the purpose of drama is catharsis.[39] The poet, by evoking pity and terror, purges the audience of similar emotions. Drama not only gets rid of emotions and hence brings relief, but also opens up sources of 'pleasure or enjoyment in our emotional life'. The

23

characters whose misfortunes make the tragedy should be neither entirely good, nor entirely wicked, he advised play-wrights,[40] for the punishment of a virtuous man excites more indignation than pity, and no one has pity for a scoundrel. They should have a moderate goodness – that is, a virtue capable of weakness – and should fall into misfortune by some fault which makes them pitied without making them detested. Brecht,[41] on the other hand, intended that those of his plays he called didactic (*Lehrstücke*) should teach social attitudes rather than arouse emotion.

In addition to the greater understanding a play gives, there is benefit from the arousal in playgoers of grief, distress and other emotions, because such emotions are shown to be part of ordinary experience and are shared. What people experience in the theatre raises their awareness of themselves and the society they live in. Being exposed to the contradictions inherent in the situations being portrayed brings self-recognition, as Hamlet expected when he said of the play within the play: 'The play's the thing wherein I'll catch the conscience of the king' (2.2.608–9). Many have learnt to understand the essence of their own relationships with their mothers and fathers, it has been said, as a result of Eugene O'Neill's laying bare of his own personal and family life in *Long Day's Journey into Night*, and have been helped to replace, like O'Neill, hatred and fear with 'deep pity and understanding and forgiveness'.[42]

All sorrows can be borne, it has been said, if you write a story about them. The dead can live on in the shadows of fantasy. Painful experiences can be reordered and given a different outcome. As Freud[43] put it: 'The ego, which experienced the trauma passively, now repeats it actively in a weakened version, in the hope of being able to direct its course.' He went on: 'Children behave in this fashion towards every distressing impression they receive, by reproducing it in their play. Changing from passivity to activity they attempt to master their experiences psychically.' Not only children do so; adults too after a disaster tend to rehearse in imagination what might have happened or have been done to reach a happier outcome – how things might have been.

Elsewhere Freud wrote,[44] 'Every child at play behaves like a creative writer' in that he 'rearranges the things of his world in a new way which pleases him'. He externalises worries in play.

24

Dolls may act out in different voices, little plays about what has been happening, one doll being naughty, another a reproving parent, and so on. This function of play is taken over by day-dreaming when language has developed far enough. An adult muses over dissatisfactions in images; in day-dreaming these are predominantly verbal, in dreaming predominantly visual. Plans are made, many of which involve communication with others, arguments are devised and sifted, and conversations are rehearsed. Putting experiences into words gives a degree of coherence and meaning to what otherwise may be chaotic and bewildering. The plans are creative in that they give promise of regaining control, relieving dissatisfactions and reaching a happier outcome.

The reordering of painful experiences as a result of their being played out on the stage helps people to come to terms with them. A character is portrayed as facing adversity with dignity and courage. Comedy provides an escape from tears by presenting even the most horrendous experiences as ridiculous and inviting laughter, the play ending in a comfortable reconciliation. In a play, but not in reality, everything works out in the end for better or worse, and nearly everything fits together without loose ends. There are of course some plays that end with an enigma.

Writing about the early theatre, Glynne Wickham makes similar points in these vivid terms.

> Song and dance come to be employed to summon those awesome beings, whether conceived of as spirits, gods or devils, into the presence of the community, to present them with suitable gifts as thank-offerings or propitiative sacrifices, and then to release them again.[45]

DISTANCING

That events on the stage are played out by characters with whom they can only partially identify distances the audience from them and makes them less disturbing. The distancing is greater when the events are presented as taking place many years ago in a far-away country, such as Illyria or Sicilia or pre-war Berlin, or affecting high-born people; these are the

SCENES OF MADNESS

ingredients of what Brecht called 'historification'. Contemporary concerns may be distanced by being played out in the setting of one of the plays of ancient Greece. Thus J-P. Sartre distanced his comments in *The Flies*[46] on political conflicts in France in the Second World War by presenting them in the guise of a story about the aftermath of Orestes' murder of Clytemnestra, the flies corresponding to the Furies in the Greek play. The emotional impact is greater when events are presented as contemporary, near-at-hand and affecting common people. One of the earliest plays to centre on the fate of a person of lowly status was Büchner's *Woyzeck*, written in 1836, Woyzeck being a simple-minded private soldier. The action in the play takes place in barracks, in the street, at an inn, in fields and in Marie's bedroom. The point is made when the play starts with the harassed Woyzeck shaving the socially superior Captain. Woyzeck, struggling to survive despite the pressures of a morality without compassion,[47] and under the influence of hallucinated voices, kills Marie after she has been unfaithful to him.

Playwrights are deliberate in their choice of time and place. Euripides' characters, as a general rule, are more ordinary, less heroic people than are Aeschylus' or Sophocles'. In his *Electra*, the scene is a peasant's cottage, whereas the scene in Aeschylus' *The Libation Bearers*, which tells a similar story, is a palace.

Shakespeare, when writing about politically sensitive issues, placed the action in a remote country at some other time. Calderón placed the action in *Life is a Dream*, not in Spain, but in the Poland of long ago. Ibsen, on the other hand, broke with the traditions governing his earlier plays, and made the events of his later plays contemporary and placed them in homes with which his audience were familiar. He broke too with the tradition, perhaps especially strong in England, of writing about prominent people. Being about the issues faced in their lives by ordinary people, and the characters in them speaking, not in verse, but in the speech forms of everyday life, his later plays have aroused intense interest and fierce and sustained controversy.

Some playwrights, notably Brecht, distance the events by using devices to remind us of their artificiality. Ibsen does much the same when he mischievously puts words into the mouth of the mysterious stranger that reassure the drowning Peer Gynt

26

and the audience at a dramatic moment: 'Don't worry; a fellow doesn't die in the middle of the fifth act.'

THERAPY FOR THE PLAYWRIGHT

Two examples will suffice to indicate what benefits playwrights gain from their writing. Goethe says through Torquato Tasso:[48]

> Nature gave me
> Above all, word and melody for grief,
> So as to tell the depths of my distress;
> Where other men must suffer grief in silence,
> A god gave me the power to speak my pain.

Ibsen remarks that 'everything I have written has a close connection with what I have experienced – not to say observed', and goes on:

> To live is to war with trolls
> In the vaults of the heart and brain;
> To write – that is to pass
> Judgement upon one's self.[49]

SUMMARY

The accounts plays give of madness differ from those to be found in textbooks of psychiatry, being made up by what the afflicted character expresses and what others express as they converse. The madness is put into the context of experiences in past and present relationships, with scant reference to the bodily or the mental mechanisms of behaviour. Plays show fresh ways of looking at the problems posed by human behaviour, and the schematic representations they provide of complex relationships form models, which make an impact on the hearts as well as the minds of the audience, especially so because they are presented dramatically.

3

MODELS OF MADNESS

Mad call I it, for to define true madness,
What is't to be nothing else but mad?
(*Hamlet* 2.2.93[1])

In this chapter I present as case-histories the plots of some well-known plays that contain models of madness. I hasten to add, in propitiation of those who disapprove, rightly so, of seeing a character in a play as a patient, that I am here concerned, not with individual pathology, but with the lessons to be learnt about how people in general behave. The character Hamlet, for instance, illustrates, in dramatic form, the turmoil or madness that may afflict a young man at a crisis in his relationships when he has not yet emancipated himself from his parents.

My sample, though not to be regarded as representative, covers a sufficient range to serve the discussion in later chapters. It includes many who immediately come to mind, such as Orestes, Hamlet, Ophelia, King Lear and Oswald.

THE PLAYS OF ANCIENT GREECE

Orestes

The Libation Bearers, the second part of Aeschylus' *The Oresteia*, tells of Orestes' vengeance on his mother Clytemnestra, whom he kills because of her adultery with Aegisthus and her murder of his father Agamemnon; he kills Aegisthus too. He has been encouraged in the killing by his sister Electra, who, unmarried and still grieving for her father, has felt bitter enmity for her mother. Devoted to her brother, she sees him as a hero.

Immediately after he has killed his mother, Orestes goes mad as a result of the pursuit of the Furies (Erinyes). As agents of the divinely appointed order they inflict madness as a form of vengeance, chiefly on those who have murdered their kindred. The first intimations are in his apprehension:[2]

> my bolting heart,
> it beats me down, and terror beats the drum,   (1020–1)

He hallucinates, screaming in terror:

> No, No! Women – look – like Gorgons,
> shrouded in black, their heads wreathed,
> swarming serpents!
>   – Cannot stay, I must move on.   (1047–50)
> No dreams, these torments,
> not to me, they're clear, real – the hounds
> of mother's hate.   (1053–5)
> God Apollo!
> Here they come, thick and fast,
> their eyes dripping hate –   (1056–8)

These vivid hallucinations, accompanied by feelings of being pursued and tormented, are referred to the spirits of the vengeful dead, who seek retaliation or justice, and thus express his fantasies about the anger of the dead mother. In other terms, they are transformations of pangs of conscience arising out of his recognition of the nature of what he has done.

His madness has the features of an acute delusional psychosis, or more specifically a paranoid reaction, as his mental illness would be described in psychiatric terms, the prominent symptoms being emotional turmoil amounting at times to terror, self-neglect, withdrawal of attention from the real world and preoccupation with vivid and horrific hallucinations. These are more visual than auditory; typically, the reverse is the case in paranoid reactions.

Another account of Orestes' illness is given by Euripides in *Orestes*. Electra describes him in terms that suggest catatonia:[3]

> There he lies, wasted by raging fever
> and whirled on to madness by his mother's blood –   (36–7)
> Six days now since our mother's murder;   (39)
> And all that time he has not tasted food

29

or wet his lips or bathed, but lies there
huddled in the blankets. When the fever lifts,
he turns lucid and cries; then suddenly, madly,
bolts from the bed like an untamed colt
bucking the bridle.   (41–6)

The writhing snakes that leap at him and drive him mad are
only phantoms in his mind. But he notches and draws his bow
in order to scare them away.

His madness is an episode in a history going back over several
generations. His father Agamemnon had sacrificed Iphigenia,
Orestes' sister, in order to raise a wind so that he could sail to
Troy and rescue Helen, the wife of his brother Menelaus, who
has been abducted by Paris. This had not been the beginning of
the feuds in the family; their origins lie in quarrels even further
back.[4]

After his victory at Troy, Agamemnon had returned to Greece
with his mistress Cassandra, and had been killed there by
Clytemnestra, his wife and the mother of Orestes and Electra.
She had acted in revenge for his sacrifice of Iphigenia, and in
order to reassert her position, which had been diminished by his
infidelities. Orestes was then 11 years old. These events are told
of in *Agamemnon*, the first part of *The Oresteia*.

In killing his mother and her lover, Orestes, acting under
Apollo's command that he should exact vengeance, recapitulates,
as the stage instructions make clear, her killing of his father and
his lover. Caught up in the feuds of the past, he is torn, on the
one hand, between his duty to avenge his father and the horrors
threatening him if he refuses to obey Apollo's command and, on
the other, his horror at the murder of his mother and its
consequences. How Orestes recovers and how the feuds are
brought to an end are told in *The Eumenides*, the third part of *The
Oresteia*. Pursuit by the Furies is called off, and he recovers as a
result of Athena's mediation at his trial at the Council of
Aeropagus. The processes in his recovery are discussed in
Chapter 8.

Ajax

The manifest cause of madness in all the plays of ancient Greece
lies in a divine agency. In Sophocles' *Ajax*, which is a study of

the despair that follows on an acute delusional psychosis, Ajax, an honourable man 'supreme in judgement' (124), but angry and jealous because the armour of the dead Achilles has been awarded by Atreus to Odysseus, butchers sheep, cattle and their drovers in a mad frenzy, having mistaken them for the human prisoners, the sons of Atreus. He is unrelenting in his frenzy although Odysseus asks him for forgiveness.

The psychological mechanism behind Ajax's mistake may be identified as the displacement of the aggression caused by frustration. Athena has used her powers as a goddess to darken his vision with a veil of delusion and fantasy and to redirect his wrath. 'Struck blind with madness in the night' (216–7), and led by his deluded fancy, he supposes he is butchering his enemies. When he regains his senses, he suffers anguish and accepts that he 'must bear the bitter torment of seeing his own hand's mischief', 'the guilt that none can share' (254–6). He feels hated and disgraced;[5]

> Hated of gods,
> Hated of all the Greeks, hated of Troy,
> And of this very soil – (457–59)
> How shall I meet my father . . . (462)
> When I come empty-handed, with no prize? (464)

Calm and resolute, he prepares to kill himself and falls on to the point of his sword. The play asks, 'how could so good a man be brought to such despair?' (411–2) – a question often put to psychiatrists.

Heracles

In Euripides' play *Heracles*, Heracles returning to Thebes from the underworld discovers that the lives of his wife and sons are being threatened by Lycus, the usurping king, whom he then kills. Madness appears suddenly as a supernatural character who, when summoned by Iris, the messenger of the goddess Hera, is responsible from outside for his mad frenzy, in the course of which he kills without rational motive his three sons and his wife. He does so while acting out, 'adrift in a storm of insanity' (1189)[6], fantasies of killing Eurystheus and his sons in the underworld. The object of his frenzy has been displaced from them to his own family. After the frenzy has passed, his mind is 'drowned in waves of turmoil' (1090), and he has no memory of what he has done.

When he recovers from the delusional psychosis and recalls what he has done, he is deeply ashamed and feels himself to be unclean. He accepts that he is guilty, yet that to kill himself 'would surely be a coward's act' (1348), and that he must 'live and suffer' (1314). He keeps by him the bow with which he killed, as the symbol of his crime: 'anguish to me, yet I cannot part with it'.

In contrast to Ajax, he accepts his frailty and suffering, being given the strength to do so by not only the concern and sympathy shown him by his father Amphitryon, but also the intervention of Theseus, who serves as a therapist.[7] Ready to pay the debt he owes him for his rescue from the 'lower world' and to share his grief, Theseus reassures Heracles: 'I am not afraid to share your deep affliction' (1220–1); 'Even the strong are crippled by misfortune' (1395–6).

SHAKESPEARE'S PLAYS

Antipholus of Syracuse and Antipholus of Ephesus

The central theme in *The Comedy of Errors* lies in the destruction of Antipholus of Syracuse's already weakened sense of identity when he is challenged by misunderstandings arising when he and his identical twin are mistaken for each other.

There are two pairs of identical twins in the play, one pair being masters, the other servants, who resemble each other in appearance so closely that the one of each pair is indistinguishable from the other, although they are of contrasting personalities. Situations arise in which what is said or done makes no sense because of the mistaking of the one for the other.

Arriving in Ephesus, Antipholus of Syracuse feels that in searching for his mother and brother he has lost his identity, and that he will only find himself when he has found them – 'I ... in quest of them, unhappy lose myself'[8] (1.2.39–40). Vulnerable for this reason and because he is a stranger, he comes to feel, when repeatedly mistaken for his twin, that the city and he are in the grip of an evil power or subject to witchcraft, and he asks:

Am I in earth, in heaven, or in hell?
Sleeping or waking? mad, or well advis'd?
Known unto these, and to myself disguis'd?
(2.2.212–4)

Antipholus of Ephesus, his twin, well-established in Ephesus, married and confident of himself, reacts differently. He comes to feel that he is the only sane one in a world gone mad, and the victim of a plot, and that his wife is a strumpet. But he is regarded by others as mad or possessed, especially after he has denied to a courtesan that he has had a ring from her. Hostility evokes hostility. His growing anger being interpreted as madness and adding to the doubts about his sanity, he is given over to the ministrations of Dr Pinch, schoolmaster and exorcist, who charges 'Satan, housed within this man, to yield possession to my holy prayers' (4.4.52–3). This adjuration having failed, he is locked away 'in a dark and dankish vault', and there left with his servant, 'both bound together'. Dr Pinch concludes:

[B]oth man and master is possess'd;
I know it by their pale and deadly looks.
They must be bound, and laid in some dark room.   (90–2)

His reaction to these disturbing events has merely confirmed others in their belief that he is mad. Such are the diagnostic mistakes that are made when the circumstances are not as they are thought to be.

Dromio, the servant of Syracuse, feeling that he is the victim of witchcraft, speaks of himself as transformed and made a fool of. The servant of Ephesus resigns himself with humorous acceptance to the topsy-turvy world and the blows of his master.

The effects of the mistakes are to disrupt the relationships of those affected, each of whom makes his own interpretations and sees others as mad, cheating, jesting, estranged, transformed in mind, or in fairy land. Antipholus from Syracuse decides to flee from Ephesus by ship, but eventually finds refuge in a priory. Some of those caught up in the confusions resort to the law in the face of the intransigence of others. Others resort to force, others to exorcism. To the audience the behaviour of each is understandable in the light of the mistakes made in distinguishing the twins, but to the characters not understandable, out of character and therefore mad.

33

Dromio and he having escaped from the cellar, Antipholus of Ephesus appeals to the Duke as the representative of justice for 'ample satisfaction/For these deep shames and great indignities' (5.1.253–4). The Duke faced by all the contradictions in the evidence thinks them all 'mated' (that is, bewildered), 'or stark mad' (282), but changes his mind as further witnesses are brought before him, the facts are uncovered and the quarrellers reconciled.

One lesson is that people are judged to be mad when their behaviour departs from expectations of how a sane person would behave in the situation as it appears to be. The judgement is liable to be mistaken when the expectations are based on faulty assumptions about the situation and the interests and motives of those responding to it. Deeming a person to be mad allows the assumptions to be held to unquestioned and uncorrected. Another is that being misunderstood is disturbing when a person's sense of identity is already weak; he may then feel under threat from mysterious powers. The lessons in the part played by the Duke when he presides over the revelations of the truth are discussed in Chapter 8.

Hamlet

Of inexhaustible interest is Hamlet's supposed madness, which has been discussed in innumerable books, critical reviews and dissertations. So pervasive has been the influence of psycho-analysis that the oedipal conflicts in Hamlet's relationships with Claudius and Gertrude tend to be regarded as the central theme. That he is a son is certainly of importance, but it should be kept in mind that there are three sons in the play, Hamlet, Laertes and Fortinbras, and three fathers, the ghost of Hamlet's father, Polonius and the old King of Norway, as well as Claudius, the step-father, who has displaced the natural father as husband to Gertrude and as king. There are other relationships of relevance, within a system that includes Ophelia, Polonius, Laertes and Horatio. Of special interest is the triangle formed by Hamlet, Ophelia and Polonius.

Various reasons are offered by other characters for Hamlet's distemper. He is first presented as continuing to mourn his father, who has died suddenly in strange circumstances two months previously. Thus Gertrude, his mother, says: 'Good

Hamlet, cast thy nighted colour off. . . . Do not for ever with thy vailèd lids/Seek for thy noble father in the dust . . . all that lives must die' (1.2.68,70–2).[9] Searching like this is a usual component of mourning.[10] Claudius tells him that 'Tis unmanly grief', and 'a course/Of impious stubbornness' 'to persevere/In obstinate condolement' (1.2.92–4).

Hamlet tells the audience, but not Gertrude or Claudius, that his distemper is more serious than mourning his father. Gertrude's behaviour has brought him to a crisis in his attitudes towards her, the world and himself. He has regarded her as a devoted wife to his father, but she has shown herself to be frail, and she has gone with indecent haste, one month after his death and with 'dexterity to incestuous sheets' (1.2.157) in a marriage, prohibited at that time, to her dead husband's brother. As a result Hamlet yearns for death, and sees the world thus: 'How weary, stale, flat and unprofitable/Seem to me all the uses of this world!' (1.2.133–4) – a cry of disillusion and despair.

His attitudes towards other women, Ophelia especially, are gravely affected, as his behaviour in the 'nunnery' scene (3.1) shows. He has become fearful of the influence of women – 'wise men know well enough what monsters you make of them' (141–2) – and sees them as deceiving – 'God has given you one face and you make yourselves another' (146–7).

His distemper has taken a turn for the worse after the ghost of his father has given him a horrendous account of 'his foul and most unnatural murder' (1.5.25) and charged him to take revenge on Claudius, 'that incestuous, that adulterate beast', but not Gertrude, who is to be left to heaven. At this point he is near to collapse. Ill-placed and in nature ill-prepared, he shrinks from the violent action demanded of him. 'The time is out of joint: O cursed spite,/That ever I was born to set it right' (187–8). Thus he recognises the powerful forces with which he has to contend. He is a young man, still a student and at a stage of growing up at which he would not expect to exercise power. His meeting with the ghost and other experiences arouse motives more complex than the sexual motives seized on subsequently by Polonius to explain his madness.

He does not tell any of this to Horatio or Marcellus, but swears them to secrecy about the ghost, whom they too have seen, and warns Horatio that he might think it meet to put 'an antic disposition on' (1.5.172) in order to disguise the strong feelings aroused in him by the ghost's revelations. By doing so he makes his behaviour strange or odd and therefore less understandable. Such a smoke-screen of obscurity and complexity is commonly used by psychotic patients.[11] Being misunderstood, deliberately or unwittingly, might be included in a list of the features of madness, although not by itself sufficient to make the diagnosis. Paranoid ideas are usually inferred, albeit unreliably, when the patient lacks frankness, shows mistrust or appears to deceive.

He tells Horatio not to make any comment, however strange his behaviour. But the marked instability in his emotions and attitudes after his encounter with the ghost goes beyond an antic disposition, as does his impulsive and inappropriate behaviour. Misunderstanding Ophelia, he misleads her, and is misunderstood by her. Misleading Claudius too, he colludes in the belief that he is mad, and he allows the hostility between them to escalate.

Polonius is quick to find an explanation of his distraught appearance to Ophelia, with 'his doublet all unbrac'd . . . his stockings foul'd,/Ungart'red, and down-gyvèd to his ankle,/Pale as his shirt . . . /And with a look so piteous . . . /As if he had been loosed out of hell' (2.1.75–80). 'He falls to such perusal of my face/As if he would draw it' (87), she reports. His behaviour is peculiar, lacks the reciprocity of normal social interaction, and gives her no help in deciding how to respond to it. 'This is the very ecstasy of love' (99) is Polonius's diagnosis. That she has repelled his letters and denied him access to her, as he had told her to do, 'hath made him mad' (107).

Polonius, confident that he has found 'the head and source' of the distemper (2.2.54–5), brushes off Gertrude's view: 'I doubt it is no other, but the main,/His father's death and our o'erhasty marriage' (56–7). 'Your noble son is mad', he tells her and Claudius. With the further evidence of Hamlet's letter to Ophelia, he describes the course of Hamlet's illness: 'he, repulsed, . . ./ Fell into a sadness; then into a fast;/Thence to a watch; thence into a weakness;/Thence to a lightness; and, by this declension,/ Into the madness wherein now he raves' (146–50).

The belief that Hamlet is love-sick and mad is strengthened after his disastrous meeting with Ophelia in the nunnery scene (3.1). This meeting has been set up by Polonius as a means of demonstrating the rightness of his diagnosis to Claudius and

Gertrude, who are to 'mark the encounter' when he 'looses' – note the veterinary term[12] – his daughter to Hamlet. His suspicions aroused, Hamlet accuses her with an extravagant and unfitting frankness, even obscenity, of being a prostitute, and tells her to get to a whore-house: 'Get thee to a nunnery' (120), for this is one of the meanings of 'nunnery' in the vernacular of the time. Dismissing what he says as unreasonable, without questioning whether there is any justification for it, she comments: 'O, what a noble mind is here o'erthrown' (153). 'Now see that noble and most sovereign reason . . . blasted with ecstasy' (160,163).

His 'transformation' has already been noticed by Claudius (2.2.5), who instructs Rosencrantz and Guildenstern, his former companions, to probe Hamlet's secret and 'to gather/So much as from occasion' they 'may glean' (15–16) about what 'hath put him/So much from the understanding of himself'(9). Claudius makes plans to send him to England to remove the danger (3.1.170–3).

Just as Polonius sets a trap for Hamlet, so Hamlet sets a trap for Claudius in the Gonzago play, which gives him the opportunity to test out what the ghost has told him about the manner of his father's death. He puts Horatio to observe Claudius: 'One scene . . . comes near the circumstance . . . of my father's death' (3.2.74–5). 'Give him heedful note . . ./And, after, we will both our judgements join' (82–4). His empirical attitude and the testing out of a belief are evidence against madness.

Claudius' reaction to the scene corroborates what the ghost has told him. Given proof of Claudius' guilt, he has to face, when he surprises him at prayer (3.3), the issue of the duty of revenge imposed on him by the ghost. He might be expected to harbour homicidal impulses towards him and Gertrude, just as Orestes did towards Aegisthus and Clytemnestra. The dilemna he faces is similar to that faced by Orestes. On the one hand, he has the duty to avenge his father and, on the other, he shrinks from the murder of Claudius.

He gives as his reason for not killing Claudius that it would then be done when Claudius' chance of salvation is greatest – better to kill him 'When he is drunk, asleep, or in his rage;/Or in the incestuous pleasure of his bed;/At gaming, swearing; or about some act/That has no relish of salvation in't' (89–92).[13]

Critics[14] tend to regard his inaction as dilatoriness, reflecting a defect in character. Freud[15] gives great importance to it: 'The play is built up on Hamlet's hesitations over fulfilling the task of revenge . . . to take vengeance on the man who did away with his father and took that father's place with his mother.' His 'inhibitions' have their origin in 'the repressed wishes of his childhood'. But the reason Hamlet gives, which is congruent with the religious ideas of his time, may be sufficient explanation without resort to oedipal conflicts.

Other points to be made about his delaying testify to his sanity. The knowledge he has gained makes him see Claudius, not as the villain of the fantasies aroused by the ghost of his father, the product of his fevered imagination, but as a real person facing his own guilt and suffering remorse.[16] To see him so makes killing him much more difficult, and he is able to resist the commands of the ghost. His forbearance may thus be seen, not as neurotic indecision, but as reflecting the restoration of judgement and return of sanity.

Claudius' precipitate departure from the hall at the climax of the Gonzago play (3.2.269) is a turning point in the plot. He knows now that Hamlet's antic disposition is a cover, and that Hamlet knows about the manner of his father's death. Alarmed by the 'Hazard so dangerous as doth hourly grow/Out of his lunacies' (3.3.6–7), and in order to put 'fetters . . . upon this fear' (25), Claudius instructs Rosencrantz and Guildenstern to take him to England and there to 'confine' him (3.1.189). Later he makes plans for him to be killed. Seeing a person as dangerous by reason of being mad or possessed or under the influence of the devil has been the common justification for sequestration and confinement.

The killing of Polonius, unseen behind the arras, brings a further escalation. Reconciliation is no longer possible, and Hamlet becomes the hunted rather than the hunter. Thereafter his behaviour is guided more by the realities than by fantasy, although the ghost does soon appear briefly to him again to 'whet' his 'almost blunted purpose' (3.4.111) to take revenge on Claudius.

Hamlet offers in the closet scene (3.4) another explanation of his seeming madness. Seeing and hearing the ghost for a second time, he realises that Gertrude is blind and deaf to the ghost, because of her adultery, he supposes. She regards his behaviour as 'ecstasy' (being out of himself) and 'the very coinage of your brain'. He then reproaches her:

My pulse, as yours, doth temperately keep time,
And makes as healthful music: it is not madness
That I have utter'd: bring me to the test,
And I the matter will re-word; which madness
Would gambol from. Mother, for love of grace,
Lay not that flattering unction to your soul,
That not your trespass, but my madness speaks: . . .
Confess yourself to heaven;
Repent what's past; avoid what is to come.

(140–6,149–50)

Hamlet's point is that to attribute madness to a person serves to deny, and defend oneself against, the truth in what he says.

Gertrude, alarmed, tells Claudius that he is as 'Mad as the sea and wind, when both contend/Which is the mightier: in his lawless fit' (4.1.7–8), and refers to 'this brainish apprehension' (11).

Claudius considers what is expedient:

How dangerous is it that this man goes loose!
Yet must not we put the strong law on him:
He's lov'd of the distracted multitude.

(4.3.2–4)

and resolves to send him to England for his 'especial safety' (39), and gives Rosencrantz and Guildenstern the commission to escort him and also to carry letters that will cause him to be killed there (64).

He leaves for England in the custody of Rosencrantz and Guildenstern, and perhaps several years pass before he returns to Denmark. He is then thirty years old (5.1), the gravedigger tells us. Whatever the truth in this, Hamlet is deemed to have made the transition from youth to maturity, and has already shown in his ruthlessness towards Rosencrantz and Guildenstern that he is capable of acting positively and taking control over what happens to him, in contrast to his passivity as a young man.

Ophelia

The evidence (in 4.5 especially) of Ophelia's madness is unequivocal. Previously she has shown herself to be prim and properly responsive to the warnings of her brother and father

(1.3). She is restrained in her response to Hamlet's disturbed behaviour (2.1), and conciliatory and sympathetic to him, although 'affrighted', in the face of his gross rudeness, she recognises that his 'noble mind' is 'o'erthrown' and 'out of tune'. That she is 'deject and wretched' is a normal response, and she expresses her distress appropriately, ending:

> O, woe is me,
> To have seen what I have seen, see what I see!
>
> (3.1.153–4)

Different is the indecency of her language and behaviour in her madness (4.5.). A gentleman describes her as 'importunate; indeed, distract':

> She speaks much of her father; says she hears
> There's tricks i' the world; and hems, and beats her heart;
> Spurns enviously at straws; speaks things in doubt,
> That carry but half sense: her speech is nothing,
> Yet the unshapèd use of it doth move
> The hearers to collection; they aim at it,
> And botch the words up fit to their own thoughts;
> Which, as her winks, and nods, and gestures yield them,
> Indeed would make one think there might be thought,
> Though nothing sure, yet much unhappily.
>
> (4.5.5–13)

This is a brilliant description of the disordered language of mental illness. Yet, though her speech is 'unshapèd' and difficult to comprehend, she presents as a person confused and suffering.[17] Her distracted behaviour and the veiled allusions in what she says, with loose associations and excessive use of metaphor, may be seen as evidence of mental illness, as does her bawdiness and overt sensuality and, especially, the unsuitable, out-of-character display of sexual preoccupations.

Claudius recognises the risk of suicide – 'Follow her close; give her good watch, I pray you' (4.5.72) – and gives Gertrude this explanation of her madness (74–85): 'this is the poison of deep grief; it springs/All from her father's death .../First, her father slain:/Next, your son gone; and he most violent author/Of his own just remove', and then making clear that she is mad:

Divided from herself and her fair judgement,
Without the which we are pictures, or mere beasts. (84–5)

Her father's death and the blight of her love for Hamlet are entwined in much of what she says.

The many sexual references in her madness suggest that the pressures put on her by her brother (1.3) have played a part. He has warned her of the dangers if 'she unmask her beauty to the moon' (37); 'Be wary, then; best safety lies in fear' (43). Her father has told her: 'You do not understand yourself so clearly' (96). Do not believe Hamlet's vows, he urges her; they 'are springes to catch woodcocks' (115). They give too little weight to her fondness for Hamlet and the distress caused her by his madness.

Portia

The reasons given for the madness of other women in Shakespeare's plays lie in the disruption of a relationship. Portia, in *Julius Caesar*,[18] denied a close relationship with her husband, asks: 'Dwell I but in the suburbs/Of your good pleasure? If it be no more,/Portia is Brutus' harlot, not his wife' (2.1.285–7). She reacts violently, slashing her thigh; highly apprehensive, she faints. Later she kills herself.

> Impatient of my absence,
> And grief that young Octavius with Mark Antony
> Have made themselves so strong,

Brutus explains,

> for with her death
> That tidings came; with this she fell distract,
> And, her attendants absent, swallow'd fire.
> (4.3.150–5)

Lady Macbeth

The onset of Lady Macbeth's mental illness as reported in the sleep-walking scene (5.1)[19] – 'a great perturbation in nature' (9), the doctor calls it – is said by her gentlewoman to have been 'Since his majesty went into the field' (3). His departure would have had two effects; her further disengagement from his

41

affairs, and the loss of whatever support she has had from him.[20] Freud[21] argues, on the other hand, that her transformation in the sleep-walking scene is from 'callousness to penitence' and is a reaction to her continuing childlessness after many years of marriage. However, the text leaves it uncertain whether she has had children and says nothing directly about the effects on her of not having had them.

There were other factors. Her psychological defences breaking down, she is preoccupied in the sleep-walking scene with memories of the horrifying experiences she has been through: 'thick-coming fancies,/That keep her from her rest' (5.3.39–40). Her continual washing of her hands is in sharp contrast to her easy assertion after the murder of Duncan that 'a little water clears us of this deed'. 'Here's the smell of the blood still', she says; from a sorely charg'd heart (5.1.48–50), 'infected minds/To their death pillows will discharge their secrets' (68–9).

The picture she presents in the sleep-walking scene is typical in many respects of an acute reactive psychosis: the obsessive attention to a particular detail, in this case to the 'damned spot' (35), preoccupation by fantasy and apparent watchfulness, in this case 'at once the benefit of sleep' and 'the effects of watching' (12). Immersion in a world of fearful fantasy is favoured by the dark, which reduces engagement with the real world – hence her command to have 'light by her continually' (26–7).

She 'by self and violent hands took off her life' (5.6.109–10). The doctor's diagnosis is sound. Despite his admission that 'This disease is beyond my practice' (5.1.56), he anticipates her suicide and instructs: 'Look after her;/Remove from her the means of all annoyance,/And still keep eyes upon her' (71–3). He knows of the history of violence and has noted her increasing agitation. She has revealed much earlier her desire for death; thus she has remarked "Tis safer to be that which we destroy' (3.2.6). Her presentiment of death is expressed in 'The Thane of Fife had a wife; where is she now?' (5.1.41). She has recognised too that there is no road back: 'what's done cannot be undone' (64).

Constance

Constance, in *King John*,[22] 'Oppress'd with wrongs, and therefore full of fears;/A widow, husbandless, subject to fears;/A woman, naturally born to fears' (3.1.13–15), is driven distracted by the loss of her son Arthur, when he is taken prisoner by his uncle, and expresses her grief at his loss in extravagant terms.

It is unclear how much her distress is due to the collapse of her plans to have him crowned as king in place of John his usurping uncle. A turning point comes when she learns of the Dauphin's betrothal to Blanche. This is a severe blow to her political hopes because it brings John and the king of France, who hitherto has given her support, into a short-lived alliance. Her hopes are raised again when they fall out as a result of the manoeuvres of the Pope's legate, but are dashed when the king of France is defeated in the field and Arthur is captured.

In a scene (3.3) reminiscent of that in which Ophelia presents a picture of madness, Constance appears preoccupied by thoughts of death: 'O amiable, lovely death!' (25). To the Pope's legate, who reproves her 'Lady, you utter madness, and not sorrow' (43), she replies, giving a definition of madness:

> I am not mad: I would to heaven I were!
> For then, 'tis like I should forget myself.
> O, if I could, what grief should I forget! . .   (48–50)
> If I were mad I should forget my son,
> Or madly think a babe of clouts were he:
> I am not mad; too well I feel
> The different plague of each calamity.   (57–60)

She has something to say about the part played by grief. Reproved again 'You are as fond of grief as of your child' (92), she replies:

> Grief fills the room up of my absent child,
> Lies in his bed, walks up and down with me,
> Puts on his pretty looks, repeats his words,
> Remembers me of all his gracious parts,
> Stuffs out his vacant garments with his form;
> Then have I reason to be fond of grief?   (93–8)

Anticipating her suicide, she remarks:

> My reasonable part produces reason
> How I may be delivered of these woes,
> And teaches me to kill or hang myself . . .   (54–6)
> And, father cardinal, I have heard you say

43

That we shall see and know our friends in heaven;
If that be true, I shall see my boy again.   (76–9)

As in *Hamlet* and *Macbeth*, the risk of suicide is recognised by the king of France: 'I fear some outrage, and I'll follow her' (106). It is reported subsequently that she has 'in a frenzy died' (4.2.122).

Titus Andronicus

In *Titus Andronicus*[23] the reasons given for Titus's madness all refer to grief and sorrow: 'grief has so wrought on him,/He takes false shadows for true substances' (3.2.79–80); 'Extremity of griefs would make men mad' (4.1.19), it is said with reference to Lavinia's madness; if 'His sorrows have so overwhelm'd his wits?/Shall we be thus afflicted in his freaks,/his fits, his frenzy, and his bitterness?' (4.4.10–12); 'Th' effects of sorrow for his valiant sons,/Whose loss hath pierc'd him deep, and scarr'd his heart' (30–1). His daughter raped and mutilated, his own hand cut off, two sons beheaded and one banished, he has been still when it has been 'a time to storm' (3.1.263). But his 'ecstasies' are also seen as 'feigned' (4.4.21), just as Hamlet's are. The sequence of bloody disasters was set in train by his insistence on sentencing Tamora's oldest son, soon to be followed by his killing of his youngest son.

He is described as 'distract' after a speech in which he makes use of rambling and obscure metaphors (4.3.1–24), like those that characterise the speech of the mentally ill. But he is able to enter into the pretence when Tamora and her two sons, supposing him to be mad, present themselves as representatives of Revenge and Rape. He is not deceived and acts decisively, cutting the throats of the two sons. Because of the stubbornness of age he has been in some degree the author of his own misfortunes and is like King Lear in this respect.

King Lear

King Lear, like Titus, goes mad after a series of disasters. His 'intent [is] to shake all cares and business from our age,/ Conferring them on younger strengths, while we/Unburden'd crawl toward death' (1.1.38–41). This is on the face of it the normal disengagement of the elderly, but it is associated with high and specific expectations of his daughters, especially

Cordelia. He 'lov'd her most, and thought to set my rest/On her kind nursery' (1.1.123–4).[24] He comes to a crisis in the first scene, when she disappoints him by qualifying her avowal of love for him by saying that the man she marries shall carry with him 'Half my love' (102).

The purpose of his plan to divide his kingdom into three, he says, is 'that future strife/May be prevented now' (44–5), but he has also a 'darker purpose' (36). Uncertain of his daughters' love for him, he makes testing demands on them, which Goneril and Regan pretend effusively to meet. Cordelia, his youngest daughter and his favourite, does not do so because of her frankness. Blind to the effects on them of his preference of Cordelia, he expects Goneril and Regan, his two older daughters, to comply with his wishes. They disappoint as soon as he requires them to make good their promises.

Reacting angrily and breaking first with Cordelia, then Kent, who speaks in her favour, and later with Goneril and Regan, he starts off a vicious circle of progressive loss of confidence in his daughters and loss of control over himself and his circumstances. Demands for love, attempts to impose control, resistance to change and loss of control are common manifestations of the 'infirmity of age'.[25] His demands for love arising out of dependency and loneliness are excessive and are not met, and his anxieties grow, so that he precipitates the strife that should be prevented.

His madness develops gradually as each new blow hits him: the foiling of his plan to divide and rule, Goneril's attack on him, his terrible curse on her, his recognition of his folly and misjudgement of Cordelia, finding Kent in the stocks, with its blow to his self-respect and as a reminder of his powerlessness, his rejection by Regan, and finally the appearance of Poor Tom. These blows destroying his conception of himself as powerful king and loving and kind father strengthen his insistence on keeping what his daughters see as an excessive number of followers; these are the tokens of power.

The transition into madness has usually been taken to be the start of the storm, this being a metaphor for his anger and disorganisation – that is, for the passions that overthrow his reason; the hovel is the metaphor for his degradation and despair.[26] The madness arises firstly when he suffers a progressive loss of control over the world he has been accustomed to rule, and secondly when he recognises that he is losing control over himself. At the height of his madness he is largely oblivious of the physical discomforts of the heath on which he finds himself: 'where the greater malady is fix'd,/The lesser is scarce felt' (3.4.8–9);

> When the mind's free,
> The body's delicate; the tempest in my mind
> Doth from my senses take all feeling else
> Save what beats there. – Filial ingratitude!'
> (11–14)

Lessons are to be learnt from comparisons between the king, the Fool and Edgar, who feigns madness due to possession. The Fool disappears as soon as the king in his madness takes over the role of expressing the unpopular truths about the harsh realities of an unjust world. Edgar has assumed the role of madman in order, like Hamlet, to preserve his life in a suddenly hostile world and thus escape from an unendurable situation.

The king recovers his sanity when he is reconciled with Cordelia. 'Pray you now, forget and forgive: I am old and foolish' (4.7.83–4)', he says to her when they are reunited. Two things have prepared him. 'He hath slept long' (18), and there has been music. That he recovers so well argues against a diagnosis that he suffers from the dementia of the elderly.

He continues, even after his recovery, and despite his suffering, to hold to his egocentric and unrealistic expectations, that she will serve his needs of her, without any acknowledgement that as a young married woman she might have obligations. Captured by his enemies, he says to her, 'Come, let's away to prison,/We two alone will sing like birds i' the cage' (5.3.8–9). The end is tragic. She is hanged on the instructions of Edmund, and the king dies of a broken heart.

Leontes

Leontes, in *The Winter's Tale*,[27] morbidly suspicious of his wife's fidelity when she becomes pregnant, becomes deluded that she has had an adulterous relationship with his life-long friend Polixenes, that Polixenes is the father of the unborn child, and that there is a conspiracy to kill him, to which his courtier Camillo too is party. These paranoid ideas, making up a pattern typical of the delusional jealousy that may arise during pregnancy, seize hold of him suddenly when Hermione gives her hand to Polixenes in a friendly gesture (1.2.108). He doubts the paternity of his son Mamillius, banishes his wife, and rejects the baby girl as a bastard, ordering first that she be committed 'to the fire', and then relenting, that she be taken to a 'remote and desert place quite out of our dominions'.

Leontes at first rejects the declaration of the Delphic oracle (3.2) that 'Hermione is chaste; Polixenes blameless; Camillo a true subject; Leontes a jealous tyrant; his innocent babe truly begotten; and the king shall live without an heir, if that which is lost be not found' (131–4). Immediately after doing so, he is told of Mamillius's death, and awakes to reality as if from a dream: 'I have too much believ'd my own suspicion' (149). Hermione faints on hearing the news and is removed as if dying. Repenting his 'profaneness' against Apollo's oracle, he beseeches that 'some remedies for life' be applied to her, and vows to seek reconciliation with Polixenes and Camillo.

Sixteen years pass, which Leontes spends in mourning and repentance. He is advised that he has 'paid down/More penitence than done trespass' (5.1.3–4). 'Do as the heavens have done, forget your evil;/With them, forgive yourself' (5–6). He recovers when he is reunited with his daughter Perdita, who is now betrothed to Polixenes' son. In the final scene the living Hermione is restored to him.

OTHER PLAYS

Torquato Tasso

Goethe's *Torquato Tasso*[28] is a study of, amongst other things, the development of a paranoid illness. It tells of a poet, Tasso, whose appraisal of his situation is so faulty that he can be regarded as suffering from a paranoid personality disorder. Introverted, socially inept and shrinking from human beings, he has tended to fear and misjudge them, and to 'mistrust a hundred people who are not his enemies'. If anything goes awry, 'he immediately thinks it is some plot to undermine him'. He has not been able to make use of the remedy for 'a sickness of the heart', which is 'best cured by trusting your sorrows to a friend'. In reaction to the events described in the play his sense of inferiority grows. The gap between his appraisal of how others are behaving towards him and their intentions widens so far that he can be regarded as mentally ill.

One model for the character of Tasso was a poet with this name who had been a court favourite at Ferrara in the sixteenth century, and who had been imprisoned after a fit of madness. The play owes much too to Goethe's own experience as a young man at the court at Weimar. But it provides more than a portrait of a poet facing 'the disproportion of talent and life', in Goethe's phrase. It can be read as a more general study of a sensitive man in a social milieu imposing constraints on him. The poet in the play is reminded that 'Nature' has given him 'word and melody for grief, so as to tell the depths of my distress', and he is eventually saved from madness because he is able to 'reach out . . . with open arms' to the help offered him. Like the shipwrecked mariner, he holds firm to the rock on which he was to have been destroyed.

The setting in the palace of Belriguardo in spring is idyllic. The surroundings are civilised, cultivated and artificial, and it can be imagined that it is the poets' golden age. But Tasso is solitary and hides away. He walks in his own magic world, and the delightful world created by the Princess and the Countess Leonora might not exist for him. He feels himself to be inferior and not enjoying esteem, despite being given by the Duke 'the clearest signs of very special treatment' and despite the Duke's patience in investigating every complaint he makes. He is an artist at odds with the world.

Hesitatingly he delivers to the Duke Alfonso the poem he owes him, although he has hardly finished it and feels it to be imperfect and unworthy, and he is embarrassed when the two ladies crown him at the Duke's behest with a laurel wreath. This adds to his sense of inadequacy. 'All my strength has gone,' he feels, and he is ashamed of the 'undeserved happiness'.

He feels oppressed, and that he is forced into a role in which his distinction as a poet is used to win acclaim for Alfonso, his poetry being seen almost as a consumer product for the delectation of the ruling classes. The genius provided for by patronage 'repays with enormously richer gifts'. Goethe is expressing through Tasso his own painful experience that patronage is not an acceptable system. Being ruled from above is not easy, nor is subordinating individual desires and ideals to a civilised social order.

The crux of the play lies in Tasso's relationship with Antonio, the Secretary of State, whose substantial achievement and approval from all sides adds to Tasso's agonising doubts about his own existence. He receives intolerable provocation from Antonio who, offended by the wreath, has become jealous of him because of the favours the ladies show him. Antonio never admits his antagonism, and never infringes the social rules, yet, parading his own authority, experience and morality, skilfully snubs him, taunts him, lectures him and puts him in the wrong. When their quarrel escalates, Tasso, belittled and angered, draws his sword. Alfonso, preferring Antonio's account of the incident, orders Tasso to confine himself to his room.

Yet Alfonso knows that when two men quarrel, one should assume that the wiser is responsible, and he tells the now regretful Antonio to invoke the help of the two ladies and to repair the discord. Plans are to be made to help Tasso. Both ladies, recognising his need for care and help, try to win him over, but their interests do not go hand-in-hand, neither with each other nor with Antonio and Alfonso.

Feeling punished, betrayed and at the mercy of his enemies, Tasso decides to leave Ferrara. Leonora agrees that he should leave, but proposes that he should do so with her when she goes to Florence to join her husband. But he is not persuaded by her to believe that no one hates him and no one persecutes him. On the contrary, he sees her as cunning and wanting to turn his plight to her advantage. No one shall deceive him, he is resolved. His fears and suspicions, now so pervasive, amount to mental illness.

He tries to get Antonio's help in getting Alfonso's permission to go to Rome where he can do further work on his poem, but Antonio refuses, leaving him, with 'the tyranny of friendship', in no doubt what he wants and thinks would be the best for him. Tasso, learning to dissemble, approaches Alfonso who, afraid of losing him to another patron, makes difficulties about letting him take back his poem.

The Princess too puts obstacles in the way of his leaving. Equivocating, she makes it difficult for him to decide. When he opens his heart to her, she gives him some encouragement to suppose that he holds a special place in her affections. In a brash gesture he embraces her and is rejected, both by her and the Countess. Once again in the wrong, regarded by Alfonso as mad, and repudiated by the ladies after this *faux pas*, he turns to Antonio for help. Banished and destroyed, an outcast in the grasp of tyrants, he has the consolation that his poetry enables him to tell of his sufferings.

In each of the confrontations, Tasso's attitudes, although innocent and idealistic, are egocentric, with both oversensitivity to the hostility of others and, at times to an absurd degree, disregard of the part played by his own behaviour in evoking the hostility. How he has seen himself has been very different from how others have seen him. The others share values and assumptions, but he is on his own, out of tune, misunderstanding others and being misunderstood. Egocentric and feeling inferior and persecuted, he responds to conflicts in his relationships so erratically and ineptly that he comes near to being wrecked.

Oswald

Ibsen's *Ghosts* is about the relationship of Oswald and his mother and their suffering. It ends with his collapse into helplessness. He 'seems to shrink in his chair, and all his muscles go flaccid, his face is expressionless, and his eyes stare vacantly'. He says 'tonelessly': 'The sun ... the sun.' As his mother stares at him in 'speechless horror', he repeats sitting motionless: 'The sun ... the sun.'[29]

Oswald, said to be 'twenty-six, twenty-seven years old', is single, a painter who has 'begun to make a name for himself', although 'things seem to have fallen off a bit of late'. For the last ten years he has been living in Paris, but has returned to his home in Norway two days before in order to attend the ceremonial opening of an orphanage built by his mother, Helene Alving, in memory of his father. The orphanage catches fire on the eve of the opening and is destroyed.

He had become ill about two years earlier when he had got back to Paris after a visit home, the main symptoms then being violent pains at the back of the head – 'like an iron band clamped tight around the neck' – and also giddiness, inability to concentrate, loss of skill in his painting and feelings of being paralysed. He had been told by a leading doctor in Paris that he had inherited a disease from a dissolute father, and that there has been something worm-eaten about him since birth; he remembers in particular that the doctor used the word 'vermoulu'. When he had rejected with indignation the assertion that his father had been dissolute, the doctor had shifted his ground and told him that his illness was the result of his own thoughtlessness. Whatever justification there may have been for the doctor's diagnosis, he has become fearful that he has contracted venereal disease, as a naïve young man may do, even when he has not had any sexual contact.

He seemed tired when he got home for the opening of the orphanage and has slept rather late, but by dinner-time he has recovered. Indeed, he makes a tentative sexual advance to the domestic servant Regine which, overheard by his mother, upsets her greatly because she sees it as a recapitulation of her husband's seduction of Regine's mother. Later that evening he drinks more than his mother thinks good for him, and tells her of 'all the torment, the anguish, the remorse and the great mental dread' from which he has been suffering, insisting that it was his mind that had 'given way and was destroyed'. He speaks also of his admiration for Regine, his hopes of finding salvation with her because of her vitality and joy in living, and his intention of marrying her. His mother declares her opposition to the match, but their conversation is cut short by the fire.

When it is resumed a few hours later, she tells him and Regine that Regine is the illegitimate child of his father. Abandoning her hopes of marrying him, and recognising also that he is ill, Regine decides to leave the house immediately. Left alone with his mother, he speaks again of the hopelessness of his disease, which he says will turn him into a helpless child, and reproaches her for sending Regine away. He then asks her to take away his life by giving him the twelve tablets of morphia he has stored up for this purpose. The attack begins a few minutes later.

Ibsen describes in *Ghosts* a case in which there is a loss of mental powers in a young adult. In 1881 when the play was written, such a case would have been regarded as an incurable dementia, with which went a progressive decline to mental feebleness and incoherence; patients have to be fed, moved and cared for in every way, it was said. Dementia like this was often attributed to syphilis, whether congenital or acquired.[30]

The critics of the time immediately seized upon syphilis as a cause.[31] Hereditary degeneracy was thought to be important.

51

This is another example of the preference of a biological explanation before a psychological explanation that might have uncomfortable implications. Oswald did not fall ill until he was 24
years old, too late for congenital syphilis to become manifest. He
has not had sexual intercourse – 'I've never done that', he says –
so that adherents to the diagnosis of syphilis have had to argue
that he had become infected when he had smoked his father's
pipe, which is unlikely.

The play was finished before any sure distinctions could be
made between the various forms of dementia. It was not until
1912 that the link between general paralysis of the insane and
syphilis was established. Maudsley wrote in 1879 of 'primary'
and 'secondary' dementia. One form of 'secondary' dementia
was called 'dementia praecox', after Kraepelin's definition of it
in 1896. Some of the mental illnesses so diagnosed then might
now be diagnosed as a schizophrenic psychosis, and Oswald's
illness might be put into this class. Little weight should be given
to such a diagnosis, however, because of the unsatisfactoriness
of the definition of schizophrenia.

The point is that Ibsen describes the psychological processes
through which the attitudes and behaviours of parents can have
disastrous effects on the mental health of a young person.
Disease, and especially venereal disease, can be regarded as a
metaphor for the evil inherent in the relationships in a family.
Ibsen was writing at a time when degeneracy of the person was
also being seen as a symptom of the sickness of society. The play
was outrageous enough when Oswald's illness was seen as the
unfortunate consequence of mundane sexual misbehaviour. It
would have been more so if the illness had been seen as arising
out of disturbed family relationships. There tends still to be
strong resistance to seeing such an illness as the outcome of
disordered interactions in the family.[32]

The scene between son and mother immediately preceding
his collapse has often been played to portray the mother as the
passive, helpless spectator of a thrust in the son's syphilitic
illness. This is how son and mother are portrayed in the
sketches Edvard Munch made for Max Reinhardt's production
in Berlin in 1906.[33] Munch identified closely with Oswald, and
while working on the sketches felt himself to be a drunken
painter doomed to suffer ruin. The furniture in the sketches
includes sofa and seats from his own childhood home. He was

well aware that the sickness of a child could be due to inheritance and what he saw as the sins of the parents, as is shown by the picture he painted of a mother and ailing child with a skin rash, to which he gave the title 'Inheritance'.[34]

Ibsen never confirmed nor denied that he had had neuro-syphilis in mind, but he did comment indirectly on the nature of the illness. Thus he said of the mother's marriage: 'Nemesis is invited upon the offspring by marrying for extrinsic reasons, even when they are religious or moral.'[35] Also, there are many similarities between his own and Oswald's experiences, and the play reflects his review of his own relationships with his parents, on which he embarked after his father's death.[36] At 26–27 years old he was passing through a period of instability and was drinking heavily. He married when he was 30 years old.

Oswald's behaviour becomes comprehensible when it is seen in the context of his interactions with his mother. The burning down of the orphanage brings his relationship with her to a crisis. The fire and her revelations after it destroy his illusions about his father, force him to review his own past, and bring to a head the conflicts in his relationship with her. The family myth is destroyed by the revelations. A comfortable fiction created by his mother, it had given Oswald a false picture of the part played by his father in the life of the family. It was to have been sustained by the orphanage built in the father's honour.

Mother and son should play the scene as a violent and destructive quarrel in the course of which they do and say ugly things to each other.[37] The way they respond to each other shows that 'they are caught in a vicious spiral of confusion, misunderstanding and mystification which thwarts all their real feelings and emotions'. 'They talk at each other and past each other, but never to each other. It is this that makes their pattern of interaction so lethal.' They fail utterly to recognise each other's needs, and make no attempt to interpret to each other what they are saying.

Oswald tries to find a way forward. His first plan, to find salvation through marrying Regine, is wrecked by his mother. After Regine has left, the quarrel comes near to violence. At one point, what he says borders on the psychotic: 'Everything will burn. There will be nothing left to remind people of father. And here am I burning down too.' Then he seeks death, but his mother refuses to help him.

Shortly before his collapse his mother presents him with a 'double bind':[38]

> What terrible ideas they were to get into your head. . . . But all just imagination. All these upsets have been too much for you . . . and now you will be able to have a good long rest. At home with your mother beside you, my darling. Anything you want you shall have, just like when you were a little boy.

This is to take control over him just as she had taken control over her husband. She goes on:

> There now the attack's over. You see how quickly it went. Oh, I knew it would . . . see what a lovely day we're going to have, Oswald. Brilliant sunshine. Now you'll be able to see the place properly.

What she offers is unacceptable. Yet there are no other courses open to him. Everything he has tried has been nullified. His capacity to choose is suspended, his will paralysed. Clinically, he has lapsed into catatonia. Existentially, he has cut himself off from an absurd and untenable situation. In the course of the quarrel he has lapsed again into dependence on her. But she fails to understand, and the play ends with her stifled scream in the face of his withdrawal from her.

The future for him has often been supposed to be hopeless, especially when his illness has been assumed to be syphilis. Ibsen has left the ending enigmatic. However, a stage instruction suggests that there is some hope: '*Sunrise. The glacier and the mountain peaks in the background gleam in the morning light.*' No notice has been taken of it in some recent productions that have offered a gloomy prognosis. Yet the psychotherapist to whom he and his mother might in due course have been referred would have found factors in the history that gave prospect of a new dawn for them both in a changed pattern of relating to each other. The mother has been reviewing constructively her relationship with her husband and son, and is ready to break out of the constraints Pastor Manders has insisted on. The family myth has been destroyed. The ghosts can be dispelled, and the future built without evasion or falsehood.

54

Ivanov

Chekhov's play *Ivanov*[39] is a study of the depression suffered by Ivanov, a 35-year-old local-government official and farmer, and a man of talent, whose marriage has turned sour, and who has got into financial difficulties through mismanaging his affairs.[40] It remains unclear in what degree his depression, amounting towards the end of the play to 'melancholia, noble grief, mysterious misery',[41] is the result or the cause of his misfortunes. He himself supposes that he has taken on too much and broken his back under the strain. He had had great plans as a young man, 'believed in different things from other people, married a different sort of wife, got excited, took risks, squandered money left, right and centre, and was happier and unhappier than anyone else in the county'.

The account Ivanov gives of his illness, that is very like that Chekhov himself suffered,[42] shows that he has had periods of expansiveness and excitement, amounting to hypomania, as well as periods of depression. His enthusiasm has made him popular and attractive especially to women. He has 'worked hard enough – has had hope enough – for ten men. I tilted at windmills and banged my head against brick walls.' But as his misfortunes have grown, there has been a vicious circle. 'Once an intelligent, educated, healthy man begins feeling sorry for himself for no obvious reason and starts rolling down the slippery slope, he rolls on and on without stopping and nothing can save him.'

His friends find simple reasons for his unhappiness. He is unhappy, they suppose, because he married a Jewess and did not get the dowry he expected, or because he is the victim of the incompetence of the manager of his estate. His various troubles have got him down, or his environment has done so. But simple reasons are dismissed at several points in the play. Thus Ivanov replies to the doctor, in a rebuke reminiscent of that delivered by Hamlet to Rosencrantz and Guildenstern:[43]

> You think I'm an open book. I married Anna for her fortune. I didn't get it, and having slipped up then, I'm now getting rid of her so I can marry someone else and get *her* money. ... How simple and straightforward. Man's such a simple, uncomplicated mechanism. No, Doctor, we all have too many wheels, screws and valves to judge each other on first impressions or one or two pointers.

His symptoms are typical of a manic-depressive illness (of 'bipolar type'), with swings between hypomania and depression. When depressed, he is irritable, bad-tempered, rude, restless, unable to relax and bored. He has headaches and cannot sleep. He feels mixed up, paralysed, half-dead, empty and exhausted, and trapped. He is unmoved by his wife's illness, and feels he has made a mess of his life. 'There's nothing I hope or care about,' he says. He blames himself, but does not know where he went wrong. His conscience worries him day and night. He feels he is deeply at fault, but cannot make out how. He despises himself, and feels that he has changed although he does not understand why. He does not understand himself, he complains.

The play tells of the tragic development of his illness. He becomes 'heavy-headed, dull-witted, worn out, broken, shattered, without faith or love, with no aim in life', and carries wherever he goes 'misery, indifference, boredom, discontent, and disgust with life'. Add 'still another enemy. That is solitude.'

One turning point is his wife's death, for which he is blamed with brutal frankness by her doctor, a facile do-gooder. He and his wife quarrelled shortly before her death, and she called him 'a rotten, contemptible creature'. He has already embarked on another affair and a year or so after her death plans a marriage that would solve his money problems, although his reasons for marrying Sasha are far more complex than that. But both she and he recognise that to marry would be wrong and would not solve anything.

By the day of the wedding he has come to 'see things in their true light' and has so lost hope that he rejects the simple, optimistic view offered by his oldest friend, his father-in-law to be. When the doctor has called him a cad in public, the final straw has been put on him. There is one way of calling a halt to the vicious circle. 'I've rolled down hill long enough, it's time to call a halt. I've outstayed my welcome.' He shoots himself.

The Father

Strindberg, having read *Othello* and noted the methods used by Iago to arouse Othello's suspicions and jealousy by playing on hidden insecurities, tells us in *The Father*,[44] as if in a guide-book written for malicious wives, of the methods Laura uses more or less deliberately to destroy her husband by driving him insane[45] and having him so declared. Husband and wife have become enemies. She needs him no longer as father and breadwinner and acts to destroy him with a ruthlessness reminiscent of Lady Macbeth.

The theme of the play is summed up in Strindberg's terms as that love between man and woman is war. She does not need to resort to such devices as stealing and planting napkins, as Iago does, but depends on more subtle methods. Thus she works on the gullible doctor and others in order to fan their doubts about her husband's sanity, spreads rumours about him, and interferes secretly in his affairs. The feud flares up in the setting of a struggle between them to gain power and then to decide on the education of their daughter. In confrontation with her wishes, he insists on his masculine superiority and his rights as a father.

Threatened by defeat, she revives his misgivings about the daughter's paternity and her faithfulness so that he develops ideas very like those expressed by Leontes in *The Winter's Tale*. A husband's uncertainty about his paternity is a theme too in Ibsen's *The Wild Duck*, written three years before *The Father*, although it is developed differently. No one can know for certain who his father is. Infidelity can be proved, but not fidelity. To be the biological father may be of great importance in contributing to a man's sense of identity and assuring him of a future. In his child lies his hope of biological immortality.

At the time the play was written there was no way in which the husband, his doubts once aroused, could remove uncertainty. These were the facts of the matter in Strindberg's time. Only during the last few years has it become possible to decide with virtual certainty through the use of the 'DNA profiling' test whether a man is or is not the father.

By treating him as if he were a child, and as if his mind were affected, she destroys his confidence and raises doubts in him about his mental stability. Also, she deceives him so that he entertains ideas of a conspiracy to interfere with him. Provoked by her, he loses control and throws a lamp at her, and thus gives credence to her claim that he is mad and should be certified as insane. In despair, he takes a revolver and prepares to shoot his daughter, but his wife, having anticipated a suicidal attempt, has ensured that the cartridges have been removed. Restraint now being justified for the protection of others as well as of himself, he is tricked into allowing a strait-jacket to be put on him. Now fully aware of what has been happening to him, he suffers a severe stroke and collapses.

At the end of the play the doctor, who has been led by the wife to interpret the husband's symptoms in her terms, recognises at least partially that he has been deceived, that he does not understand the illness, and that there is nothing more that his skill can do. Yet the playwright has described with brutal clarity the steps in the development of the husband's madness.

Blanche Dubois

Blanche in Tennessee Williams' *A Streetcar Named Desire*[46] has come to a crisis in her life. Having left The Flamingo in another city, where in a life of despair she has had 'many intimacies with strangers', she has turned, 'washed up', to her sister Stella in the forlorn hope of finding some sort of love and a degree of security.

The circumstances of her life have prevented her from developing a sense of identity. While still young and innocent, she married a poet, who shot himself after she had told him of her disgust at his homosexuality. Returning to the family's home, she looked after her elderly relatives. As one by one they died, financial difficulties increased, and eventually the home had to be sold. She survived precariously while still good-looking and sexually attractive, but as she has lost her beauty there has been no role remaining to her, and she has become dependent on disabling illusions that deny the realities. The crisis starts with her dismissal from her post as schoolteacher, and then eviction from her hotel, when it is discovered that she is having sexual relations with a pupil.

She has been struggling to preserve in fantasy a fragile image of herself as a gentle and well-bred lady, a Southern belle, in a setting in which the image has been continually under attack from the coarse realities. Her name, Blanche Dubois, she tells Mitch, her suitor, means 'white woods', like 'an orchard in spring'. Stella, in contrast, survives by accepting without restraint the demands of her sexuality and abandons herself to passion with her husband Stanley.

Blanche is lonely and at sea in a world dominated by Stanley's realism. One by one the illusions sustaining her have been destroyed. The loss of the mortgaged family home and plantation, Belle Rêve (which means 'beautiful dream'), has been a serious blow to her. She has lost youth, husband, inheritance, employment and nearly all her family. Mitch, who has shown interest in her, and who she hopes might offer marriage, strips away the mask of gentility and forces her to recognise that she has lost her beauty. 'I don't want realism,' she says. 'Magic, I try to give that to people. I misrepresent things to them. I tell them what ought to be the truth.' He turns the light on to her face in order to have a good look at her, and thus exposes the lies in what she has told him of herself.

The proud but insecure Stanley has felt threatened by her. His confidence has been impaired, and he has become deeply resentful after he has heard her speaking of him as 'sub-human, ape-like'.[47] He humiliates her by forcing her to have sexual intercourse with him. This is a further blow to her self-esteem, and in despair, she enters into a world of confusion, chaotic memories and fleeting wish-fulfilling fantasies which together amount to mental illness.

On her own, rejected by her sister, and forced by Stanley to leave the home, she accepts the kindness of the doctor who has come with a nurse to remove her to a state hospital. She is on her knees, her arms pinioned by the nurse, when the doctor, *personalised* as the playwright's notes instruct, speaks gently and reassuringly to her, addressing her as 'Miss Dubois'. Her terror subsides. In a courtly gesture he offers her his arm and guides her, as if a bride, towards the door. Responding thus to her, he restores her dignity, her illusions of gentility and her sense of personal worth, while she recognises that she has 'always depended on the kindness of strangers'. The ending is one of triumph over disaster, as she leaves the stage with her gentleman caller.

4

THE STORIES PLAYS TELL

Better to shrug worry off if you can,
And try not to think too much about it,
So either you take to the bottle, or lies;
That's it; we made do with fairy stories
About princes and trolls, and birds and beasts;
And bride-stealing, too.

(Henrik Ibsen[1])

Plays are parables, which have an educative purpose. Brecht's play *Mother Courage and her Children* tells of the struggle of ordinary people to survive despite adversity, and his *The Life of Galileo*, of the struggle of scepticism and reason against faith and power. The stuff of plays is story-telling; they tell stories and have plots, in which are contained the themes the playwright wishes to explore. The plot imposing on events a pattern that in real life would tend to be casual and haphazard shapes them into a story that has a degree of coherence.

A theatre group has been described as a 'multi-headed story-teller'.[2] The story does not unfold smoothly, as it tends to do in a novel, but is punctuated by crises when, as a result perhaps of some revelation or event, conflicts between persons over social or political issues come to turning points, which are often marked by the ending of an Act. Much of a play's effects on attitudes depends on the way in which the story is brought to an end. This may be disaster, or order may be restored, conflicts resolved, or evil contained or vanquished.

The stories in plays are about how people behave towards one another, how they communicate and how they interact. Being about relationships and crises, they are of particular interest to those who look for explanations of madness in disorders of relationships,[3] that is, in interpersonal, or social, processes. They illuminate intrapsychic, that is, mental, processes as well.

PATTERNS OF COMMUNICATION

The playwright speaks through the characters, what they have to express being mediated through directly observable speech, movement, gesture and body-language. What is spoken is qualified through the choice of words and their coherence, metre, rhyme and rhythm. During rehearsals the actors, advised by the director, try out different ways of bringing out the meaning in the text without departing from it. Thus they experiment with different positions in relation to one another, or postures, tempos, points of emphasis and so on.

The playwright and/or the director provides a visual commentary by prescribing how the scenery and props should be disposed and lit and by other devices. Reference to continuous rain in *Ghosts*, for instance, with its sound or visual realisation, contributes to the atmosphere of oppression engendered by the text as a whole. The gleam of the light on the glacier and mountain peaks as the sun rises revives optimism at the end. Also, there is a sub-text that is inferred from what is not said or the allusions and pauses in what is said. Other characters or a chorus or narrator may comment on what is being said or done.

Acting and language are the essence of the theatre, spectacle and design being subservient. Modern techniques of acting make possible a more sensitive representation of the playwright's intentions than used to be possible.[4] The inner life of a character is revealed through what the actor does or says, as well as how he is dressed. The playwright thus conveys something of the quality of the experience of madness. Of course not all the representations of madness are authentic in the sense that they are based on sound observations or sound ideas.

The characters in plays tend to speak more to the point and at greater length than people do in real life. The relationship between two characters is defined by what they say to each other and what other characters, or the chorus in the plays of ancient Greece, say about them. Almost all the meaning is conveyed in the language. This is true especially of the plays of ancient Greece and Shakespeare.

Since the second half of the last century, with the introduction of ensemble acting in the 1870s,[5] playwrights have developed increasingly sophisticated techniques, so that more is conveyed in the sub-text than is contained in the words alone. Actors have learned to use posture, gesture, intonation and pauses as pointers. What they say is then closer to what people say off the stage or in the consulting room.

What is not said may be crucial. Esslin[6] takes this example from Chekhov's *The Cherry Orchard*. In the last Act, at the climax of the play, Lopakhin is on the point of proposing marriage to Varya just as they are all leaving, but does not bring himself to do so, and the fateful moment passes. What is said instead is:

V. It's strange. I just can't find . . .
L. What are you looking for?
V. I packed the things myself, yet I can't remember.

The cherry orchard, for Varya's family the symbol of the happiness and stability of their former life, has just been sold, and a new future has to be faced. But neither Varya nor Lopakhin has been able to break out of the constraints derived from the differences in their social position, she as the mistress of the estate, which he, the son of a former serf, has just bought. The audience are left in no doubt about what has happened – something very important, although no word in the text refers to it. The conversation seems to be about some unspecified and irrelevant articles that have been mislaid.

This is surface dialogue. Chekhov's characters tend to talk past the point, hints of the sub-text and the underlying feelings being conveyed through gesture, tone of voice, hesitation or trivial comment. Much is left below the surface, and there is an iceberg of hidden meaning, just as there often is in conversations in the consulting room.

Ibsen too in the plays of social criticism he wrote after 1873 depended on ensemble acting. He left much to be read between the lines. Here is an example given by David Thomas[7] and taken from *Ghosts*. Mrs Alving confronts Pastor Manders, reproaching him for his rejection of her when, nearly thirty years ago, she had come to him in distress after leaving her husband. The incident was crucial in deciding the pattern of each of their lives subsequently.

He: Was that a crime? Never once . . . not in my most secret thoughts – have I ever regarded you as anything other than another man's wife.

She: Really.
He: Helene . . .
She: It's so easy to forget one's own past.

Much has not been said about the misunderstandings between them, his denial of his feelings, and her hurt at his rejection of her. Neither is prepared to run the risk of expressing unequivocally the pain at the heart of the matter.

Harold Pinter, notably in *The Caretaker*,[8] shows how communication, like that between the two brothers, Mick and Aston, and the old man, Davies, is perverted by digressions, irrelevancies, banalities, tautologies and pauses as devices for evading or disguising what bothers them.[9] Words may hide feelings and intentions better than silences by serving as a smoke-screen. The conversations in his plays provide dramatised versions of the very characteristics of what patients say while freely associating that led Freud to speak of resistance, repression and other defence mechanisms.

Pinter is economical in the information he gives the audience, but, though occasionally mystified, the audience are not deceived, even when the characters deceive one another, because the underlying ideas and feelings are indicated by the context and the actors' postures and gestures, as indeed they are indicated similarly by patients.

Pinter's purpose, without deference to psychoanalysis, is not to provide amusing parodies of the speech of the ill-educated or disadvantaged, but to illuminate the contrasts between what is spoken and the underlying feelings, what is spoken being intended not to inform, but to restore or preserve a comforting myth. Although communication may be blocked and vitiated, the characters struggle to convey feelings, which may shine through their inarticulacy. Davies has come to the end of the road and is to be extruded by the two brothers, perhaps a mortal blow to him. The impact of his keen despair is mollified because what is spoken preserves a comforting myth and evokes laughter.

Other playwrights, such as Beckett and Ionescu, have put illogical, confused or banal utterances into the mouths of their characters in order to express the absence of meaning in life or life's futility. Creating thus a surrealistic drama, they initiated in the 1950s what came to be known as the theatre of the absurd.[10]

PERSONIFICATION

The characters in plays are not real persons, though they resemble them. They are the playwright's creations, although he may claim paradoxically that they take on their own existence and speak through him. In writing a play, as in day-dreaming and dreaming, ideas are 'personified' to give the illusion of being autonomous characters. C.G. Jung introduced the term when he wrote of the personification of unconscious thoughts or complexes or ideas. It 'always means autonomous activity of the unconscious', he said.[11] The personification of the feminine nature of a man's unconscious he called 'anima', 'animus' being the masculine nature of a woman's. Through personification, intrapsychic are converted into interpersonal conflicts.

For this reason he encouraged his patients to conduct dialogues with figures from the unconscious as if they were real people in the external world. There are contemporary schools of psychotherapy which propose the technique that the 'I' should stand outside himself and observe as a spectator the images of his experience as if they were being played out by actors on a television screen. It is only a short step forward to propose that the 'I' should likewise observe hallucinations as containing meaning, and not dismiss them as insane as is often advised.

The characters in a play are the products of 'decomposition', through which a group of attributes of a person of complex make-up is dissolved and replaced by two or more characters who are complementary to one another. Formed by rearranging the attributes as if in a kaleidoscope, each is also a 'composite' incorporating two or more ideas through 'condensation',[12] and each is a component of a system of relationships.

Playwrights tend to be well aware of these processes. Thus Ibsen claimed: 'My task has been to create human beings.' His habit was to go through a period of day-dreaming about a new play, perhaps for a year or more, before he started to give it form. Characters gradually established themselves in his imagination. Attributes might be switched from one character to another, the character called Hjalmar in the final version of *The Wild Duck*, for instance, being called Gregers in some of his earlier notes. Halfdan Walle becomes Gregers Werle.[13]

Bernard Shaw, when telling of his method of working, wrote of 'conversations that come into my head unaccountably. It is hallucination; and sane hallucination is what we call play or drama.' Arthur Miller in an interview on television remarked: 'I can't write a character I can't hear,' and elsewhere: 'One learns to listen to what a developing play is saying.'[14] A playwright or novelist may feel elated when taken over by one of his characters, hears him talking, and finds it difficult to write fast enough to get down all he is saying. Karl Miller quotes this comment by an unnamed writer:[15] 'Writing is the passage, entrance, exit, sojourn in me of the other that I am and am not.'

An actor too may feel that he is possessed by the character he impersonates; that is, gives life to. Acting is more than impersonation. It is to recreate and express the experience of the character. In doing so the actor discovers new things about himself.

The playwright converts his imagery into a written text, which in turn is converted by producer and actors into a play. The processes through which characters formed in the playwright's imagination achieve the appearance of reality on the stage are dramatised in Pirandello's play *Six Characters in Search of an Author*. They may be short-circuited, the writing down then being left out.

The personification of imagined ideas to form a fictive character is one of the distinctive techniques of the playwright, but one he shares with other artists, such as novelists or painters. Peculiar to drama are the actor's impersonation of the character and the communication of the ideas to the audience as if felt and expressed in the present by a real person.[16] He plays a person, not a set of ideas. The essence of drama is the actor. The audience attend to what the fictive character says or does, but know that it is a real person who is pretending. Even young children know that the character they see on the stage is a pretend king or a pretend witch.

In the medieval morality plays, virtues and vices are each represented by an actor who engages in the fight between the forces of good and evil. In *The Castle of Perseverance*,[17] written in the fifteenth century and perhaps the earliest surviving play in English, actors represent, amongst other qualities, Lust-liking, Folly, Pride, Wrath and Gluttony, on the one side, and Chastity, Industry, Meekness and Patience, on the other, and also Good Angel, Bad Angel, Shrift, Death and Peace. Good Angel and Bad Angel appear too in Marlowe's *Doctor Faustus*, with Mephostophilis, Lucifer, Belzebub and spirits representing the Seven Deadly Sins.

The characters of more modern plays, especially those written in the seventeenth and eighteenth centuries before the Romantic movement, tend to portray such types as the controlling father, the unruly son, the cunning servant, the deceived husband, the braggart soldier, the buffoon, the would-be poet, the delicate daughter or the warm-hearted whore.

The other self

The different sides of the conflicts engaging the playwright, when personified, are represented or symbolised by seemingly autonomous whole persons. One character represents one side of a conflict, another linked more or less closely with him, another side. Linked characters, if broadly similar, may be described as doubles or multiples;[18] if they differ, but are complementary, one is described as 'the self', the other as the 'second' or 'other self'. The likenesses of self and other self are often but not always as impressive as their differences. They may be twins or companions of similar age and background. Leggatt, in Conrad's story 'The Secret Sharer',[19] who is often cited as an example of a second self, is 'an independent sharer of the mind' of the Captain. Both he and the Captain are seafarers, of the same age, height and build, and they wear similar clothes, as if mirror images of each other.

Gregers Werle in Ibsen's *The Wild Duck*, 'the apostle of truth', and 'an acute case of inflamed scruples', is linked with Hjalmar Ekdal, whose job is the retouching of photographs, and who lives comfortably in a world of half-truths amd make-believe. Both are fully formed, objectively independent characters, but they show a special affinity with each other. They make their first appearance on the stage together, are of the same age and have shared childhood experiences, having regarded themselves as best friends, but the facts of where Gregers has been during the last sixteen years and where he has come from are left unclear.

Objective independence and subjective continuity have been given as the two criteria for regarding two characters as self and other self.[20] Gregers, the outsider who intrudes into the life of the Ekdal family, is a typical other self. He seeks to promote the welfare of the self, or even bring about his salvation, seeing himself as the dog who dives down to rescue the maimed duck. He initiates the action in the relationship with Hjalmar, who registers its effects. At the theatre we tend to identify with the self, our interest being held by what is done by the other self, and what happens in consequence to, or within, the self. Similarly, Hamlet and Laertes are linked.[21] Of like age, both are students, the one a disaffected son, the other a loyal, submissive one. Hamlet is linked too with Horatio, his confidant; both are students at Wittenberg. In *King Lear*,[22] the foolish old king is shadowed by a wise old fool. In *The Seagull*, Treplev and Trigorin, though of different generations, represent the conflicting views towards the theatre that were exercising Chekhov at the time. Some productions of Beckett's *Waiting for Godot* have reinforced the idea that Vladimir and Estragon are complementary and inseparable by making striking contrasts in their physical appearances and clothes.

Gregers and Hjalmar represent the opposed ideas – the dilemmas – that were preoccupying Ibsen after the intense public attacks on *Ghosts*. He had first written *An Enemy of the People* as a riposte. In this play Dr Thomas Stockmann, who is linked with his pragmatic brother, Peter, represents one side of Ibsen – Ibsen was born in Stockmannsgaarden in Skien – and like Oedipus is a determined seeker after the truth about the sources of pollution in society. The injudicious Thomas, showing a troll-like self-sufficiency,[23] comes near to disaster, isolation and madness. The pragmatic, moderate Peter survives. *The Wild Duck*, his next play, is a study of the consequences of Gregers' insistence on bringing home the truth to the Ekdal family; one consequence is Hedvig's death.

Ibsen's plays provide many other examples of linkages. In *A Doll's House*, Nora Helmer and Kristine Linde, friends over many years, show contrasting attitudes towards marriage. Gunhild and Ella in *John Gabriel Borkman* are twins, and in their relationships with Borkman and Erhart (Gunhild's son with Borkman) represent opposed viewpoints, Gunhild setting store by duty, and Ella, by the expression of feelings.

Linked characters are often presented as identical twins,[24] that is, twins alike in their physical appearance, their behaviour then being contrasted in the confusing situations arising when one is mistaken for the other, as in *The Comedy of Errors*. In *Twelfth Night*, Viola and Sebastian, although not identical twins, and of different gender, are alike in appearance and are mistaken for each other. Carlo Goldoni used a similar device in

The Servant of Two Masters, the two, Pantaloon and the merchant, being identical twins. In *The Venetian Twins*, composed too in the tradition of *commedia dell'arte*, the two lovers are contrasted, the hot-headed, foolish Zanetto with the elegant, manly and wise Tonino.

The darker side

The darker side of a person may be represented through decomposition as the other self, which has been 'dissociated' and appears as a more or less independent character. In Euripides' *The Bacchae*, Dionysus serves as Pentheus' other self. They are opposites linked with each other, Pentheus representing grief or sorrow, or *nomos* (law) or the superego, order and control. Dionysus, the teacher of the art of viniculture, and Pentheus' cousin, who was born beyond the pale of Greek society, represents joy or *physis* (that is, the natural) or the id; he embodies split-off, denied or unconscious impulses and fears as well as emotional abandonment and licence.

What happens to Pentheus is as if in a nightmare, being both capricious and miraculous, and as if directed by the god Dionysus, who coming as a stranger and tempter induces madness by encouraging him to express the repressed hedonistic aspects of himself. In his madness he is like an actor in a play within a play. He tries to preserve his sense of identity and authority, but discovers that he has no power to control events. Yet he scorns Dionysus, refuses to recognise his power, and, disturbed by the cult of Dionysus and his worshippers, tries to incarcerate him, in doing so tying up a bull, which is one of the forms in which Dionysus manifests himself, then as rampant with fertility and power.

Although representing denial and repression, Pentheus is a voyeur, at first at a safe distance. While engaging in erotic fantasies, he shows horror for the sexuality of the Bacchic women. Repression failing, he lapses into wildness and sickness, and is killed by his mother and aunts. They too have become mad through the influence of the gods.

The abstemious Pentheus has been advised by Teiresias not to fight against a god, but to participate modestly in the dance and revels in honour of Dionysus. Wine brings benefits, soothes pain, 'stops wretched men from suffering', and is poured as a libation to the gods. To deny any expression to the forces of the other self – the unconscious – invites disaster, he is warned, in terms similar to those in which the nurse warns Phaedra in *Hippolytus*: 'It's not for us to struggle after tiresome perfection.'[25] Not heeding this counsel of sane moderation and of nothing in excess, Pentheus is destroyed. He has failed to strike a balance between reason and passion.

Other plays lending themselves to analysis along these lines include Marlowe's *Doctor Faustus, Othello, Macbeth* and Ibsen's *Hedda Gabler*. Dr Faustus is linked with Mephostophilis, Othello with Iago, Macbeth with Lady Macbeth, or perhaps with Banquo, and Hedda with Eilert Løvborg. The latter in each pair is the other self. On such an analysis the conflict between self and other self is intrapsychic. Iago's power, it has been said, is that 'he represents something that is in Othello'. 'The essential traitor is within the gates.'[26] Freud seized on the idea (which he attributed to Ludwig Jekels) that 'Shakespeare often splits up a character into two personages, which, taken separately, are not completely understandable and do not become so until they are brought together once more into a unity'. The Macbeths are just such a pair, he added.[27]

The rejection of Dionysus is a theme in Ibsen's later plays. Oswald, like his mother, is denied the joy of life. Rosmer rejecting Dionysus brings about the death of Rebecca, his other self, with whom he has a special affinity. Ibsen himself, middle-aged like Faust and at the peak of a career that had given him little satisfaction, did not enter into any contract with the devil, as Faust did, and succeeded in separating himself from the Dionysian attractions and dangers of Emilie Bardach, his companion while on holiday in the summer of 1889. His controlled intellectual side won over the indulgent sensual.[28] Having broken off his correspondence with her, he returned to the writing of *Hedda Gabler*.

Hedda Gabler

Hedda and Eilert are linked with one another. Denial of sexuality has often been seen as the key feature in her personality. Eilert, her other self, represents Dionysus for her, and she imagines him as 'crowned with vine leaves'. Vine leaves in his hair are referred to in the text on no less than nine occasions,[29] and

Tesman talks of Bacchanalia when he tells her about Judge Brack's stag party. But there is a striking contrast between the Dionysus she imagines him to be and how others see him. The stage instructions specify his hair as dark brown, whereas Dionysus has flaxen locks, and describe him as 'the same age as Tesman, but looks older and a little haggard'. Other characters see him as a drifter who has wasted his talents.

Hedda, trapped in domesticity, is a spectator from a safe distance, a voyeur, of the Dionysian revels. Her strange power over Eilert has led him to tell her of his exploits while 'out on the razzle for whole days and nights', and she has been able to find out at second hand, vicariously as Helene Alving does from the Chamberlain, about 'a world she isn't supposed to know about'. 'Too much a coward' to risk a scandal, she has also been fearful that the danger would become a reality.

She speaks of 'this secret intimacy' with Eilert, 'this companionship that no one even dreamed of', but denies that there is any love in her relationship with him. He is her animus who personifies her masculine nature. What he represents for her is both fascinating and frightening. She cannot do without him, yet wants him to die a beautiful, noble death. In the event he dies a sordid death, in which she has played little part, except as the provider of the pistol.

His death leaves her incomplete, her sense of identity and integrity destroyed, and at the mercy of Judge Brack, who combines law and control with licence (and indulgence), and she can no longer resist the impulses of what Ibsen calls her 'demonic substratum',[30] and shoots herself. Suicide, when one self kills or is killed by the other, provides irrefutable evidence of the duality of a person.[31]

FANTASY AND REALITY

Some plays claim to be, and are accepted, not as wish-fulfilling fantasies, but as naturalistic representations of reality. They create the illusion of reality, the impression being given of something that is really happening,[32] though a reality that has various levels of meaning. Other plays are like dreams. Reality testing is in abeyance, though less so than while dreaming, distinctions not being made between fantasy and reality.

That events and objects have meanings going beyond their

manifest characteristics is made plain in the theatre. The masks worn in the theatre of ancient Greece were devices for causing the actors to be seen not as individuals but as personifying a more universal theme and, paradoxically, favouring the expression of mental conflicts that would otherwise remain hidden.

In Ibsen's *Ghosts*, the burning down of the orphanage at the end of the second Act, an event in a story, is shown to mean much more; it is also the destruction of the false picture the mother has given the son of his dead father. The white shawl Rebecca is seen crocheting at the beginning of *Rosmersholm*, real enough at one level, has also a symbolic connection with the white horse that is later spoken of with fear as presaging death; it is later to become a wedding veil, then a shroud.[33] In *The Lady from the Sea*, the pollution of the waters of the inner fjord, in which Ellida bathes each day, represents the deceptions poisoning the life of the Wangel family. In Osborne's *The Entertainer*, the dacaying music hall is a metaphor for Britain, the comedian keeping his despair at bay by sentimental appeals to the glories of the past.

In some plays the illusion is closer to dreams than to reality. This is especially so in the plays written for the small, experimental, intimate theatres that sprang up in many European cities at the end of the nineteenth century in reaction to the commercial theatre. These theatres, which allowed a closer contact between actors and audience, dispensed with theatre drops and footlights, and properties were kept to a minimum.

The intention of the new theatres, such as Antoine's 'théâtre libre',[34] had been to foster naturalism and realism, but paradoxicaly encouraged illusion when further devices were used, as they were in Strindberg's 'Intima Teatren'.[35] In *A Dream Play*, he used a magic lantern to project what he called 'dissolving views'.[36] Set and dialogue left out the details that would create a framework of realism. Actors, with a minimum of make-up, were encouraged to improvise. Monologue, mime and ballet helped to maintain the illusion. Examples of his plays intended to be experienced as dreams are *To Damascus*, *A Dream Play* and *The Ghost Sonata*.[37]

In the theatre of the absurd, of which Strindberg was a pioneer, there is no clear distinction between fantasy and reality. An inner landscape replaces the outer world; mental conditions are represented on the stage in the form of visual and auditory metaphors. The outer world is absurd because it is without justification or purpose and inexplicable.

Bertolt Brecht

Brecht created a different illusion. The boundary between self and non-self, ego and non-ego, is preserved. The audience should be not participants through identifying with characters on the stage, but spectators who, being constantly reminded of the artificiality of what happens on the stage, distance themselves from it – the *'Verfremdungseffekt'*.[38] His intention was to foster emotional coolness and detachment, although that is not always how it works out.

Falling under the spell of the play, the audience are jarred into wakefulness by reminders that it is a play. Disconcerting events, contradictions and incongruities contribute to the strangeness and create through wonder a new understanding of the human situation. The audience are thus made to think and reflect on the lessons to be learnt from the events depicted – hence the idea of the 'didactic' play. Brecht, fascinated by exceptional individuals, tended too to put the events into the past and gave his plays an 'epic structure', the narrative being interrupted with a dialectical commentary or song and dance. At times he entertained hopes that his plays would not only enlarge understanding, but actually contribute to the reshaping of society. The people in many of his plays are the poor and disadvantaged.

In Brecht's theatre the actor does not impersonate a character. His approach is not psychological, but critical. Thus he demonstrates and comments on those elements of a person's behaviour that are relevant to the situation being described. The play does not recreate past events; it gives a report on them. The audience do not identify with any of the characters; they interest themselves not in the characters, but in the story – the fable – in which the characters are involved. The story is more like a report told at a clinical meeting about the patient and his family than reports told by the patient and his family about their experiences.

The play studies not human nature, not the inner life of the characters, but human relations and the way characters behave towards one another, and also 'Gestus' – the outward signs of social relationships such as deportment, intonation and facial

72

expression. Behaviour is then viewed in its context of events and circumstances and is not reduced to factors within the person.

Brecht was of course not alone in his emphasis on the context of behaviour; nor was he the first to remind the audience of the artificiality of the events portrayed. Again, it has become commonplace in recent years for the audience to see the actors before the play begins, moving about informally on the stage or in the auditorium as ordinary people and chatting with one another. The actors then put on their masks, figuratively though seldom actually, and the audience are thus encouraged to enter with the actors into a world of make-believe.

At the end of the make-believe the actors destroy the illusion, declaring the play to be at an end, and present themselves as now out of character and seeking the applause of the audience. These are old devices. Thus Puck (Robin) at the end of *A Midsummer Night's Dream* turns to the audience and says:

> If we shadows have offended,
> Think but this – and all is mended –
> That you have but slumber'd here
> While these visions did appear. . . .
> So, good night unto you all.
> Give me your hands, if we be friends,
> And Robin shall restore amends.
> (5.1.414–7; 426–8)

SYSTEMS THEORY

In considering the context of behaviour, particular attention is given to the part a person plays in his relationships with other persons within a system – that is, an organisation of two or more other persons interacting with each other in such a way as to regulate each other's behaviour. The concept of a system is given meaning by a specialised psychological theory derived from cybernetics,[39] that treats behaviour not as discrete reactions to stimuli, but as exchanges in the interaction between a person and a machine or one person and another, one's response serving as a stimulus to the other. A husband and wife form such a system. This is open in the sense that it is also part of one or more other systems, such as a nuclear family, which in turn is part of an extended family, and that, part of a community.

A system gives a degree of stability to its members because it reacts to external events homeostatically – that is, in such a way as to preserve unchanged the relationships of its members to one another. Homeostasis fails, and the system is disrupted, if something happens of such force or significance as to compel a change in the terms of the relationships. This brings a crisis or turning point.

A family may come to a crisis when the myth governing their attitudes towards one another has to be abandoned. A family myth[40] is a fiction that provides a comfortable formula for regulating and explaining how individual members relate to each other. It is made up by what they say about how they relate. This may be very different from what they are observed to do.

The crisis is followed by a period of disequilibrium,[41] or instability, while the members explore the implications and consequences of what has happened. There is then a further turning point when decisions are taken. This in the Greek play is the 'peripeteia', which may be preceded by 'anagnorisis' – that is, the recognition by a character of his true state. Sometimes the result is reconciliation, although then usually on different terms from before. That is, the system is reorganised, with perhaps the extrusion, or sacrifice, of one or more of its members. Sometimes the system breaks up more or less completely, with estrangement of its former members. Sometimes events move towards disaster.

A simple example – the ways in which a couple behave towards each other – are governed by unwritten rules and expectations. A quarrel brings their relationship to a crisis, and there follows a period of instability, during which they explore, separately or together, the implications and consequences of what has happened. Perhaps they then separate, or there is reconciliation on terms different from before. The unwritten rules have been revised, and expectations modified, to provide a sounder basis for a continuing partnership. Indeed, quarrels often serve to ensure that the basis evolves to their mutual satisfaction and is up-dated from time to time – hence the general acceptance that 'the course of true love never did run smooth'. Others may be implicated in the quarrels between two lovers, as they are in *A Midsummer Night's Dream*.

The sequence can be summarised in a formula which supposes there to be three phases, corresponding roughly to the beginning, middle and end of the play: crisis (or challenge), exploration and reorganisation. There are three similar phases in traditional pre-Reformation drama: fall from grace, redemption through repentance and atonement, and return to grace, followed by salvation. In a comedy the three phases may be separation, tribulation and reunion. Comedies end in reconciliation. Villains are unmasked and repent in the last minutes of the play, and are restored to their place in the community as redeemed members.

A modern critic writing about Ibsen's *Pillars of Society*, *A Doll's House* and *Ghosts* uses different terms: 'All three plays document a process of emancipation by ordeal; and all three principals are driven on from some earlier and more rudimentary stage of personal integrity and freedom to a more advanced and enlightened one.'[42] That is, the challenge to the system results, after an intermediate stage, in reorganisation on more progressive or more enlightened terms. The phases in another modern formulation have been called confrontation, reordering and renewal.[43] As a general rule, a play is about one or more crises in the relationships forming a system, and what happens can usually be covered without undue stretching by the three-phase formula.

In Shakespeare's *Macbeth*, the terms on which Macbeth can relate to the king, Malcolm, Banquo and others change when the campaign against the Norweyan lord has ended in victory. His role as trusted general and valiant warrior has come to an end. This is the first crisis. His encounter with the witches starts off, or perhaps reflects the start of, his exploration of the consequences of his demobilisation; these he discusses with Lady Macbeth. The system at the royal court is disrupted irreparably when the king is murdered. The investment of Macbeth as king in his place does not restore stability, and the system disintegrates, with dispersal of its members, some of whom go abroad. At the end of the play, Macbeth being dead, Malcolm, now named as king, states in the closing speech of the play the terms on which a new order is to be established; these include 'the calling home' of 'our exil'd friends abroad, That fled the snares of watchful tyranny' (5.6.105–6) and his crowning at Scone.

There are many plays in which there is a similar sequence. In

Othello, one crisis starts with Desdemona's attachment to Othello, another with Cassio's promotion, and a third with the departure from Venice to Cyprus, which is the centre of disorder. The threat of invasion by the Turks and the storm at sea are symbols of disorder. The return of the survivors to Venice at the end of the play represents the restoration of order in the third respect. In the first and second respect, events end in disaster, without reconciliation.

SUMMARY

Characters are created out of the imagination of the playwright. Each represents a more or less complete person – that is, 'personifies' the thoughts and feelings the playwright wishes to explore. Also, each is a product of 'decomposition', by which the complex make-up of a person is dissolved and replaced by two or more complementary or 'linked' characters, who may be described as 'doubles' or 'self' and 'other self'; the other self tends to represent the darker side of a person. The characters in a play are akin to those in a dream, but are filled out with more detail and put into a more realistic context so that they convey the illusion of being real. Intrapsychic conflicts are played out in plays as in dreams indirectly as conflicts between people. Plays are about crises in systems of relationhips between people. Three phases can be recognised: crisis or challenge; exploration of the implications and consequences of the crisis, and reorganisation of the system on new terms.

5

REALITY AND ILLUSION

Lovers and madmen have such seething brains,
Such shaping fantasies, that apprehend
More than cool reason ever comprehends.
The lunatic, the lover, and the poet
Are of imagination all compact:
One sees more devils than vast hell can hold;
That is the madman.

(*A Midsummer Night's Dream*, 5.1.4–10)

THE ILLUSION OF REALITY

This chapter continues the discussion started in the last under the heading 'Fantasy and reality'. Plays differ in the degree to which they provide a realistic setting for the action on the stage, but, however realistic it is, much that is portrayed is in the realm of fantasy. In Ibsen's social plays, written between 1877 and 1890, from *Pillars of Society* to *Hedda Gabler*, the characters, relatively few in number – five in *Ghosts*, for instance – all give the illusion of being fully formed persons, presenting themselves as real although their reality is illusory. The illusion is supported by a realistic setting in that the action goes on in a reception room in a home, for instance, furnished with tables, chairs, portraits, flowers, a stove, lamps and ornaments, and very different from the spaces in which plays are acted out in our dreams.

Especially after a play has been seen several times, the characters in it come across as almost as real as the people met in everyday life. Hedda's husband, Jörgen Tesman, is almost as real as the teacher met in a university common room. More than shadows, the characters in these plays are more or less distinctly defined by reference to their histories and roles. Also, they relate realistically to the objects in the physical environment, Tesman fussing over his slippers and his learned journals, or Hedda handling pistols, in *Ghosts*, Regine watering flowers, Manders disapproving of Helene's books, or in *Rosmersholm*, Rebecca crocheting a shawl.

They are coloured too by the names they are given, and these in turn take on colour from the characters they are attached to. A journalist in *An Enemy of the People* is coloured by being called Billing. The colour given to Rector Kroll, Rosmer's harsh brother-in-law, or to Ulfheim, the earthy landowner and bear-slayer in *When We Dead Awaken*, is hardly spoilt in the translation from Norwegian to English. In the other direction, such names as Hamlet, Peer Gynt and Hedda Gabler have come to evoke the ideas associated with the characters.

The action in Ibsen's social plays is firmly rooted in time and place. Helene Alving's home is sited on a fjord in the west of Norway. In *The Wild Duck*, Haakon Werle's spacious and well-appointed house and the Ekdals' modest home, similar in many respects to the house at Venstøp where Ibsen spent much of his childhood, are both realistic representations of homes with which the audiences of the time were familiar.

Yet in the Werle house there is a concealed and unseen realm, the office, from which the clerk and the old father embarrassingly emerge in the middle of a celebratory party. The studio in the Ekdal home is a realm both of fantasy, in which Hjalmar day-dreams about the castles in the air he will build when he has achieved his invention, and of reality, where the everyday activities of the family take place. Also there is the unseen and mysterious realm of the loft in which Old Ekdal can indulge in fantasies of happy days spent hunting in the woods, and from which disturbing influences emerge, just as they do from the unconscious.

Rosmer's study has bookshelves and cupboards and an old-fashioned sofa, and the house is reminiscent of a particular house on the edge of Molde, where Ibsen had spent the summer of 1885.[1] One may speculate about the location in Kristiania (now Oslo) of the house of the privy counsellor's widow that has been bought by Tesman with the help of his aunts to satisfy Hedda's whim. Her world is where the respectable live, a few hundred yards higher up Drammensveien, one may suppose, from Vika, where Madamoiselle Diana's establishment is situated.[2] Judge Brack, Eilert and Tesman move freely from the one world to the other as if there is no frontier between them. But Hedda stays out of the world inhabited by Diana and her like.

In the plays after *Hedda Gabler* the action tends to move out of rooms in a house and to take place in a garden or on a hillside. In *John Gabriel Borkman*, the first move is from the realm of reality downstairs to the realm of fantasy upstairs, Act One being in Mrs Gunhild Borkman's realistic sitting room, Act Two on the storey above where the recluse John Gabriel lives out his life dreaming of what might have been been or might be. The last scene is on the edge of a wood. The ground has a deep covering of freshly fallen snow, from which the only light is dimly reflected. Occasionally the pale moon is visible. This is the scenery not of real experiences, but of dreams.

Typically in Ibsen's late plays the human characters become aware of the powerful forces outside them which govern the world. John Gabriel and Ella contend with the cold and the snow and ice on the mountainside, the 'dreamland' of their lives, but the hand of ice clutching at his heart, which presages his death, is a symbol for the love he has killed in Ella.

Likewise in *When We Dead Awaken*, the set for Act One is a realistic representation of the outside of a spa hotel, with tables, chairs, newspapers, drinks and so on, and with views of trees, the fjord, promontories and islets. But Rubek, waking at night, sees from the window 'a white figure in among the trees', accompanied by another figure – 'like a shadow'. This is the first appearance of Irene, a stranger, with a relation to him like that of the Stranger to Ellida.

Whereas Ellida dismisses the Stranger, Rubek and Irene in Act Three enter into another realm together. This is 'a wild precipitous place high in the mountains'. Dawn is breaking; the sun has not yet risen. Rubek and Irene, facing the raging winds on the mountainside, and refusing to take refuge in the safety of a hut until help can arrive, are caught up and overwhelmed by the powerful forces of an avalanche. Ulfheim and Maia, the other couple who are more closely tied to reality, choose to clamber down to the safer and less glorious life of the valley.

Similar distinctions between the realms of reality and fantasy are made by Shakespeare although he uses little or no scenery. His audience are aware that what is being enacted is on a stage, the location being conveyed through the dialogue. The first Act of *A Midsummer Night's Dream* is said to take place in Athens, with which his audience would not have been familiar, though they might have heard certain things about it. The time and place of the second Act, with the move to 'the wood, a mile without the town', is conveyed in Puck's comment, 'The King doth keep his revels here to-night' (2.1.18).

This is the setting for experiences with no more than loose ties to reality. Here, in the freedom of the natural world, emotion rather than intellect rules, just as it does in the loft or on the mountainside. There is a return to Athens (4.2), with restoration of order and sanity, but a sanity which is commented on by the mechanicals' play *Pyramus and Thisbe*. There are four worlds interacting with one another: the worlds of the court, the lovers, the fairies and the mechanicals.

In *As You Like It*, there is a similar contrast between the court of the usurper Duke Frederick and Arden, to which Duke Senior and his 'co-mates and brothers in exile' have moved, and of which it can be asked: 'Are not these woods/More free from peril than the envious court?/Here feel we not the penalty of Adam' (2.1.3–5). The woods are a place of wish-fulfilment and healing.

Strindberg's dream plays

Ibsen's later plays anticipated the changes in the audience's attitudes that came about in the experimental theatres opening at the end of the last century. Strindberg, exploiting the new opportunities, encouraged his audience in 'Intima Teatren' to follow the action on the stage as if it were a dream. Not seeing the whole room on the stage, the audience's imagination is set in motion, he argued, and completes its own picture. There should be no interruption in the action and no interval therefore.

He had deliberately written the parts of the protagonists in his earlier plays, such as *The Father*, as somewhat lacking in character; split and vacillating, they are agglomerations of past and present culture, he said, to be filled out as characters by the imagination. Minor characters, on the other hand, such as the priest and the doctor, are to appear as everyday human beings.[3] In the later 'dream' plays, the characters, with few exceptions, are not named, other than as types, such as father, mother, old man, the poet, a naval officer and so on. Several of his plays were written to imitate dream experiences. The characters are given little definition. Hardly more than shadows, they make a fleeting appearance. In *A Dream Play*, there are forty-one characters; in addition there are dancers, singers, clerks, children, schoolboys and sailors, who move in a kaleidoscopic way in front of 'a background of banks of clouds like crumbling slate mountains, with ruined castles and fortresses' – the landscape of a dream.

About the characters in *A Dream Play* and *To Damascus*, Strindberg wrote:[4]

> Time and place do not exist; on an insignificant basis of reality the imagination spins, weaving new patterns; a mixture of memories, experiences, free fancies, incongruities, and improvisations. The characters split, double, multiply, evaporate, condense, disperse, assemble. But one consciousness rules over them all, that of the dreamer.

In *To Damascus I*, many of the seventeen characters, such as the Beggar and a Madman, are aspects of the Stranger, who represents the playwright himself. Products of the Stranger's imagination, perhaps dream images, they appear on the stage as figures rather than characters or real people. They engage in soliloquies. Ibsen's social plays, in contrast, contain no monologues and no asides.

To Damascus I is a jumbled review of the playwright's own experiences during the 'Inferno' period,[5] not only his life with Frida, his second wife, and his separation from her that had brought on the turmoil of the inferno, but also his strife with God and his grudging acceptance of God's existence and of punishment from a just God. These last ideas reflect what he had learnt from Swedenborg, whose writings had given him solace, and had thus played a part in his recovery from madness. Also, there are versions of his honeymoon with Frida in Heligoland, his borrowing of money, his inability to support his children, and his stay in hospital in Paris. Of specialised interest is his account of a *déjà vu* experience in the gorge near Dornach.[6]

Dream plays have distinctive features. The characters are not rounded, full persons, but figures – representatives or even stereotypes, sometimes grotesque. Time and place are ill-defined. The action in the play is episodic rather than continuous. The spotlight of attention moves erratically from one figure to another, but the dreamer, like the madman, sees 'himself as the pivot of all that happens',[7] or, as Strindberg puts it, the dreamer's consciousness 'rules over them all'.

Peer Gynt

Strindberg had learnt from Ibsen's *Peer Gynt* about the representation of dreams. What happens to Peer in Act Two of this play, especially while he is in the kingdom of the trolls, is nightmare or psychosis, for there Peer sees almost 'more devils than vast hell can hold'. It provides a more vivid description than any other play of the experience of acute psychosis. There are of course many other examples in plays of acute and severe psychotic breakdowns, such as those of Orestes, Ajax, Heracles and Ophelia.

Some scenes in *Peer Gynt* can be seen as presenting reality, the wedding party at Haegstad Farm in Act One, for instance, with its many features of country weddings in Norway. Ostracised by his peers at this party, Peer Gynt abducts the bride, Ingrid, ravishes and abandons her. Pursued by her family and angry villagers, he meets, now as if in a dream, three sexually inviting saeter girls with whom he dances across the hills. The scene changes and he imagines himself to be the honoured guest at a banquet in his wealthy father's house, where he is proclaimed as born out of greatness and destined to become great himself. Peer's father, like Ibsen's, had suffered financial disaster, and the reversal in the dream in the father's fortunes and his own aggrandisement can be seen as wish-fulfilment.

At this point, rushing forward, he collides with a rock and falls motionless. One critic has argued that what happens afterwards is 'delirium following this blow on the head'.[8] An alternative, and I think, preferable explanation is that he has entered into a world of psychotic fantasy as a result of his guilt over his ravishing of Ingrid and his exclusion from the community. 'Sin binds us together,' Ingrid claims. But he feels bound to Solveig.

Whatever is the explanation of the sharp change in his mental state, Peer, guilty, frightened and unsure of himself, enters into a dream world in which his recent experience is transformed and recapitulated. Meeting a 'woman in green', whom he lusts for, courts and marries, he enters into the kingdom of the trolls. She being the daughter of the troll king, he presents himself boastfully as the son of Queen Aase. Although received as an honoured guest, he has to submit to the scratches, teasing and threats of the troll children and other indignities, amongst them, being given a tail to make him acceptable as a suitor. He is to be cured of his tyrannical human nature, but refuses to submit to operations on his eyes which would make him see everything askew yet bright and fair. He is in a topsy-turvy world, in which everything has another meaning, and black seems white, ugly seems fair, great little and foul clean. He fights to escape, but not before he has been told that he will be the father of a 'cub'.

He is challenged by the Dovre-master, the troll king, to assent to the creed among the trolls, not 'to thine own self be true', as for men 'under the radiant sky', but 'to thine own self be – enough'. He demurs, but agrees although not understanding what the creed implies. One of the themes to which the play returns on several occasions is Peer's search for understanding of what it means to be oneself.

Some of the elements in his dreams are wish-fulfilments. Whereas the girls at the wedding spurn him, those at the saeter and the woman in green accept him as he is. Some elements reflect guilt over what he has done, some, uncertainty about himself. Others are threatening and arouse fear and horror. He tries to flee, first from the kingdom of the trolls, where he is fenced round by the young trolls, and then from the great Boyg, whom he encounters when he has escaped from the troll kingdom. He tries to break free, but is prevented from doing so, in a way typical of an anxiety dream, by ill-defined forces, against which he struggles, but in relation to which he finds himself powerless. He does not get an answer to the question he puts to the Boyg, who puts it back to him, 'Who are you?'

The Boyg, for whom there is a counterpart in the folklore of the Norwegian valleys, is a large, invisible, slippery, shapeless monster, who blocks his escape, but cannot be conquered because he will not fight. He personifies the forces that prevent the anxious from taking any effective action. Feeling smothered and exhausted, Peer is saved when church bells and hymn-singing are heard. The Boyg's voice shrinks to nothingness, gasping: 'He's too strong. There are women behind him.'

He has rejected the degraded life of the trolls, and has accepted that he has lusted after the woman in green and is dependent on women. Yet he has shown an exclusive pre-occupation with self, as well as uncertainty about who he is, and has hallucinated the voice of the Boyg. These characteristics are shared by dreamers and the mentally ill.

In the scene after he has got away from the Boyg, he is seen building a wooden hut, into which he invites Solveig. Jubilant, he goes to fetch some wood for fuel, but meets – hallucinates – a woman with an ugly, lame child, who claims him as father. 'Shamefaced and ugly', he feels unable to go to Solveig – 'to meet her like this – just as I am – would be sacrilege'. His happiness destroyed, he takes flight – 'to go round about' – and sets out on a long journey. He must bear the burden alone, and try and forget Solveig. 'Repentance? Why it might take me years before I won through.'[9]

At the wedding party Solveig has been given a degree of reality as a member of a family, with her parents and sister, and she has had a brief conversation with Peer's mother, Aase, but in the hut scene and later she exists for Peer alone; there is little to define her in reality, and she can be seen as largely if not wholly a creature of Peer's imagination.

At the beginning of Act Four, Peer, now middle-aged, is seen as a host at the lavish entertainment of businessmen. This scene, with its many ironic comments on the commercial and political issues and habits of Ibsen's time, marks a partial return to reality. The scenes that follow blend reality and dream. After being saved providentially from the explosion on the yacht, on which his guests have embarked, he becomes elated – hypomanic, one might say – develops grandiose ideas about his special position, and, first as Sir Peter and then as prophet and emperor, enters into an erotic adventure with Anitra. He has her in his power but she eludes him, as so often happens in the dreams of the hypomanic; these tend to start as wish-fulfilments and to end in bewilderment and frustration. In the scenes that follow, more nightmare than dream, he is plagued again by doubts about who he is – 'Wer bist du?' the echo behind the Sphinx asks him in a Berlin dialect – then finds himself as a visitor in the lunatic asylum in Cairo and a witness to the desperation of the inmates.

The account in Act Five of his return and reminiscences as a shipwrecked old man to familiar places in Norway can be regarded as a reverie in which a drowning or dying man reviews his life. He meets the Dovre-master again, and is given the same advice as before – 'to yourself be enough'[10] – which he rejects, blaming the trolls that 'My royal Ego's in hock'. Nearing the end of his life he accepts that he has lived like a troll without recognising it. He has owed his success in hoisting himself to the top of the ladder to following the creed of self-sufficiency that distinguishes trolls from mankind. In his reverie he returns to Solveig and asks her:

> Then say, if you know!
> Where was I? Myself – complete and whole?
> Where? With God's seal upon my brow?

and she replies:

> In my faith, in my hope, and in my love.

ALTERNATE PERSONALITIES: THE FAUST LEGEND

Another model of psychosis is to be found in the Faust legend. Doctor Faustus, in Marlowe's play, a middle-aged pedant at the peak of his academic career, which has given him little satisfaction and brought disillusion, and, like Marlowe himself, a renegade student of theology and an apostate, agrees a contract with Lucifer and enters through the exercise of necromancy into a fantasy world in which he is able to carry out as a changed person actions he would have repudiated in his normal state, in order to achieve in fantasy the satisfactions he has been denied in reality. It is the power that attracts him.

> O what a world of profit and delight,
> Of power, of honour and omnipotence, is
> Promis'd to the studious artisan![11]

But he gives power over himself to Mephostophilis, who may be seen as his other self. Once he has done so, he feels he is damned, his soul forfeit. The Good Angel and the Bad Angel fight for his soul. They are the counterparts of the Virtues and Vices personified in the morality plays of the Middle Ages. He becomes the target of the violence of temporal forces, and is tempted to destroy himself: 'then swords and knives, poison, guns, halters and envenomed steel are laid before me to despatch myself'. In the end he dies violently, with his 'limbs, all torn asunder by the hand of death'.[12]

The play is about the struggle between the two sides of Doctor Faustus, the controlled intellectual side giving way in what may be seen as a mid-life crisis to the indulgent sensual. When the latter is in the ascendant, he betrays his ideals of pursuing knowledge. His manner is jocose and exuberant, his antics ludicrous or mad buffoonery, and he is driven by ambition. He pursues riches and pleasures, as if acting out day-dreams, but the demands he makes are seen by Mephostopholis as 'frivolous'; what he achieves is trivial. He overreaches himself,[13] his ambition for rich rewards and power driving him into wild, dangerous and ultimately tragic actions.

When the controlled intellectual side is dominant, he tends to be cast into deep despair and to feel himself to be beyond pardon. The other side shows reckless ambition. The two sides may be seen, the one as depressive, and the other as manic. His pranks are then like those of patients suffering from hypomania, in which form of illness the reckless pursuit of power and pleasure, with delusions of grandeur, serves to cover despair. The sense of being beyond pardon is felt in both phases: 'The serpent that tempted Eve may be saved, but not Faustus.' In both Marlowe's *Doctor Faustus* and Goethe's *Faust*, the scholar turns to supernatural powers in the search for fulfilment and lives out in hallucinatory experiences what he has failed to live out in reality.

The Faust legend provides a model for functional psychosis of manic-depressive type, especially for that form of mental illness seen in a person, typically middle-aged, who has depended on intellectualisation as a defence against forbidden impulses. Ambitions for power and sexual needs not being met in other ways, he gives expression, at least in fantasy, to impulses previously held under control. As a result the person, like Doctor Faustus, feels damned and in the power of or even possessed by the devil, who is hallucinated as a tempter. The devil reconciles hidden and hitherto unexpressed hedonist wishes with a persona as a reasonable and disciplined person.

It is too simple to see such a person as caught up in a struggle between the forces of good and evil or ego and id. Doctor Faustus, the scholar and idealist, is egocentric, greedy and ruthless, whereas Mephostophilis, the fallen angel, with experience of both heaven and hell, is the ironic realist and critic who exposes self-deception. In Goethe's play, Gretchen, who is seduced by Faust, can hardly be seen as a symbol of innocence, for she sells herself for jewellery and kills her baby. Splits in personalities do not create neat antitheses.

Variations of the Faust legend are to be found in several plays. *The Blue Angel*, a film made famous by Marlene Dietrich between the two world wars, tells of the moral destruction of the professor who, like Faust, looks for hedonistic satisfactions he has hitherto been denied in his academic life. Vaclav Havel's *Temptation*[14] tells of the moral and perhaps physical destruction of Doctor Foustka, a disillusioned scientist in a state institute in an unidentified country, perhaps in Eastern Europe, who engages in forbidden studies of the hermetic, or the occult, and in doing so puts himself into the power of Fistula; that is, Mephistopheles.

STRANGERS AND INTRUDERS

In many plays a shadowy figure, an alien or a 'stranger', appears who, although outside the main action, exerts a strong influence on the course of events by expressing hitherto hidden or unacknowledged thoughts. He may be seen as the other self[15] or as an intruder from the unconscious. Dionysus presents himself to Pentheus as a stranger.

Another example is the ghost of Hamlet's father, who appears to Hamlet on the battlements and utters the disturbing ideas: 'Revenge his foul and most unnatural murther' (1.5.24); that is, kill his step-father, but leave his mother 'to heaven'. He vanishes into the ground, and his voice is later heard again from 'beneath'. Personifying ideas residing in the unconscious, he expresses the son's oedipal anger towards the person who has displaced him in his mother's affection.

Another example: the witches at their first meeting with Macbeth put into words the ambitions already in his mind and set him on the course toward his killing of Duncan. At their second meeting they confirm his delusion that he is invulnerable, but also represent the hidden forces who determine his fate. Other examples in Shakespeare's plays of strangers or outsiders who articulate hidden thoughts are the Fool in *King Lear* and Touchstone and Jaques in *As You Like It*.

Similar strangers intrude in several of Ibsen's plays. In *Rosmersholm*, the disturbing outsider Ulrik Brendel articulates the hidden thoughts of Rosmer and Rebecca, and puts them on the course that ends in the millstream. In *Little Eyolf*, the Rat-Wife articulates for Rita her hidden desire to be quit of her crippled son and for Alfred his rejection of him. Alfred has just returned from a walking tour in the other unseen realm of the mountains, and is still preoccupied by his dream-like adventures there.

Of particular interest is the Stranger in *The Lady from the Sea*, who appears to Ellida when she is severely depressed because of her rejection by her husband and step-daughters. He represents her one-time fiancé. Daring to break free from the shackles of convention he has had an adventurous life at sea, with which she too has a 'special affinity'. She has felt that 'he was somehow of the same kith and kin as those sea-creatures'. 'I too almost felt as though I were one of them,' she says. 'He belongs out there in the open sea.'

Her fiancé had died in mysterious circumstances, but has come back as a drowned man from the dark sea to claim her. Talk by minor characters about rumours of the return of the mysterious sailor have aroused her expectations. Like Leggatt in 'The Secret Sharer', he is an outcast and a stowaway on the run after killing a man. He represents for her something of what Eilert represents for Hedda Gabler, her Dionysus, though without vine leaves in his hair. He has a mysterious power over her and represents for her something that 'draws, tempts, lures me into the unknown! That contains all the concentrated power of the sea!' She speaks of him as within herself, as demonic, and who 'scares and attracts'. When her husband offers to protect her, she replies: 'There is no external power or force threatening me. The pull is within my own mind. And what can you do about that?'

The audience first see the Stranger as a shadowy figure on the other side of the fence of the family's garden, but he does address Ellida and her husband, and on two occasions climbs over the fence. Ibsen leaves the audience in doubt whether the Stranger has any existence in reality, and objected to any description that specifies who he is. 'Nobody is to know *who* he is or what he is actually called,' he wrote. 'Precisely this uncertainty is the main thing in the method I have chosen.'[16]

Anthony Storr,[17] in his short biography of Jung, discusses him as an example of what Jung meant by 'animus', her inner being, or the personification of the masculine nature of her unconscious.

FROM INTERPERSONAL TO INTRAPSYCHIC: HALLUCINATORY EXPERIENCES

The return of the dead as tormentors

There are many other examples in plays of a shadowy character who, like the ghost of Hamlet's father, returns from the dead as if hallucinated, and who is a tormenting intruder. The gorgons (Furies) hallucinated by Orestes represent the mother he has killed. They are not seen by the audience although to Orestes 'they're clear, real – the hounds of mother's hate', and he 'screams in terror'.[18]

In many instances the hallucinations are visual rather than auditory. In Euripides' version,[19] Orestes cries out, with reference to his mother, 'She'll kill me – where can I escape?', and the herdsman comments that 'no such sights were to be seen'.

In *The Family Reunion*, a modern version of the Orestes story, Harry hallucinates his tormentors ('Eumenides') as always there, very close, spying on him, although he does not see them. He complains: 'Why do you play me, why do you let me go, only to surround me?' 'They were always there', he tells his uncle, 'but I did not see them.' And then: 'They are here, I tell you. . . . Are you so imperceptive that you could not see them?'[20] They make a brief appearance on the stage.

The ghosts of those he has murdered appear to Richard III in his dreams on the eve of the battle of Bosworth and bring him despair. Brutus, in *Julius Caesar*, while he sits reading at night before the battle at Philippi, sees the ghost of Julius Caesar as a 'monstrous apparition' that makes his 'blood cold' and his 'hair to stare'. The ghost of the murdered Banquo appears to Macbeth, 'the very painting' of his fear. Macbeth accepts him at first as real, and then dismisses him, saying 'Hence, horrible shadow! unreal mock'ry, hence!' Clarence, in *Richard III*, tells on the eve of his own murder how one whom he had 'stabbed in the field by Tewksbury' appeared to him, and 'shrieked': 'Seize on him, Furies, take him into torment.' In *The Changeling*,

Alonzo's ghost, showing his hand with the severed finger, appears to his murderer De Flores, who in denying him any significance remarks: "Twas but a mist of conscience.'

Perhaps the commonest hallucination met with in clinical practice is the return, as a short-lived wish-fulfilment, of someone who has died or been lost. The dead person is seen or heard, or his presence is felt in some way. A more elaborate wish-fulfilling fantasy is told of in Shakespeare's *Pericles, Prince of Tyre*. *'Diana appears to Pericles as in a vision,'* the stage instruction says (5.1), just after Pericles has been reunited with his daughter, whom he had supposed had been killed. He hears 'most heavenly music', and then Diana appears to tell him where he will find his wife, whom he had supposed to be drowned.

Sometimes the person hallucinated is not dead, but estranged, with intense guilt being attached to him. Phaedra, tormented by her guilty love, hallucinates Hippolytus as calling her 'filthy bawd' and 'traitress to her master's bed'.[21]

Other hallucinations

Many plays tell of hallucinatory experiences. The source of a hallucinated voice may not be identified. The tormented Woyzeck in Büchner's play, harassed by powers he has no control over, asks of the voices he hears from below the ground: 'What are you saying? Louder, louder! Stab, stab the she-wolf to death?' 'Does the wind say it too?' In the barracks he hears a voice speak from the wall and say, 'Stab, stab, and flashes between my eyes like a knife.' On the following morning he tells a companion of his dreaming. 'Wasn't it of a knife? What silly dreams one has.' But he buys a knife and stabs the woman, Marie, who has been unfaithful to him. Similar 'command' hallucinations are occasionally experienced by the mentally ill, and are warnings of violence.

Waiting for Godot

One further example will suffice to show the wide variety of the hallucinations described in plays. Ibsen's characters contend against what are represented as the impersonal forces of nature. The forces Estragon and Vladimir in Beckett's play are dimly aware of are equally capricious, but are imagined as persons. Pozzo declares himself to be demonstrating to them his power over Lucky. Godot, although awaited, does not appear. At the mercy of capricious and mysterious forces Estragon and Vladimir cannot change their situation because they are waiting for Godot. The scene is 'a country road'. There is a tree and a mound as the only definition of the reality. Estragon (also called Gogo) and Vladimir (Didi) converse, so passing the time when there is 'nothing to be done', the situation being hopeless. 'It would have passed in any case.' They lack any sense of purpose, other than trying to find some meaning in the confused world they are on the edge of. This is the reason why the play is seen to belong to the 'theatre of the absurd' – absurd because the ideas they express reflect the helplessness and futility of struggle in a world without purpose.

Unwilling subjects of what others say to them, they play games, and keep talking about trivialities in order to drown out the voices that assail them. The veil their chatter draws over their preoccupations is transparent although it disguises. They talk of the comments being made about them by persons with 'dead voices' who have no representation in the real world, but come from a world hidden to them and the audience. For this reason their imagery, although they share it, is hallucinatory. Here are some extracts from a passage in which they talk about what they are experiencing.

> E.: It's so we won't think. ... All the dead voices.
> V.: They make a noise like wings.
> E.: Like leaves.
> V.: Like sand. ... They all speak together.
> E.: They rustle.
> V.: What do they say?
> E.: They talk about our lives.
> V.: To have lived is not enough for them.
> E.: They have to talk about it ...
> V.: (in anguish) Say anything at all.[22]

They personify what they hallucinate; those who talk about their lives are persons, albeit dead persons. The voices are intrusive; if they are disturbing they are only mildly so. They are disowned. We are not told what they say. That belongs to the sub-text and has to be inferred.

Hallucination in mental illness

It is not uncommon for those who are impoverished in their mental lives, such as some vagrants, to tell of vague auditory hallucinations like those of Estragon and Vladimir. The mentally ill who hallucinate tend to be as reticent, puzzled or ignorant as Estragon and Vladimir are about whose are the voices that talk about them and what the voices say. The voices tend to be intrusive and preoccupying. They are usually referred to one or more persons, who may or may not be identified, occasionally to an animal. Sometimes the voice is recognised as that of a parent or grandparent or lover, sometimes that of a foreigner. What is heard is not always a voice. Strindberg heard on one occasion a musical tune, on another, a turning wheel, but attributed what he heard to the player or operator, whom he thought to be a former rival.[23]

Jung[24] remarked of the imagery of dreams: 'the affect of the traumatic complex is typically represented as an enemy or as a wild and dangerous animal'. The mad are sometimes represented in plays as birds or beasts; for example, the inmates of the madhouse in Middleton and Rowley's *The Changeling* so dressed themselves (3.3.197) for the entertainment at Beatrice's wedding.

On one occasion during her mental illness in 1904, Virginia Woolf heard King Edward VII lurking in the azaleas 'using the foulest language possible'; on another, the voices came from the birds outside her window talking Greek.[25] Edward VII probably represented her imperious and recently dead father. Greek, although perhaps not birds, had a special significance for her because of the importance attached in her education to prowess in it.

As another example of hallucinated voices not being human: Margot Ruddock, an admirer of W.B. Yeats, tells how a dog had said suddenly to her: 'Run, run for your life. . . . It did not speak with a voice, but I heard it in my mind. I thought it meant the bliss was dangerous and I must run to shake it off.'[26]

A dog when hallucinated may have a more specific significance, whether for a patient or a character in a play, especially if it is black, for it may then represent the devil or a witch's familiar, as it does in Dekker, Ford and Rowley's *The Witch of Edmonton*. In this play the dog eggs Frank on to kill Susan, and induces madness in Ann Ratcliffe, as well as laming a horse, nipping a sucking child, and stopping churned cream from setting. These mischiefs are typical of the repertoire of witches.

A mysterious black poodle appears to Faust in Goethe's play, and undergoes transformation, as a result of Faust's incantation, to become Mephistopheles. Peer Gynt in the storm at sea at the start of the last Act shows some confusion between the devil masquerading as a passenger and the ship's dog. In *Little Eyolf*, the 'broad black nose' of the dog, Mopseman, who accompanies the Rat-Wife as her familiar, gives the clue to the magical part the dog is to play in luring the children to destruction. Occasionally a mentally ill patient when telling of hallucinating a black dog refers to it as Satan or his/her own darker side.

Mysterious forces we have no control over may be represented in folklore as an animal. Nøkken in Norwegian folklore,[27] who may be seen at dusk in rivers or in the mist of a waterfall, personifies the demonic powers of water, which can overturn boats or lure a person into the water so that he drowns. Emerging as a white horse he presages death, as he does at Rosmersholm. In Lorca's *Blood Wedding*, the horse that takes Leonardo straight to the door of the Bride's dwelling almost against his wishes, symbolises sexual drives,[28] as does the white horse that plays a key role in Peer Gynt's attempts to seduce Anitra.

An important point about any instance of hallucinating is how far the person tests the reality of the imagery. Banquo questions the reality of the witches, when Macbeth does not. Are they 'fantastical' (1.3.53), he asks, or 'bubbles' of the earth (79)? Have Macbeth and he 'eaten of the insane root'? Macbeth holds to the ideas derived from his meeting with the witches. Such ideas persist if they are not corrected by testing. The therapeutic task in such cases is to create the conditions in which they can be reviewed in the light of other experience.

Hallucination has traditionally been regarded as a disorder of perceiving, being so defined in dictionaries; for example, as 'apparent perception of an external object not actually present'.[29] But it is better to regard it as a form of thinking or imagining. Its imagery is a fragment of a day-dream or dream – day-dream rather than dream since in the functional psychoses it is auditory more often than visual. Its similarity to dreaming has been recognised over many centuries.

AGENTS AND PROCESSES

Note that a person when hallucinating personifies ideas and attributes them not to intrapsychic processes within himself, but to a living agent, either to the other self or to intruders, whether human, divine or satanic. 'The other self is the basis of an hallucination,' it has been said,[30] but this is perhaps too general a statement.

The distinction between agents and processes is crucial. Explanation in terms of agents has a long history. In the plays of ancient Greece the manifest cause of the madness in every case is a divine agency – that is, lies in action by the gods, who are metaphors for powerful natural forces affecting behaviour, some with their origins in the unconscious. Mortal men had to recognise and propitiate them or otherwise come to terms with them.[31] Homer described the inner life as a personified interchange between a man and his parts or as initiated from a source other than the person: a god, part of the person or another person. The soul – the psyche – is a part person capable of a more or less independent existence. There was then a widespread belief (animism) that spirits pervade and control the world.

As a result of the growth of science in the Renaissance in the sixteenth and seventeenth centuries, explanations of mental events changed from attributing them to agents, as capricious, even as mischievous, in their behaviour as the gods, to attributing them to natural processes subject to discoverable laws. Thus contemporary psychologists explain hallucinations in terms of mental, intrapsychic processes. Patients, on the other hand, may insist on describing them in terms of external agents. Even in the enlightened 1990s there are some who attribute the manifestations of madness to agents outside the patient, such as evil spirits, thus providing a rationale for the practice of exorcism as a technique for expelling them. Ordinary people too may see their behaviour as out of character and attribute it to something – or a puck – that has got into them.

Plays describe experiences in terms of agents. Their stories follow a tradition of giving coherence and organisation to experience and thus conceptualising and commenting on it by personifying processes and ideas; that is, by representing them as persons who are given an existence on the stage. In this way they are externalised, and intrapsychic conflicts are converted into interpersonal conflicts. The ghost of Hamlet's father externalises the fantasies Hamlet entertains about his father and the manner of his death. These fantasies are shared in some degree by his companions.

DISTINCTIONS BETWEEN REALITY AND FANTASY IN RECOLLECTIONS

Old Times

Plays explore the relation of fantasy to reality in other ways. In Pinter's Old Times, a study of 'the highly compressed stage poetry of recollected experience',[32] Deeley and his wife Kate, now in their early forties, recall experiences they shared twenty years or so ago. One theme then was the rivalry of Deeley and Anna for Kate's affections.

Their relationships turn out to have been more complicated than this simple theme suggests. There are doubts whether Anna is a real person or a fantasy in a dream shared by Kate and Deeley while they review their marriage. Kate taunts him by telling of Anna's imminent visit. Anna, the intruder, is the ghost who returns to haunt them. Was it he who twenty years ago had intruded into Kate and Anna's relationship, not only as a rival with Anna for the possession of Kate, but also making a pass at Anna? Had they ever freed themselves from Anna? Has she come to reclaim Kate?

The mismatching of their reminiscences shows the vagaries, blurring, evasiveness and ambiguity with which they distinguish in their memories between what was real and what was fantasy. Anna makes the point: 'There are some things one remembers even though they never have happened; but as I recall them so they take place.' The versions they give of events change kaleidoscopically as they explore and interpret what they recall as if in a dream, which for Deeley becomes a nightmare since it ends with his extrusion as the odd man out, while Kate remains as self-sufficient and as unattainable as before. How people come to see one another thus depends as much on fantasy as reality.

SUMMARY

The theatre creates the illusion of reality, but much of the action lies in the realm of fantasy. This may have its special place, such as the loft in the Ekdal home (in *The Wild Duck*). 'Intruders' may represent hidden thoughts, such as the Witches in *Macbeth*, Ulrik Brendel (in *Rosmersholm*), the Stranger (in *The Lady from the Sea*) and the Rat-Wife (in *Little Eyolf*). Scenes that have a degree of realism may be followed by scenes in a dream world, as in *A Midsummer Night's Dream*, in which the action moves from daytime Athens to a wood at night, or in *When We Dead Awaken*, in which the realistic setting of the outside of a spa hotel is followed by the dream-like landscape of the mountainside. In 'dream' plays, like Strindberg's, there are many shadowy figures, rather than rounded characters, and the action is episodic, with erratic shifts of attention and kaleidoscopic transformations. 'Memory' plays like *Old Times* show how unreliable are the distinctions made between reality and fantasy when past experiences are recalled.

Of special interest are plays like *Peer Gynt* and *Doctor Faustus*, because they provide models of psychoses. Peer's experiences as the baffled victim of devils in the form of trolls are like those of a nightmare or a psychosis. In a sequence like that in manic-depressive disorders, the disillusion and despair of Doctor Faustus, a middle-aged pedant and renegade, is replaced, with the help of the devil's representative, by the indulgence and jocosity of his search for riches and pleasure, the end being a hideous death. There are many examples in plays of the return of the dead in the form of ghosts or hallucinations: the Furies appearing to Orestes, as representatives of his murdered mother, his murdered father to Hamlet, Banquo to Macbeth, and their victims to Richard III and Julius Caesar.

6

FAMILY FEUDS

The fiercest anger of all, the most incurable, is that which rages in the place of dearest love.[1]

Plays are interpreted in the light of the ideas prevailing at the time. Sevententh-century audiences saw Hamlet as a malcontent, comically mad as all lovers are.[2] For David Garrick, he was a prince caught up in a web of intrigue. Eighteenth-century audiences discovered his psychology, but without medicalising his contemplative melancholy, which they saw as part of his character; he was a man habitually afraid of spectres. For the Romantics, he was caught between thought and action. In the nineteenth century the melancholy was seen by the newly emerging profession of psychiatry as evidence of a deficiency in brain or mind, for which there is also evidence in his suicidal tendencies (the product of an excessive melancholy), as well as his impulsive loss of control, moral weakness as shown in his capricious and obscene behaviour towards Ophelia, blunted emotional response, and indecisiveness and incapacity to act.

Modern interpretations have been strongly influenced by psychoanalysis, which has deemed him to be neurotic, his indecisiveness and incapacity to act, his intense emotional response to his mother's remarriage, his hostility to his father, and rejection of Ophelia, all seeming to reflect unresolved oedipal conflicts. Particular importance has been given to his vacillation in the prayer scene when he might have been expected to kill Claudius, had he not been restrained by oedipal conflicts, which Freud identifies as the essential process underlying Hamlet's neurotic behaviour.[3]

In some recent productions he has been presented as either a bungler or a pawn caught up in the power games being played by Claudius, as the usurper of the crown, Polonius, the main minister, and Fortinbras, who brings forces to bear from outside.[4] Polonius, now an adept political schemer in a corrupt society, is very different from the 'weak, pedant, minister of state' of Samuel Johnson.

Also of interest is the use other playwrights have made of themes they have seen in *Hamlet*. Heiner Müller, the East German, has abstracted in his fragmentary script *Hamletmachine* the theme of the intellectual struggling in vain after a failed revolution to come to terms with a world on the brink of annihilation.[5]

In this chapter I put illnesses into the context of destructive quarrels or feuds, within or between families, which tend to be sustained in some degree by struggles for power, in some degree by more complex drives. The antagonisms being sustained and not readily modified, I prefer the word 'feud' to 'conflict'. Feuds expressing rivalries and revenge may lead to disaster or death. Romeo and Juliet are victims destroyed by the feud between their families.

In many of the cases I have offered as models, the madness has arisen out of persistent hostilities between members of families. This is true too in the Indian epic poem *The Mahabharata*, recently dramatised by Peter Brook,[6] which tells of the rivalrous feud between two branches of a family, the Pandavas, who are the sons of Pandu, and the Kauravas, the sons of Dhritarashtra. Pandu and Dhritarashtra are half-brothers. The feud affects several generations and has enormously destructive results.

Plays tell how processes which in some circumstances knit individuals together into a harmonious and beneficent family become distorted in other circumstances so that individuals act violently and destructively toward one another. Intense, even murderous feelings may be generated and endure when there are quarrels between family members – between parents and children, or husbands and wives, especially so when children are implicated. In half the cases of murder in contemporary Britain, the victim is a member of the family; in many of these the victim is a child of the murderer.[7]

This flux between the constructive and destructive tendencies in relationships is the central theme of many plays – between love and hate or 'the hatred of love', as Strindberg calls it, which is 'born in hell'.[8] 'No wound strikes deeper than love that is turned to hate' is Creon's warning to his son about Antigone, his son's betrothed.[9] The essence of tragedy lies in the turning of love into hate, with the consequent destruction, moral or physical, of one or more of those implicated.

In many cases the quarrels at the heart of the play may be seen as being between one generation and another. Orestes, Hamlet and Oswald quarrel with their mothers. In *King Lear*, the quarrel is between father and daughters. In others, the core of the dissension, although expressed as a quarrel between generations, lies in conflicts in a marriage, such as that of the parents of Orestes, Hamlet and Oswald. On the other hand, Lady Macbeth, Leontes, Ivanov and the Captain (in *The Father*), all become ill in the setting of marital discords without reference to the parental generation. However, as a general rule, discords in one relationship tend to be associated with discords in others. In some cases it is the children who suffer, as does Perdita, Leontes' daughter, and Bertha, the Captain's daughter. Conversely, a sound partnership between the parents tends to be associated with harmonious relationships between parents and children and also between the children.

Nevertheless, a broad distinction between vertical and horizontal relationships is convenient for purposes of exposition. A vertical, or in the jargon of social psychology an intergenerational, relationship is one between a person of an older and a person of a younger generation, such as parent and child, uncle and nephew, step-parent and step-child, or parent and child's lover, and a horizontal relationship, one between persons of the same generation: sibs and step-sibs, or married or other partners.

To refer to either a vertical or a horizontal relationship is to pick one component out of a complex pattern. To focus on Hamlet's relationships with his mother and step-father may be a good way of summarising what happens in *Hamlet* because it brings out a particular pattern, but the story so told is but a biased version since it draws attention away from the conflicts in the horizontal relationships between Hamlet and Ophelia and Hamlet and Laertes.

The Oedipus complex is a convenient rubric for the discussion of the relationship between a parent and a son. Likewise the names Lear, Phaedra, Don Carlos or Cain, for example, may be attached to other patterns of relationships, but without

99

intending to reduce their stories to particular attitudes to be regarded as crucial.

The point in the life cycle at which a story is started is chosen for its convenience in serving the playwright's purpose. How the child sees his parents is determined by how they behave towards him, and how they behave towards him reflects their experiences as children. How one thing follows from another is vividly illustrated in the story told of the Pandavas and Kauravas in *The Mahabharata* or of the Atreus family in *The Oresteia*. To pick out the son's anger toward his mother as the essential underlying process starts the story at an arbitrary point.

VERTICAL RELATIONSHIPS: PARENTS AND CHILDREN

Broad patterns of feuds have been identified, special importance being given by Freud and his followers to the combination of a son's jealous hostility towards his father and his erotic interest in his mother. Ernest Jones,[10] in his account of *Hamlet*, puts the love for the mother first, when he sums up the play as 'a highly elaborated and disguised account of a boy's love for his mother and consequent jealousy of and hatred towards his father'. St Mark (13.12) is more even-handed: 'Now the brother shall betray the brother to death, and the father the son; and children shall rise up against their parents, and shall cause them to be put to death.'

Not all the enmities between fathers and sons are accompanied by rivalry for the mother's affection. Some reflect struggles for power in other respects. The prize won by Oedipus for solving the Sphinx's riddle was the throne. For some psychopathologists – for example, Fromm[11] – the essence of the Oedipus complex lies in the son's rebellion against the authority of the father rooted in the patriarchal structure of society; incestuous strivings towards the mother are then an inessential component. In the prophet Teiresias' view, Oedipus is first 'father-killer' and then 'father-supplanter'.[12]

Prince Hal, a rebellious son

Prince Hal's attitude towards his father the king in Shakespeare's *Henry IV, Part 1*[13] serves as an example. The son's rebellion is but one component of a complex pattern. The king is pained by the waywardness of the young prince – 'See riot and dishonour stain the brow/Of my young Harry' (1.1.84–5) – which he sees as punishment for his own 'mistreadings' (3.2.11). The prince, gaining maturity through 'education in a tavern', where he meets Falstaff, accepts the need to rehabilitate himself in the king's eyes, so that when the king, who sees him as 'my near'st and dearest enemy', tells him 'thou hast lost they princely privilege/With vile participation' (86–7), he replies, 'I shall hereafter . . ./Be more myself' (92–3).

Rebellion, followed by emancipation and then reconciliation on new terms or, less happily, estrangement, is a common pattern in adolescence, reconciliation being achieved in early adult life. Having established independence, the young person can see parents in less idealistic, more realistic terms, and is then free to transfer his or her affections from the parent of opposite sex to a person of the same generation. The parent may resent this transfer.

The reconciliation of Prince Hal and the king is completed when the prince saves the king's life in battle. The king, recognising the regard the prince has for him, assures him that his reputation has been redeemed. On his death bed (in Part 2) the father is able to hand over gracefully to the son the power symbolised by the crown.

King Oedipus

Freud's version of the Oedipus legend puts the emphasis strongly one way: on the son's jealous hostility towards his father and his erotic interest in his mother. 'Being in love with one parent and hating the other', Freud supposed, are among 'the essential components of the stock of psychical impulses'[14] formed in childhood and important in determining the symptoms of later neurosis.

Freud wrote about the impulses reported by patients of themselves as sons. He discovered the Oedipus complex in 1897, the year after his father's death, in the course of the self-analysis which he had then begun, and which included the study of his own dreams.[15] He selected from them the themes that reflected his own feelings towards his parents. His version of the legend, leaving out the attitudes of the parents towards sons and each other, shows, it has been said, 'a scotoma for the less creditable aspects of the conduct of fathers'; the son is seen as the sinner.[16] Psychoanalysts were slow to recognise the part played by the father's hostility to the son.[17]

At the centre of Sophocles' play is the prophecy at the oracle that the child will kill the father, hence the father's fear of him and his instruction to the mother to kill him at birth. Little weight is put on the son's sexual interest in the mother. Jocasta remarks of it: 'Nor need this mother-marrying frighten you; many a man has dreamt as much. Such things must be forgotten, if life is to be endured' (ll.980–1). Freud too, in his earlier writings, pays less attention to this component than to the son's hostility to the father.

As much psychopathological interest lies in the father's fear of the son.[18] The father fearful of his son is a stock character in the theatre. In Shelley's *Prometheus Unbound*, as in the Greek myth, the secret that Prometheus will not reveal is that if Jupiter marries Thetis he will beget a son more powerful than himself. Jupiter had previously ousted his father. The fear may be greater in royal families when the son is the heir apparent.

Laius' fear had started before the son was born as a result of the oracle's warning. Men are met with in clinical practice who fear that a son as yet unborn will oust them from the affections of the mother. This fear may become more acute after the child's birth, and interfere with the incorporation of the child into the family triangle.

There are important themes in *King Oedipus* other than those Freud picked out. One is the demonstration that efforts to escape from what fate has decreed may have a paradoxical effect and bring about what has been most feared. Thus Oedipus' departure from Thebes, intended to frustrate the prophecy that his father would die at his hands, puts him on the road to Thebes where he meets and kills him.

Another theme is Oedipus' insistence on searching out, without regard to the warnings about the dangers of doing so, the truth about the causes of the pollution in the community. 'O never live to learn the truth!' (l.1067) is Jocasta's plea to him. The results of his uncovering of the truth are that she hangs herself in 'desperate passion' and bewailing her sins, and Oedipus blinds himself.

Freud's thesis has nothing to say about her suicide, nor his blinding, although this has been discussed as a symbolic castration. The playwright writes of 'eyes that should see no longer his shame, his guilt'. His distress after learning the truth arises out of the nature of what he has done rather than his intentions, which have been innocent.[19] Yet acting on his personal responsibility he has compromised in his obedience to the gods. Exiled from Thebes he wanders from country to country, accompanied by his daughter Antigone, eventually coming to Colonus, where he is hounded to death by the Erinyes, who have a grove there.

Hamlet: a son displaced from his mother's affections

Freud chose *Hamlet* to illustrate the effects of oedipal impulses, arguing that 'the child's wishful fantasy' of the father being dead remains repressed, and 'we only learn of its existence from its inhibiting consequences', whereas in *King Oedipus* it is 'brought into the open and realized as it would be in a dream'. The consequences seizing Freud's attention lie in 'Hamlet's hesitations over fulfilling the task of revenge that is assigned to him'. Hamlet cannot kill Claudius because Claudius in killing the King and marrying Gertrude has realised the very wishes of his own childhood, now 'repressed', to kill his father and marry his mother.[20] But there is evidence in the 'To be, or not to be' soliloquy that his indecisiveness is not special to his task of revenge and affects other matters as well.

Shakespeare called his play *Hamlet*, and not *Claudius*, although it is as much about the step-father as the son. The title has led critics into seeing the conflicts as arising from the son's attitudes, but in *Hamlet*, as in *King Oedipus*, the aggression of the parent-figure towards the child is at least as marked as that of the child towards the parent-figure. The aggression is not simply the reaction of the one to the other, but is mutual and arises out of the interaction between them.

Hamlet's anger and resentment are directed towards the step-father, whom he sees as murderer and usurper and as displacing him from his mother's affections. He expresses no antipathy to his father and speaks well of him – 'So excellent a king' (1.2.139) and 'He was a man, take him for all in all, I shall not look upon his like again' (187–8). But he has been put on the path of revenge by his ghost, who represents motives of which he is unconscious.

His courting of Ophelia is obstructed by Polonius, a father-figure and ally of his step-father, and his feelings for Ophelia are confused by his conflicted attitudes towards his mother and hence women in general. On the other hand, Claudius, made aware by the Gonzago play of Hamlet's beliefs about the death of his father, and fearful lest he becomes violent, takes steps to protect himself and 'will fetters put upon this fear' (3.3.25), invoking the help of Rosencrantz and Guildenstern to have him detained and confined.

The mother, although worried, is less pressing. Ophelia too has been affrighted by Hamlet's strangeness. He has been teasingly rude to her father. The crisis in the system of relationships has been brought about not only by Hamlet's father's death and his mother's o'erhasty marriage, but also by Claudius' assumption of the throne and Hamlet's quarrel with Ophelia.

Hamlet entertains fantasies, on the one hand, of avenging his father by killing his step-father and is preoccupied, on the other, with his mother's trespass in going with 'most wicked speed' and 'such dexterity' to his step-father's – 'my uncle's' – bed. The two are close to the two components of the Oedipus complex. In consequence, he abandons his life as a student in Wittenberg, to stay at the court in Elsinore, and brings his courtship of Ophelia to a disastrous end. Why does he not return to Wittenberg after the funeral, and disengage from conflicts with his family? He is easily persuaded by Claudius not to leave Elsinore. Is it that he shows the strong fixation to the complex that Freud regarded as typical of the neurotic? Or does he stay because of his love for Ophelia? His attachment to her argues against the view that he has a strong sexual interest in his mother.

Displacement from his mother's affections contributes to a son's anger. Much of Orestes' anger towards his mother is due to her adultery with Aegisthus, much of Hamlet's to his mother's going to Claudius' bed. In Chekhov's The Seagull,[21] Treplev, like Hamlet, an introspective student, resents Trigorin, his mother's lover. Preoccupied with his mother he does not return to his studies. The rivalry intensifies when Trigorin displaces him in the affections of Nina, a young girl – a theme that does not appear in *Hamlet* – and he challenges him to a duel. He kills himself when he recognises his failure in art as in life.

Another theme in *The Seagull* not apparent in *Hamlet* is the mother's (Irina Arkadina's) jealousy of the son's girl-friend, whereas Gertrude had 'hop'd thou [Ophelia] shouldst have been my Hamlet's wife' (5.1.238). The mother's displacement from her son's affections by his girl-friend, and hence her jealousy and possessiveness, often highly sexualised, is a theme in several plays; for example, D.H. Lawrence's *A Collier's Friday Night*.[22] The rivalry between mother and girl-friend is more likely to arise when mother and father are estranged.

Hamlet differs in this respect from most of those who show in adult life a preoccupying attachment to the mother. His parents' marriage had been loving. 'So excellent a king, . . . so loving to my mother . . . she would hang on him/As if appetite had grown/By what it fed on,' he tells us (1.2.143–5).

King Basilio and Prince Segismundo

A father's fear of his son is a theme in other plays, such as Calderón's *Life is a Dream*,[23] the fear in this case being shared by the mother. The son, Prince Segismundo, is born in special circumstances. 'His mother time and again, between reality and raving', dreams that she is giving birth to some montrosity in human form, who, stained in her own blood, is killing her by being born, 'the human viper of the century'.

Here described is the transformation of her fear of the child into psychotic ideas. Also, there is an eclipse of the sun, an earthquake and storms, and the mother dies. The father, Basilio, then consults a horoscope and, learning that his son would rule with tyranny both for other people and himself, imprisons him in a tower.[24] Shutting him away from the court, he withholds from him any information about his identity.

Basilio's cruelty towards his son causes confusion, frustration, anger and violence, the very behaviour the horoscope has predicted, and he has tried to prevent. This is another illustration of the paradoxical effect that, as the adage puts it, 'dangers breed fears, and fears more dangers bring'. In the course of the play he decides to subject Segismundo, now a grown man, to a test of his capacity to rule, the test being carried out under conditions in which the son is deceived about what is dream and what reality, his misinterpretations being matched by the self-deceit and deception of many others.

The feud between father and son divides the people into two factions. The son being victorious acts generously toward the father who, as the son says, 'made me a brute, a human beast'. 'This way of life and strange upbringing were enough to make my whole behaviour wild: a fine way to prevent me being so.' The father being enlightened about the error of his ways, the play ends in reconciliation.

THE FEAR OF THE OLD FOR THE YOUNG

Count Cenci

Among other plays portraying a father's destructive impulses towards his children is Shelley's *The Cenci*,[25] which has been called 'dramatised autobiography',[26] and which is based on a story Shelley had heard in Rome of a rich and noble family brought to extinction. The father had conceived 'an implacable hatred toward his children', with 'an incestuous passion for his daughter', who had plotted with her mother-in-law and brother to murder their common tyrant. Despite most earnest prayers to the Pope the three criminals were put to death.

Shelley puts the fears of the villainous father into the wider context of 'the great war between the old and the young'. Count Cenci, like Basilio, a character more out of a nightmare than the real world, gloatingly celebrates the deaths of two disobedient and rebellious sons. He has ruined a third by squandering his wife's dowry, and commits 'wrongs darker than death or night' on his daughter Beatrice. Having raped her, he curses her in terms as horrible as those Lear uses in cursing Goneril, wishing her to be polluted by evil, which is symbolised as a syphilitic disease.[27] He hopes that she will die 'plague-spotted'. He is himself murdered by assassins hired by his son Bernardo, his daughter Beatrice and his wife Lucretia. It is Beatrice, the daughter, who takes the decision that he should be killed.

Cenci is a less tragic figure than he might be because the play gives no explanation of his actions and motives. Beatrice's actions arise out of her horrendous sufferings. Cenci's death she sees as the only way she, Lucretia and Bernardo can save themselves, not only from physical destruction, but also moral corruption. Shelley comments: 'No person can be truly dis-honoured by the act of another.' 'Revenge, retaliation, atone-ment, are pernicious mistakes.' 'The fit return to make to the most enormous injuries is kindness and forbearance, and the resolution to convert the injurer from his dark passions by peace and love.'[28] So to respond denies any direct expression to anger. In *The Winter's Tale*, Leontes, suspicious of the paternity of not only his son but also the infant girl newly delivered by his wife, rejects her as a bastard and orders that she be destroyed. The infant, like the infant Oedipus, is abandoned in a deserted place. Similar doubts about the paternity of a child are portrayed in many plays, not only in *The Father*, but also in Schiller's *Don Carlos*, in which the father rejects his daughter after his suspicions have been aroused. Hjalmar in *The Wild Duck* shows signs of rejecting Hedvig when he becomes suspicious of his wife's fidelity.

Paranoid ideas aroused when a wife is pregnant may take other forms. In Eliot's *The Family Reunion*, the father wants to get rid of the mother and plots to kill her, but is stopped by the mother's sister. Otherwise the son whose birth is due in three months would have been killed; later the sister comes to regard the son as her own. Mothers too may show destructive impulses towards their children, as did Segismundo's mother. Another example is Rita's rejection of her son in *Little Eyolf*, and her resentment of her husband's interest in him.

DAUGHTERS AND MOTHERS

Electra

The term 'Oedipus complex' has also been applied to the combination of a daughter's hostility towards her mother and sexual impulses towards her father. Less often, but following C.G. Jung,[29] the term used is the 'Electra complex'. In Aeschylus' *The Libation Bearers*, Electra, unmarried and still grieving for her father Agamemnon, killed long ago by her mother Clytemnestra and Aegisthus, feels bitter enmity for her mother and encourages her brother Orestes to kill them in retribution. She has been described as a female Hamlet.

In Euripides' *Orestes*, written fifty years later, Electra plays a more active part, and Orestes, guilty, desperate and frenzied, acts brutally and with hatred in a feud extending beyond that with his mother and her lover. Courts of justice already existed to which Orestes might have had recourse instead of taking revenge himself. His depravity and desperation is further shown in the plan he makes with Pylades to kill Helen and take Hermione as a hostage. The play ends with Orestes and Pylades on the roof, holding a drawn sword at Hermione's throat. Helen has been saved from death by the gods. Electra is on the point of firing the roof. Menelaus and his men watch in horror.

The impasse is complete until Apollo intervenes as *Deus ex machina*, and thus reaffirms law and order in a way that marks a striking change in the mood of the play. In Euripides' *Electra*, Castor and Pollux hand down *ex machina* a similar but less comprehensive judgment.

Apollo's judgment seems an impossible wish, a futile hope. Orestes, after a year in exile, shall return to Athens and render justice to the Eumenides for his mother's murder. 'Gods shall be your judges, sitting in holy session, and acquitting you by sacred verdict.' He shall marry Hermione and reign in Argos.[30] Menelaus shall reign in Sparta, and the two kingdoms shall be reconciled. Electra shall be given in marriage to Pylades. Helen is to be a goddess, enthroned for ever as a star for sailors. Order is thus restored.

Orin and Lavinia

O'Neill's *Mourning Becomes Electra*[31] transfers the story to America under the shadow of the Civil War, from which Orin (that is, Orestes), returns to his home soon after his father has been murdered by his mother and her lover. He has had a psychotic illness following a wound to his head. He and his sister Lavinia (namely, Electra) kill the lover and are responsible indirectly for the death of their mother, who shoots herself. Lavinia, dominating Orin, plays the active part. She has been closely attached to her father and rivalrous with her mother in her position both as wife and mother. After the deaths Orin becomes haunted and guilty and, on his return home after a year of travel, or exile, with Lavinia, shoots himself. In this tragic interpretation without the benefit of gods, there is no restoration of law and order, no reconciliation.

Points of interest in Orin's schizophrenia-like illness are that he has grown up in a skewed, schismatic family,[32] with a close relationship with a possessive mother and a shallow relationship with his soldier father. Mother and son have shared fantasies of a secret little world of their own, from which father and sister have been excluded. Orin has not emancipated himself sufficiently from his mother to pay more than casual attention to Hazel, whom his mother resents as a potential rival. Already disturbed by his war experiences, he becomes more so when he discovers his mother's relationship with Captain Brant. He allies himself with his sister, who is motivated by both revenge for her father and rivalry with her mother for Captain Brant.

On his return home Orin is thin, haggard, confused and emotionally flat. He has become as dependent on Lavinia as he has been on his mother, and is disturbed further when he learns of her plans to marry Peter. Profoundly guilty, he writes a confessional history of what he calls the family's crimes in order to face the ghosts of the past: 'If I could see it clearly in the past, I might be able to foretell what fate is in store for me.' But he finds no peace and kills himself.

Peter and his sister Hazel, standing outside the feuds affecting Orin and Lavinia, are unaware and uncomprehending, but puzzled, like many are who observe the madness afflicting one or more members of a family.

FATHERS AND DAUGHTERS

King Lear

The possessive love of a father for his daughter has been called after King Lear. His wrath is aroused by Cordelia's unequivocal assertion of the need to share:

> Haply, when I shall wed,
> That lord whose hand must take my plight shall carry
> Half my love with him, half my care and duty.
> (1.1.100–2)

And he disclaims 'all my paternal care', and declares that she shall be 'a stranger to my heart and me'. She has emancipated herself from him and become more independent than he has recognised or is ready to accept.

Brabantio in *Othello*, in contrast, accepts, although reluctantly, Desdemona's 'divided duty'. She has learnt to respect her father, but her preference must go to her husband, she tells him, as her mother's had done to him. Another example of a possessive father is Polonius. He discourages Ophelia from forming an attachment with a man of her own generation, warning her of the dangers. No mention is made of her mother, and he, like Lear and Brabantio, is presumably a widower.

A father may entertain hard feelings for a potential son-in-law; Polonius warns his daughter against Hamlet, and causes her to rebuff him. Brabantio accuses Othello of being 'a practiser of arts inhibited, and out of warrant' (1.2.78–9). The legend tells that Offa killed Ethelbert, his prospective son-in-law. Jonathan Peachum in John Gay's *The Beggar's Opera* (likewise Brecht's *The Threepenny Opera*), betrays to the police Mac the Knife, his daughter's husband.

A girl brought up in a household, whether a natural daughter, adopted, or a niece, may gain the father's interest, and he, becoming possessive of her, may then put obstacles in her way when she shows signs of becoming attached to a man outside the family.

Eddie Carbone and Catherine

Eddie in Arthur Miller's *A View from the Bridge*[33] betrays Rudolpho, his niece Catherine's fiancé, and an illegal immigrant, to the immigration officers. Catherine, the 17-year-old daughter of his wife's sister, has lived with Eddie and his wife, Beatrice, since her childhood. In the course of the feud between them, Eddie becomes highly suspicious of Rudolpho's motives and suspects him of not being 'right' – that is, of being homosexual. The feud stretches and breaks the bonds of loyalty in the family and the community and ends in Eddie's death.

The feud forces Catherine to come to a decision to let her relationship with Rudolpho move towards marriage, and emancipate herself from Eddie. In deciding to leave home, she is encouraged by Beatrice. As she has become more independent and more attractive sexually, Eddie's interest in her has grown, and his interest in Beatrice has declined, so that Beatrice has worried about what has gone wrong between them. The conflicts affecting Catherine, Eddie, Rudolpho and Beatrice epitomise those activated in a family when an adolescent daughter begins to break away. Eddie, like King Lear, refuses to compromise.

STEP-MOTHERS AND STEP-SONS

Phaedra

Another pattern of family feud is illustrated by the story of Phaedra. Her love for Hippolytus, her husband Theseus' son by a previous marriage, leads to both her own and the step-son's destruction. This complex of a woman's love for a step-son may be called after her. The essential story, how a married woman falls in love with a young man, has her advances rejected, and pre-empts denunciation by accusing him to her husband appears in various forms – for example, in the *Genesis* story of Potiphar's wife,[34] as well as in plays by Euripides, Seneca and Racine.

When a step-son shows sexual interest in his step-mother, his desire being then rather for his father's wife than the mother, the complex may be called after Don Carlos, with reference usually to Schiller's play. The attraction may be mutual, the difference between the two complexes being little more than one of emphasis.

The stories recur in plays separated by many years, and interest lies in the differences between one version and another because these show what brings the play to bear on the preoccupations of the time. Raymond Williams[35] discusses the differences between Euripides' play *Hippolytus*[36] and Racine's play *Phèdre*.[37] In Seneca's play,[38] the emphasis is more on the destructiveness of Phaedra's uncontrolled passions, less than in Euripides' play on Hippolytus' abhorrence of sex.

In Euripides' play the course of action is determined by the gods, Aphrodite, the goddess of sexual love, and Artemis, the huntress goddess of virginity. For the modern audience they are personifications of unconscious impulses. In the Racine play, the gods are not present dramatically, although characters attribute disordered thoughts and feelings to them. Phèdre thus cries out: 'Oh, I am mad! Where are my thoughts, my wandering mind? Lost, for the Gods have taken it away.'

The step-mother's heart is gripped by a terrible love for

Hippolytus as a result of the contrivance of Aphrodite, who wants to take vengeance on him because she is insulted by his abhorrence for the bed of love and his honouring of Artemis. Keeping silent about her love for Hippolytus, Phaedra lies sleepless, sick and longing for death, driven mad by the goads of a guilty and defiling love, which she has tried to ward off with prayers, vows and offerings, and even drugs.

No one knows what troubles her until she reveals her passion while in delirium – that is, in psychosis – first to the nurse and later to Hippolytus, speaking then with such shame and confusion that her passion has to be regarded as punishment from the gods rather than the impulse of a free will, or, in other terms, as reflecting processes in the unconscious. 'My madness speaks the thing it should not.' She tells how she has tried to endure, first by hiding her suffering, then by mastering the madness by self-control, and finally when she has failed to subdue 'the goddess', by ending her life.

The nurse chides her, just as a psychotherapist might do: 'to keep faults out of sight is mortal wisdom; it's not for us to struggle after tiresome perfection' (ll.469–70). Phaedra accuses Hippolytus on her death-bed, angrily and falsely, of having violated her. In Racine's play, the accusation of intending to violate her, a calumny too base and evil to put into the mouth of a princess, is made by the nurse in order to save her mistress's honour and life; later the nurse drowns herself.

Hippolytus has turned away from love and engaged in hunting, partly because of his oedipal fear of his father's anger, and partly because, wanting to keep his body pure, he shies away from following the example of an adulterous father.

In Racine's play he has been obsessed against his will by his love for Aricie, the daughter and sister of his father's enemies. He is not, as in Euripides play, 'a philosopher exempt of all imperfection'. His relationship with Aricie makes him a rival for the father's throne, just as his supposed violation of Phèdre makes him a rival for her.

His jealousy and anger aroused, the father challenges him to kill himself in retribution, taunting him with accusations of adultery and incest. Destined to kill him with curses, he banishes him and calls on the gods to undertake his doom. The son, so accursed, dies in a horrific accident when the horses drawing his chariot become panic-stricken in reaction to strange, unnatural events. Phèdre, then remorseful, takes poison and dies. In Euripides' play, Phaedra hangs herself before Hippolytus is killed.

In Racine's play, the father (Theseus), who has descended into the underworld to rescue Prosperpine, is rumoured in the first Act to be dead, and is described as having been a tyrant and reckless adulterer. These things release Phèdre from her obligations to him and allow her to declare her love for Hippolytus. An additional theme, not in the Euripides play, is Phèdre's jealousy of Aricie. In the end the father, grieving for his dead son, adopts Aricie as his daughter, thus settling the inheritance of his title. In Euripides' play the gods take control over the future. Racine changed the way in which Phèdre's behaviour is to be understood. In the Euripides play, 'the whole course of human action and passion is seen as essentially determined by the deliberate but often competitive or conflicting impulses of a diversity of gods', as Williams puts it, whereas Racine sees Phèdre's 'ungovernable sexual passion' as arising in the context of complex psychological, social and political conditions, and displays the passions to show 'all the disorders of which they are the cause'. The daughter of a mother who had been cursed with unnatural desires, she has all the qualities demanded in the heroes of tragedy that excite pity and terror. Neither entirely guilty nor entirely innocent, Racine remarks, she is driven by an unlawful passion, for which she is the first to feel horror.[39]

A SON'S LOVE FOR HIS FATHER'S WIFE

Don Carlos

Otway's Don Carlos[40] is about the rivalry of the King of Spain with Don Carlos, his son by a former marriage. At first the king approves of Don Carlos' courtship of Elizabeth, but then takes her away for reasons of pride. Although in love with Don Carlos, and he with her, she marries the king for political reasons and, as a person of integrity, resolves to be faithful to him. The jealousy of the austere, lonely king, fearful lest she prefer the son, is inflamed by Ruy Gomez, an elderly courtier whose role is similar to Iago's in Othello. He does not consummate the marriage. His jealousy and suspicion escalating, and becoming delusional, he plans revenge on the 'false' queen and son.

Don Carlos feeling that the father has 'robbed' him of her persists in his courtship although she is unobtainable. Denied scope for his energies he starts to intrigue against the king, sparing his life because he sees him as father rather than king. But he is led into a trap by Gomez. The king, morbidly jealous, murders 'a loyal wife and guiltless son', giving her a deadly poison. Don Carlos cuts his veins in a bath. Discovering too late that he has been grievously misled, the king repenting seeks forgiveness from the dying lovers.

The essentials of Otway's play recur in Schiller's version.[41] In this, Don Carlos lost his mother at birth; 'My birth was the murder of my mother,' he says. Until he was 6 years old he had not seen his father, and still feels terror when he does so. He is deeply resentful of his 'new mother' as having cost him his father's love, although in love with her. He is in poor spirits, the symptoms of his 'unhappy sickness' being paranoid. Thus he feels that he is surrounded by traitors and is the subject of 'ignoble whisperings'. His 'elaborate display of silence' is a source of distress to his father. He recognises that the queen is 'forever beyond [his] reach'. In her view it is 'spite and bitterness and envy, pride too' that draw him to her.

Confused by angry feelings for his father and love for the queen, he fails to respond to the loving advances of the Princess Eboli, who, jealous of the queen because of his rejection, decides to seek revenge by informing the king that the queen and Don Carlos have been deceiving him. The king, his jealousy inflamed, and uncertain of the paternity of his young daughter, becomes fearful lest the queen has abandoned herself to the son's 'incestuous embraces'. Don Carlos then becomes caught up in political intrigue that threatens the king, who invokes the help of the Grand Inquisitor. The play ends with the death of the queen and the son. The central theme in Schiller's play, as in Otway's, is the rivalry of father and son for the affection of the father's wife; out of this rivalry develops the political intrigue.

Abbie and Eben

O'Neill's *Desire under the Elms*,[42] set in nineteenth-century New England, contains another version of the Phaedra or Don Carlos

FAMILY FEUDS

complex, in which the motives are as much to do with power
and possession as sex. Not least is rivalry for the possession of
the ageing father's farm. Abbie, his new wife, seduces his son
Eben in order to conceive a son who will inherit the farm. Eben's
lust is restrained by his memories of his dead mother. In the
event she kills the infant in order to prove her love for Eben and
to preserve her relationship with him, and both are arrested.

HORIZONTAL RELATIONSHIPS: THE RIVALRY OF SIBS

A description of a family as a system includes the interactions of
the children. A son's struggle for power may be more with his
brother than his father. The rivalry of one brother with another
has been named after the biblical story of Cain[43] who, jealous
because his younger brother Abel's offerings to the Lord are
favoured, slays him. In *Hamlet*, Claudius, the younger son, kills
his older brother and gains the throne, having already seduced
his wife. He recognises the nature of his offence when he says,
'It hath the primal eldest curse upon't,/A brother's murder'
(3.3.37–8). Macbeth's killing of Duncan is condemned in similar
terms.

In *As You Like It*, the younger brother, Duke Frederick,
becomes jealous, and banishes his older brother, Duke Senior.
His anger is extended to Rosalind, his niece. He 'Hath ta'en
displeasure 'gainst' her for no other reason than that the people
praise her for her virtues and 'pity her for her good father's sake'
(1.2.254–5, 267–70). 'I trust thee not', he says to her; 'Thou art
thy father's daughter, there's enough' (1.3.53, 56). In the same
play, Oliver, the older brother, hates the younger Orlando and
plots his death; 'my soul, yet I know not why, hates nothing
more than he,' he says.

The rivalry of one son with another may lead to the destruction of one or both. Oedipus' twin sons, Eteocles and Polynices,
rebel, when Oedipus has gone into exile, against the regent
Creon, not in alliance, but in ambitious rivalry with each other.

Other examples of brothers whose rivalry leads to the destruction of one of them are Edgar, the legitimate son, and Edmund,
the illegitimate son of Gloucester in *King Lear*. Edmund, jealous
because of Edgar's favoured position, plots against Edgar and
his father. Similar are Jamie and Edmund in Eugene O'Neill's

115

Long Day's Journey into Night. Jamie, the older brother, tells Edmund of his mixed feelings. 'Wanted you to fail. Always jealous of you. Mama's baby, Papa's pet.' 'I can't help hating your guts.' 'I love you more than I hate you.' 'I'll do my damnedest to make you fail. Can't help it. I hate myself. Got to take revenge.' The rivalry between close friends may also become destructive; for example, Leontes, who becomes jealous of his life-long friend and rival Polixenes and suspicious of his wife's fidelity.

The rivalry of women

In several plays, women, rivals in claiming the love of a man, compete for a possessive relationship with his child. The assumption of the maternal role by the unmarried one is a theme in two of Ibsen's plays. The 16-year-old Asta in *Little Eyolf* takes over the mothering of Eyolf from Rita, her sister-in-law. In *John Gabriel Borkman*, Ella treats Erhart, the son of her twin sister Gunhild with Borkman, as her own son. In Eliot's *The Family Reunion*, Agatha develops strong maternal feelings for Harry, whose life she has saved when she stopped the father from killing her sister Amy when pregnant.

Brothers and sisters

In some relationships between brothers and sisters there are strong mutual interests and comradeship, without competition, sexual impulses being held under control; for example, Orestes and Electra (Orin and Lavinia), Antigone and Polyneices, Laertes and Ophelia, and Alfred and Asta. Some plays, such as John Ford's *'Tis Pity She's a Whore*, portray the tragic consequences of an incestuous relationship.

Marriage partners and other couples

There may also be rivalry between marriage partners. In *The Father*, each parent fights for the daughter's affection. But feuds take many forms. In Strindberg's *The Dance of Death*, husband and wife, having failed each other, have developed a murderous, mutual hate for each other, all the more so because of their social isolation and therefore dependence on each other. Their one visitor proves ineffective as a mediator.

In *Ghosts*, the feud between husband and wife arises out of the unsatisfactory reasons for which they married. In *The Lady from the Sea*, a husband and wife are estranged after the death of a child; neither had become free to marry after the loss of a previous partner. In *The Oresteia*, Clytemnestra kills her husband, Agamemnon, in revenge for his sacrifice of their daughter Iphigenia, and because of his unfaithfulness. Modern examples of feuds in marriage are Sartre's *Huis Clos*, Albee's *Who's Afraid of Virginia Woolf?*, and Whitehead's *Alpha Beta*.

Strindberg attacked Ibsen for his scandalous attacks on the male sex. There are indeed few or no husbands in Ibsen's plays who do not fail their wives in one way or other, or who do not act destructively towards them. Helmer, Captain Alving, Hjalmar, Rosmer, Doctor Wangel, Tesman, Alfred Allmers, Solness, John Gabriel Borkman and Arnold Rubek are all destructive in their relationships with their wives or other women. There are many tyrants, who exercise their power while being unresponsive to the needs of others, and who expect their women to hold to high standards of conduct without compromise. Brand's refusal to compromise brings misery and disaster to Agnes and others. Rosmer's insensitivity and inability to respond to the needs of first Beata and then Rebecca bring disaster to them all.

Helene Alving recognises that she has been responsible for destroying her husband and is in danger of destroying her son. In Strindberg's plays, in contrast, are to be found women who are outrageously destructive of their husbands; for example, Laura in *The Father* and Alice in *The Dance of Death*.[44] In this play, Edgar and Alice, imprisoned in marriage, engage in a bitter and destructive struggle, with no holds barred. He, the victim, has done little in his marriage to earn his wife's respect or good-will and has destroyed the peace of all in contact with him as he staggers from one death throe to another. Kurt serves as a referee.

Dürrenmatt in *Play Strindberg*[45] reworks Strindberg's play in order to present the exchanges between them as if they are in a contest with rounds in a boxing ring, thus converting the tragedy of a conventional marriage into comedy. The protagonists in Albee's *Who's Afraid of Virginia Woolf?*, a comedy owing much to Strindberg, who are prepared to wound, but not deeply, show a tender forbearance towards each other, and the play ends in a precarious reconciliation.

117

COUPLES AND FAMILIES

So far, feuds have been considered as the way in which two people interact with each other. But a couple or a 'dyad' are usually part of a larger system of a family or other social group, how the two behave towards each other being determined in part by other relationships within the larger system.

In *The Lady from the Sea*, Doctor Wangel's older daughter, Bolette, has taken over the place in the household previously held by her mother, who has died. This makes it difficult for Ellida to assume the roles she as the wife and step-mother would expect to play; hence arise her feelings that she is being excluded. Bolette's engagement to Arnholm gives promise that she will relinquish the place in favour of Ellida. It is then easier for Ellida to decide to stay.

The events in Act One of David Hare's *The Secret Rapture*[46] take place on the day of, or soon after, the funeral of the father. In the state of flux following his death, dormant conflicts are awakened in the relationship of the two sisters, Isobel and Marion, who, having developed different styles of life, disagree about what practical steps should be taken. Marion, the dominant one, imposes her views on the more compliant Isobel, and Isobel assumes some responsibility for the widow, her step-mother, Katherine, with whom the sisters have hitherto had little to do, but who has now to be incorporated into a new, reorganised system of relationships. Isobel's relationship with Irwin, her lover and partner in a design office, is strained and then thrown into disorder as a result. The play might be seen as being about simply the feud between the two sisters. The conflicts are more intricate for, at the climax, Irwin, angry and resentful because he, displaced by Katherine, feels rejected by Isobel and murders her.

The father's death has set in train a sequence of changes in the system, which do not bring stability and end in disaster. Isobel is the unexpected victim. The victims of family feuds are a mixed lot. They are not usually scapegoats and as a rule do not deserve their fate. They tend to have been relatively passive as protagonists. Among them are Iphigenia (in the Atreus family), Polonius, Ophelia, Banquo, Hedvig (in *The Wild Duck*), and Little Eyolf.

The conflicts between two people are more readily understood if they are put into the context of a larger system. *Hamlet* tends to be seen as a play about the rivalry between Hamlet and Claudius, all the more so because of Freud's emphasis on the Oedipus complex. But the play is also about the quarrel between Hamlet and Ophelia. The fatal difficulties in this relationship have to be seen in the light of their relationships with their parents. Not emancipated from parents, they are handicapped in relating to each other.

SUMMARY

A start is made on the description of a family feud by identifying the main protagonists, such as father and son, or mother and daughter. The feud is 'vertical' when they belong to different generations, 'horizontal' when to the same generation, such as two brothers, or brother and sister, or marriage partners.

The essence of the feud may be rivalry, as in the Oedipus complex, when the son challenges the father for the affection of the mother, and, in the case of Cain and Abel, and Edgar and Edmund, when they vie with each other for recognition by the father. The essence of other feuds is anger at rejection, as it is in the case of King Lear and his daughters, or anger at the unfaithfulness of the mother, as in Orestes' case.

A step-son may become a rival with his father for the affection of his step-mother or for political power, as in the case of Don Carlos. A step-mother may be angry because of her rejection by her step-son, as in the case of Phaedra. A mother and father may fight each other for the affection of their child, as in the case of Laura and the Captain. There are many patterns. Terms like 'the Oedipus complex' tend to leave out key elements. Hamlet is subject to the hostility of not only Claudius but also Polonius, who sees him as a rival for the affection of Ophelia, with whom he quarrels.

Interest lies in both the origins of the feud and the reasons for its persistence. In some cases, the origins lie in the birth of a child, as in the case of Laius, who fears that he will be killed by his son. The birth of a child arouses Leontes' suspicions of his wife's faithfulness. The persistence of a feud may reflect the failure of a son or daughter to break free from the past. Hamlet and Ophelia, neither emancipated from parents, are not free to establish an enduring relationship with each other. What prevents a person from breaking free is to be discussed in the next chapter.

7

BREAKING FREE FROM THE PAST

I give you the original script of this play of old sorrows,
written in tears and blood. I mean it as a tribute to your
love and tenderness which gave me the faith in love that
enabled me to face my dead at last and write this play –
write it with deep pity and understanding and forgiveness
for *all* the four haunted Tyrones. These twelve years,
Beloved One, have been a Journey into Light – into love.

(Dedication of *Long Day's Journey into Night*[1])

FACING THE GHOSTS

Destructive feuds have their roots in the past, those implicated
in them tending to repeat – recapitulate – the damaging mistakes
of the previous generation, and thus to add to their suffering. In
some instances this vicious circle is interrupted, and some break
free from the past. What can we learn from them?

In *Long Day's Journey into Night*, published in 1941, O'Neill,
then 53 years old, faced the ghosts from twenty-five years
previously, as if conducting an inquest. He had already written
The Iceman Cometh, published in 1939, of which he said, 'I felt I
had locked myself in with my memories'.[2] Such an interval is
not unusual. Flaubert's autobiographical novel *The Temptation of
Saint Anthony*, planned in the shadow of his father's death in
1842, was not published until 1872, when he was 51. Ibsen was
53 when he completed the writing of *Ghosts*, which dealt with
experiences of some twenty-six years before. Virginia Woolf was
43 when she gave in her novel *Mrs Dalloway* an account of the
mental illness she had suffered in her teen years and twenties.

Often it is not until middle age or later, after many years of suffering, that people come to face the realities of their lives; that is, they gain 'insight' in psychiatric terms. Krapp, in Beckett's *Krapp's Last Tape*, who is elderly and decrepit, has defended himself against 'the suffering of being' by 'drink, bananas and slapstick'.[3] He listens with a mixture of fascination, boredom and revulsion to the tape he had recorded when he was 39. In clinical experience, many years may pass before a person who has committed a serious offence, such as murder, begins to review what happened and work through the feelings of anger and remorse associated with it.

Orestes, Orin, Harry, Hamlet, Oswald and Trofimov stand out among the several discussed in previous chapters who are haunted by their past. They have in common that they have returned home after a voyage or respite elsewhere: Orestes and Orin from exile, Harry from abroad, Hamlet from Wittenberg, Oswald from Paris, and Trofimov from Moscow. Staying away has postponed the facing of the conflicts and imperatives of the past, but has not reduced their force.

Sometimes the metaphor is a voyage of discovery, a search for understanding or enlightenment about the origins of the sense of evil conveyed at the start of the play. In other cases, a voyage may stand for madness and signify a flight into a world of fantasy: for example, Peer Gynt's journey, first into the mountains, then into the kingdom of the trolls; likewise Alfred Allmers' walking tour in the mountains, where he gets lost and faces death. Hamlet, on the other hand, having had confirmation of the causes of his father's death, pauses in his search for revenge against his uncle. During the voyage to England forced on him by Claudius, his attitudes undergo change, with restoration of his capacity to take control over his situation.

HARRY

The central theme in T.S. Eliot's *The Family Reunion*[4] is Harry's unhappy marriage and the loss of his wife. Pursued by the Eumenides after his wife's death in a storm at sea, about which he feels guilty because he thinks he may have pushed her,[5] he has returned home for a family reunion on his mother's birthday. He is told by his aunt Agatha about his father's wish to kill his mother while she was carrying him. This disclosure, most needed by him and most feared, is the key event in the play.

Once he has found out the truth about his early life, and has recognised the Eumenides as real, significant and outside him, he is released from them. 'The past is irremediable', Agatha says, 'because the future can only be built upon the real past.' What he has learnt means 'the end of a relation'. But 'where does one go from a world of insanity?', he asks, and decides to leave his home on a journey of uncertain destination. 'I know that I have made a decision – and I know that I must go.' He has found a special role: 'Why I have this election, I do not understand. . . . I must follow the bright angels' – that is, seek personal salvation, not through reconciliation with others but on his own.

By reviving the painful conflicts of the past, returning home makes progress possible in the painful process of self-discovery. As is said of Harry, 'the man who returns will have to meet the boy who left'. The Eumenides become troublesome again, and he seeks out the facts of his childhood. Orestes on his return home calls out to his murdered father at his grave. Orin returning from exile writes a history of the family's crimes and, like O'Neill, faces his dead. Hamlet is shocked by the revelations of his father's ghost. Oswald, who has returned home for the ceremonial opening of the orphanage built as a memorial to his father, is forced by his mother's revelations to abandon the myths that have made his father a model for him.

THE CHERRY ORCHARD

Trofimov, the perpetual student in *The Cherry Orchard*,[6] has this to say about the effects of the past:

> We still have no real background, no clear attitude to our past, we just philosophize and complain of depression, or drink vodka. Yet it's perfectly clear that to begin to live in the present, we must first atone for our past and be finished with it, and we can only atone for it by suffering, by extraordinary, unceasing exertion.

The cherry orchard is the family's symbol for the happiness, stability and innocence they remember of their former life, and they return to it with nostalgia as a refuge after the distresses of life in Moscow. For the reason Trofimov gives, they cannot face parting with it or altering anything. The play starts in the nursery, which like the other rooms in the house is just as it was when they had left it five years before, soon after the 7-year-old son had drowned. The sale of the orchard, forced on them by their financial circumstances, obliges them to confront realities and take decisions about the future, although they appear to do so more by default than by firm intention.

As Ranyevskaia, the owner, points out, the young, like Trofimov and Ania, her 17-year-old daughter, are able to look ahead boldly, but she has returned home because of the breakdown of a relationship with a lover, and has not hitherto been able to conceive of life without the cherry orchard. 'Before the cherry orchard was sold everybody was worried and upset', her brother Gayev says, 'but as soon as it was all settled finally and once for all, everybody calmed down and felt quite cheerful.'

Already looking and sleeping better, she plans to go to Paris for a while, and then return to renew her relationship with Ania. Varia, her adopted daughter and the housekeeper, having broken with Lopakhin, is to move to be the housekeeper for another family. Only for Feers, the elderly man-servant, is there no future other than death.

The end of the play confirms that the nostalgic preoccupation with the cherry orchard has reflected recent disappointments and failures to face and decide on the immediate problems. When forced by its sale to do so, each is largely freed from the past, and can engage with the future.

RESTORATION OF RELATIONSHIPS

Arkady and Yevgeny

A common pattern is for young people to leave home in order to emancipate themselves from the parental generation and, returning after a few years, to restore their relationships with their parents on new terms that are more fitting for equals. The sequence is rebellion, estrangement and reconciliation. One example is Prince Hal. Other examples are to be found in Brian Friel's play *Fathers and Sons*,[7] which is based on Turgenev's novel. Two young men, Arkady Kirsanov and Yevgeny Bazarov, linked to each other as close friends, but very different in their attitudes – Yevgeny perhaps as Arkady's other self – return to their parental homes after years away as students. Arkady, compromising his principles, giving up his ambitions to remake the world, and coming to agreeable terms with his father and his father's mistress without rivalry, takes on the management of the family's land, settles down and marries. Yevgeny, struggling to stay true to his principles as a nihilist, fails in an attempt to make a relationship with a young woman and enters into a partnership with his father in caring for those stricken in a typhus epidemic, of which he becomes a victim.

The significant events in the past tend to emerge piecemeal. A few plays adopt the style of a narrative and report them in chronological order, but most are both retrospective and prospective, as they show how the past impedes adaptation to the present. Notable is Harold Pinter's *Betrayal*, in which the story of an adulterous couple is told in reverse order, the first scene being a reunion after the affair is over, the last, its passionate beginning. This is often the order in which a story unfolds in the consulting room.

IBSEN ON BREAKING FREE

Halvdan Koht[8] in his biography comments on the tendency of Ibsen's plays to deal with the problem: how is one to escape the heritage of the past? He refers to *Pillars of Society*, *A Doll's House* and *Ghosts*, in particular, and adds: 'The past avenges itself on Catiline, on Lady Inger, on Hjørdis, and on Sigurd', all characters in earlier plays. *Brand*, written in 1866, and his first popular success, is described by McFarlane[9] as 'an act of repudiation and avowal, a passionate denial of earlier assumptions and beliefs, a vehement apostasy', requiring the scrutiny of 'his earlier life and career'.

After *Peer Gynt*, he spent almost a decade reviewing his dramatic policies and methods, one result being that he abandoned verse, and another, that he turned to 'dramas of contemporary life', such as *Pillars of Society*, which was the first of several plays of social criticism. In these, the characters speak in the language of everyday life, with broken sentences and irregularities in their construction, instead of the fluent verse expected in the theatre of the time. He insisted nevertheless that he was a poet and not a social reformer.

The publication in 1873 of *Emperor and Galilean*, which is about the career of Julian the Apostate, marked the first of three turning points in the development of his ideas. This play was the first to break with many of the traditions that had governed him. A second turning point came soon after he had finished *A Doll's House*, published in 1879. His father, from whom he had long been estranged, died in 1877. Soon afterwards he began to review his earlier life, as Freud did twenty years later after his father's death. Thus he proposed to his publishers in 1880 that he should write prefaces to two of his earlier plays – *Lady Inger*, written in 1855 when he was 27, and *The Vikings at Helgeland* (1858), in which he would describe his life in Bergen when like Oswald in *Ghosts* he was 26, 27 years old. Also, in the autumn of 1880 he started on an account of his childhood in Skien, but in March 1881 broke off this autobiographical essay to make a start on *Ghosts*, which he finished in a burst of activity over the four days 21–24 October, the 24th being the fourth anniversary of his father's death.[10]

In 1880 there was what has been called a 'caesura' in his work, with a greater recognition thereafter of the constraints imposed by the past.[11] Hitherto he had seen hope of improvement in mankind, but he became a fatalist. 'Retribution for faults committed in the past is inevitable,' he wrote. Note the pessimism of the endings of his later plays, except *The Lady from the Sea* and *Little Eyolf*.

There was a third turning point in 1891 when he returned to Norway after having lived abroad for twenty-seven years. His return brought a change in his plays. *Hedda Gabler*, published in 1890, proved to be the last play of social criticism. His next play, *The Master Builder*, published in 1892, was the first of three plays in which he examined the destructive effects of the artist or reformer on those related to him, the second and third being *John Gabriel Borkman* and *When We Dead Awaken*. These plays share a theme that has an obvious reference to Ibsen's own experience. The theme had been anticipated in *Brand* and *Rosmersholm*. In the latter play Rosmer, the artist, who wants to ennoble mankind, demands of Rebecca that she sacrifice herself for art. Rubek, in *When We Dead Awaken*, demands a similar sacrifice of Irene.

HALVARD SOLNESS

In *The Master Builder*, Solness, threatened by the growing strength of the younger generation[12] and the decline in his own powers, reviews the disasters he has brought on his wife through the death of their twin sons, and his crimes against his business partner. Amongst other things, the play contains an account, worthy of a textbook, but unlikely to be found in one, of the effects on parents and their marriage of the death of children in an accident in the home. Also, he is afraid that he will be broken by his partner's son just as he broke the father. His guilt and fears contribute to the phobia for heights he has suffered for many years, but hitherto has been able to overcome.

Challenged by Hilde Wangel to carry the wreath to the top of the church tower in a topping-out ceremony, he becomes dizzy and falls to his death. She has arrived in his house as a youthful admirer, but she should perhaps be seen as a figure of fantasy, perhaps a troll who, offering him the prospect of redemption, restores his belief in his powers to climb to the top and there to build for them a castle in the air. But his past catches up on him and causes his destruction.

GHOSTS

The action in many of his plays of social criticism occurs over a relatively short period of time, condensed for dramatic purposes. Events are then told of that are the late consequences of family conflicts going back over many years. Ibsen finds various ways of showing how the past exerts its powerful influence.

Of all his plays Ghosts[13] is the one that deals most directly with the shackles of the past, the salient metaphor in it being ghosts. 'Ghosts', like the German 'Gespenster', is a misleading translation of the Norwegian 'gjengangere', literally those who return; the French 'les revenants' is much closer.

Many elements in Ghosts are related more or less directly to his own experience. The Alvings, like the Ibsens, had been obliged by the financial ruin of the father to move out of town to a house[14] where they felt socially isolated and of lowered status. The playwright was then 7 years old. It was when 'getting on for seven' that Oswald was put out to strangers. Oswald was 16 years old when he moved to Paris, Henrik a little less than 16 when he moved to Grimstad.

Ibsen at 26, 27 years old had been drinking heavily, and had got into difficulties in his job at the theatre in Bergen. His plays were failing, and he was neglecting his duty as a producer. Yet a few years later he had made a marriage, at 30 years old, and some years afterwards had left Norway.

It was not for many years that he could free himself even partly from the ghosts of the past. His father's death started him off on a review of his earlier life, just as his father's death had started Freud off on his own self-analysis, which Ernest Jones described as 'his most heroic feat, a psychoanalysis of his own unconscious'. This led to the writing of *An Interpretation of Dreams*, which Freud, then 43, completed three years after his father's death. *Ghosts* was for Ibsen what *The Interpretation of Dreams* was for Freud.

The audience is suddenly made aware in *Ghosts*, just before the curtain falls at the end of Act One, of the influence of the past and the tendency to recapitulation, when the mother overhears her son making a sexual advance to the maid-servant Regine, just as his father had done to Regine's mother. Soon she recognises that she might destroy her son just as she had destroyed her husband by denying him outlets for his energies and his sexuality. Regine would take her son away from her, she fears, just as Regine's mother had taken away her husband. Also, the son has been drinking. Is the son to recapitulate the tragedy of the father, who died as a debauchee and drunkard? The mother says to Pastor Manders:

> When I heard Regine and Oswald in there, it was just like seeing ghosts . . . but then I think that we are all ghosts . . . every one of us . . . it is not just what we inherit from our mothers and fathers that haunt us. It's all kinds of old defunct theories, all sorts of defunct beliefs. It's not that they live on in us; they are simply lodged there, and we cannot get rid of them. And here we are, all of us, abysmally afraid of the light.

By showing the steps towards tragedy, and the reasons why they were taken, Ibsen shows how tragedy might have been averted; the tragic end was not inevitable. The mother, psychologically crippled by her upbringing and the failure of her marriage, has not faced the issues after her husband's death. Instead she has built an orphanage idealising him, although his name would be more fittingly attached to the seaman's home to

127

which Regine the maid-servant is to go as hostess and star attraction when the mother has sent her packing.

She has tried to find understanding through reading what Pastor Manders, the spokesman for a conventional morality, condemns as 'these disgusting free-thinking pamphlets'. She regrets that she has kept secret, in order not to shatter her son's ideals, the kind of life his father had led. But the truth when it is told does not set Oswald free.

Oswald has planned to find salvation through Regine's vitality and joy of living. The evil in his past can be expelled through love, just as in Shelley's play, in which Prometheus is unbound through his love for Asia. After the fire and the symbolic destruction of the illusions, this plan is wrecked when his mother reveals the truth about his father, and that Regine is his half-sister. The relapse in his illness follows on this revelation.

She has considered allowing him to become independent and saying to him, 'Marry the girl, or come to some arrangement between yourselves,' but does not have the courage to do so in the face of the Pastor's condemnation. The conflicts between mother and son escalate. The 'real past' cuts short his courtship of Regine and his hope of a new life, and he has then to face the prospect that the softening of the brain the doctor has spoken of will turn him into a helpless child. No role appears to be open to him except one of dependence on his mother, but there is a gleam of hope, as I argue in Chapter 3.

THE DANGERS OF THE TRUTH

Ibsen returned in his next three plays to the consequences of revealing the truth. His preoccupation with this topic reflected the 'persistent and anxious questioning' at the end of the last century: how much truth, how much reality, can a person bear?[15] This question, that psychotherapists face every day, recurs many times in plays in one form or another, with its related questions: how do people break free from the myths, the illusions, the lies that sustain them? T.S. Eliot's answer was that humankind cannot bear very much reality.

Ibsen was well aware that the truth may be difficult to bear, as the quotation from *Peer Gynt* at the head of Chapter 4 shows, and that it may be better to make do with the consolation of fairy stories. Later in the play Peer says to his dying mother:

Forget what's unpleasant and vexing,
The things that bruise and hurt us.

A central theme of *King Oedipus*, on the other hand, is Oedipus' insistence on searching out and revealing the truth about the sources of pollution in the community. The blind prophet Teiresias tries to withhold the truth in order to spare Oedipus: 'I refuse to utter the heavy secrets of my soul – and yours' (1.334).[16] Jocasta, discouraging Oedipus in his obsessive search for the truth against the wishes of the gods, advises; 'Best live as best we may, from day to day', and says of man's dreams of 'mother-marrying': 'Such things must be forgotten, if life is to be endured' (ll.980–1). Oedipus insists on pursuing 'this trail to the end, until I have unravelled the mystery of my birth'. 'Let all come out.' 'I must unlock the secret of my birth.' 'I ask to be no other man than that I am and will know who I am.'

Having learned the truth, Jocasta hangs herself in 'desperate passion'. Oedipus' ruin is due to his loyalty to the truth. Yet he has the strength to bear it, and the courage to accept the dire consequences and with them the punishment he deserves.

It is a strange irony that Freud, who found so much of interest in the story of Oedipus, did not comment on the warnings given of the dangers of searching out the truth. In the early days of psychoanalysis it was the leading idea that 'neurotics suffer from reminiscences', and that neuroses have their roots in past experiences, with which patients have to come to terms if they are to recover. To search out the truth was the essential purpose: making conscious the unconscious, removing the repressions, filling in gaps of memory. It was much later that Freud came to write in *The Future of an Illusion*[17] that countless people can only bear life with the help of illusions.

In psychoanalytic treatment the revelation of the truth goes no faster than the patient can bear. He keeps control over the progress of the sessions, and is protected by defences that ensure that any distress is bearable. But gaining insight is painful, and the light (that is, the truth) is something to be 'abysmally afraid' of.

The truth is brought out, not only to satisfy Oedipus' need to know who he is, but also, as he sees it, for the sake of the well-being of the community. This latter motive is prominent in Ibsen's next play, written very quickly in reaction to the intense hostility evoked in some sections of the public by *Ghosts*.

AN ENEMY OF THE PEOPLE

Dr Thomas Stockmann earns the appellation in the play's title when he insists on making it known to the public that the water supply to the baths, which are the source of the wealth of the community, is poisoned. Pollution of the community's water supply is a metaphor for what was seen at that time as the distortion of the truth of scientific discovery by self-interest. Although as a physician he should have known better, he is surprised that the truth should evoke such hostility and prove so destructive. At the end of the play his insistence on the truth has isolated him. Unreconciled, he makes 'a great discovery', which he reveals to the consternation of his family:

Now I am one of the strongest men in the whole world. The thing is, you see, that the strongest man in the world is the man who stands alone.

He wills what is right with respect for the law, and refuses to bow to external influence or compromise. This degree of self-sufficiency, with the element of grandiosity, amounts to madness. His pragmatic brother Peter, for whom the suppression of the truth is the more comfortable course, preserves the illusions and his capacity to influence people.

At the end of the earlier play, *Pillars of Society*, Karsten Bernick admits that he has felt poisoned by the guilty secrets of his past. After confessing to the lies on which he has built his career, he is able to say: 'Now I feel as if I had come to my senses,' and 'I can be young and strong again.' He is freed to restore his relationships with his family and friends on new and more honest terms, and the play ends with the assertion that the pillars of society lie in truth and freedom.

THE WILD DUCK

Ibsen returned in his next play after *An Enemy of the People* to the theme of the dangers of the truth. Gregers insists on bringing home to Hjalmar and his wife the truth about their marriage although warned about the dangers by Doctor Relling, who sees the world as a wretched place made tolerable only by 'romancing'. The effect is to destabilise a family whose romancing and refusal to face the realities have preserved a precarious equilibrium. The doubts aroused in Hjalmar about the parentage of Hedvig, his supposed daughter, causes a rift between them, and she shoots herself as a symbolic sacrifice of the wild duck. This is the result of Gregers' breach of the principle enunciated by Doctor Relling: 'I take care to keep the life-lie alive.' Doctor Relling says of the life-lie: 'It's a tried and tested method. I have used it on Molvik as well. I have made him a demonic.' Otherwise, 'the poor devil would have succumbed to mortification and despair long ago' – 'just a bit of silly nonsense I thought up to keep him alive', he adds.[18] 'Manic-depressive' might be the modern equivalent of 'demonic'. The drunken Molvik survives. Blanche Dubois, on the other hand, lapses into madness when Mitch and Stanley destroy one after the other the illusions, the lies, that have sustained her.

Chekhov too recognises the dangers. Through one of the characters in *Ivanov* he says this about the blunt, honest Doctor Lvov, with his 'phoney sincerity': 'You've meddled in his private life, made his name dirt and set yourself up to judge him.' 'In the name of honesty you, a doctor, didn't spare even his sick wife, you pestered her with your suspicions. There's no outrageous, rotten, cruel trick you couldn't play while still thinking yourself an unusually honest and progressive man.'[19]

In *The Wild Duck*, as in most of Ibsen's plays, there are other characters, realists, who search for the truth and believe frankness to be best. Berta Sørby has told Haakon Werle 'everything'. 'It was the very first thing I did, when he began to make his intentions plain,' she says to the sceptical Gregers. 'Frank is something I have always been. It's the best policy for us women.' In *A Doll's House*, Kristine Linde urges Nils Krogstad not to withdraw his letter: 'This unhappy secret must come out. The two must have the whole thing out between them. All this secrecy and deception, it just can't go on.' No psychotherapist would have said otherwise.

ROSMERSHOLM[20]

Doctor Kroll, Rosmer's brother-in-law, insists on revealing to Rebecca that Doctor West, with whom she had been living up to his death, was in all probability her father. The revelation does much to destroy her courage, and she has it in mind, as well as her complicity in the suicide of Rosmer's wife, when she says:

'My own past bars my way. It confronts me like a barrier.' She and Rosmer, united in the struggle for political freedom in a world without God, and opponents of Kroll's repressive conservatism, are trapped.

Rosmer, landowner, one-time clergyman and now an apostate, and his wife Beata had taken Rebecca West, who had recently come from the north, into their home. Beata had become infatuated with her and increasingly disturbed as she sensed Rosmer's growing interest in her. He had a horror of physical sexual relationships, whereas she had expected him to reciprocate the emotional and physical attraction she felt for him. She had even considered a ménage-à-trois. These were the circumstances in which she had fallen to her death in the millrace.

After her death Rosmer and Rebecca try to work out terms on which to relate to each other. He defends himself by his belief that Beata had been 'a sick unhappy woman of unsound mind', and speaks of her 'wild fits of sensual passion . . . she expected me to respond to' and her self-reproach and 'dreadful agony of mind about something' (her childlessness) 'that wasn't her fault' and her 'disordered mind that drove her to those wild aberrations'. He has developed an 'ennobled' (that is, desexualised) relationship with Rebecca, which has meant keeping tight control over feelings. They have shown no grief, no remorse, and have protected their precarious relationship by shutting themselves off from others.

That Rosmer is no more free from the past than is Rebecca is shown in the first few minutes of the play when he is seen by Rebecca to make a detour in order to avoid crossing the footbridge from which Beata had fallen. Also, on the walls of his living-room are hung past and recent portraits of his relatives, who preside over events at Rosmersholm, just as the portrait of General Gabler presides over events in the Tesman home.[21]

Life at Rosmersholm is controlled by its traditions. These are represented by the white horses to which mysterious references are made. *White Horses* was the original title of the play, and in the second draft, Rebecca comments:

> All the emancipated people I know – all those who fancied that they had emancipated themselves – all of them somewhere or other had a white horse, which they never stopped believing in! Emancipation is to be quit of one's white horses . . . we must have light.[22]

Their restricted life together lasts for about 18 months until Beata's brother, Doctor Kroll, reveals two truths about the past, and brings them to a crisis. The first revelation makes untenable Rosmer's belief that Beata had been mentally ill. He has then to recognise 'her despair and quite alone . . . and then in the end her triumph . . . that agonising indictment in the millstream'. He had laid that flattering unction to his conscience, just as Hamlet accuses Gertrude of doing, that it was not his trespass but her madness.

He has to accept too that his feelings for Rebecca have been more than platonic, despite the horror he had experienced when Beata had expected him to reciprocate her sexual desire, and that Beata's awareness of his feelings for Rebecca had contributed to her suicide. Doctor Kroll's second revelation gives Rebecca the facts that make it probable that Doctor West was her father, and that their putative relationship was incestuous.

After these revelations Rosmer asks Rebecca to become his wife in terms indicating that she is to take the place vacated by Beata, and she refuses, although she admits that her passion for him has been overwhelming and had played a part in Beata's death. Her passion has subsided, she says, and she now loves him in an ennobled way.

Freud, asking, 'how could it come about that the adventuress with the fearless free will should now refuse to pluck the fruits of success that would come to her through marriage with Rosmer?', points out that her relations with her mother and Doctor West are recapitulated in her relations with Beata and Rosmer.[23] Hence arises the guilt that paralyses her. But his answer is incomplete, and says nothing about the circumstances in the here-and-now that prevent her from breaking free.

Uncovering the truths about Beata's illness and the character of Rebecca's relationship with Doctor West does not free them to build a future. Neither Rosmer, emotionally crippled by his upbringing at Rosmersholm, nor Rebecca, oppressed by her belief of her incest with Doctor West – and both aware of their complicity in Beata's death – can face the realities of marriage.

At this point the strange Ulrik Brendel, Rosmer's former tutor, now down-at-heel, comes on the scene, and goes straight to the heart of the matter. Trust can only be restored, he tells them, on one unavoidable condition, 'That the woman who loves him goes gladly out into the kitchen and cuts off her dainty, pink little finger ... and furthermore – likewise gladly – cuts off her incomparably moulded left ear'.[24] Note that it is the woman who is to be unsexed.

The components of the final solution are now assembled: the dismissal of sexuality, spiritual marriage, death together in the millstream, and reunion with Beata. After a token marriage service, in which Rosmer is both priest and bridegroom, they go together, the way Beata went, on to the foot-bridge and into the millstream. The last words are the housekeeper's: 'No, no help there. The dead woman has taken them.' The past has reasserted its hold over them.

THE LADY FROM THE SEA

At the core of *Ghosts* are the changes in the relationship of mother and son, which have reached a deadlock when the curtain falls. There is no therapist to mediate. Pastor Manders talks with the mother, but hardly at all with Oswald, except for an exchange in which they disagree about the morality of artists in Paris. Rosmer and Rebecca are put into quarantine, as it were, by Doctor Kroll and his allies, and they protect their precarious relationship after Beata's death by shutting themselves off from others; that is, by 'self-enclosure'. They do not themselves discuss the terms of their relationship.

In *The Lady from the Sea*, the outcome is different. Ellida is as much impeded as Rebecca by her past, but she confronts and dismisses the stranger, who appears to her as a hallucination in the form of her former fiancé. 'Your will no longer has any power over me at all,' she says. 'To me you are a dead man, one who came back from the sea and now returns there. But I no longer fear you. Nor am I swayed by you.' Freed from her past she can make a marriage with Doctor Wangel, and return to his bed.

The crucial part played by Arnholm as a mediator or third party is to be discussed in Chapter 8, Formerly a tutor in the family, his help is invoked by her husband, Doctor Wangel, a doctor practising in a small seaside community. Doctor Wangel has regarded her as mentally ill because of her changeable mood and upredictable and erratic behaviour, and he has remembered that her mother had died in a mental hospital. Able to under-stand physical illness, he claims, he is bewildered by her mental symptoms, which he has tried to control with drugs. These, as his older teen-age daughter remarks, will do her very little good in the long run. The clinical picture is that of a depressive illness, brought on, it might be argued in conventional psychiatric terms, by the death of her child and her estrangement from her husband.

Husband and wife have been on poor terms since the death of their only child about three years before. She has been preoccupied by memories of a fiancé, a sailor, who deserted her, and who is thought to have drowned, and is obsessed by thoughts of the sea, in which she feels compelled to bathe every day. She feels oppressed in the home, 'stifled', of no use, and on the outside of everything. Her fantasies indicate a risk of suicide by drowning. Ibsen gives us the symbol of 'a beached mermaid, lying between the dangerous freedom of the sea', the sea being a symbol of powerful forces, and capitulation to the comforting security of the land.

Matters come to a head on the birthday of Doctor Wangel's first wife, who had died about eight years before. It is celebrated ostentatiously by her two daughters. Ellida, feeling excluded, becomes obsessed with the idea that the stranger is coming to claim her.

Arnholm intervenes. The turning point comes when Doctor Wangel, who has hitherto insisted on taking decisions for her as ill and irresponsible, gives her the responsibility to decide for herself when the stranger comes to claim her. He thus abandons his professional attitude towards her and responds to her as a person deserving his respect and affection. Given freedom to choose – 'freedom with responsibility' – she decides to stay with him. She gives credit to him: 'You have been a good doctor to me. You found ... and had the courage to apply ... the right remedy.'[25]

LITTLE EYOLF

Asta in this play[26] decides to break away from her life with Alfred and Rita, and to share a new life with the road-building engineer Borgheim. Ibsen contrasts the steps that enable her to reach this decision with those taken by Rita and Alfred which trap them in a dance of death.

The system of relationships composed by Alfred, Rita, their

9-year-old crippled son Eyolf, Alfred's supposed half-sister Asta, and her suitor Borgheim is already under strain. Alfred has been on a walking tour in the mountains during which he has confronted thoughts of death, symbolically coming out on the other side of the Stygian lake, and has resolved to devote himself to the care and education of his son. On the evening of his return he responds to Rita's sexual advances by enquiring about Eyolf's digestion, and then falls asleep. 'Champagne was yours, but you touched it not' is her bitter comment as she recognises once again that Alfred has used Eyolf as a pretext for avoiding her sexual advances.

Asta has just discovered the truth of her parentage from some letters Alfred has given her. These reveal that her mother had been made pregnant by a lover, and that there is no blood relationship between her and Alfred. At this point the witch-like 'Rat-Wife' arrives with her black-nosed dog and, like the Pied Piper, lures Eyolf into the fjord, where he drowns.

The Rat-Wife has acted out Rita's wish to be rid of Eyolf. Alfred, tortured by guilt for having married Rita for 'the gold and the green forests', and for allowing Eyolf to fall and cripple himself as a baby while he was making love to Rita, has longed for the peace of death, just as rats do, the Rat-Wife tells him, when they are enticed into the water. Eyolf's drowning at the end of the first Act, as well as Asta's discovery, bring the system to a crisis.

The second Act explores the history of the relationships and the implications and consequences of Eyolf's death: especially how Alfred, then 20, had assumed the care of the 9-year-old Asta after his father and step-mother had died, how he had encouraged her to wear boys' clothes, and had called her by the boy's name Eyolf, and how in spite of this disabling defence he had become in fantasy both father and platonic lover.

This pattern, fixed and hardly changing over sixteen years, has not been subject to, in Ibsen's term, 'the law of change'. Forbidding any expression of what is desired, the incest taboo has created an impasse from which neither has wanted or been able to escape. Both, like Eyolf, have been crippled emotionally. Their relationships have been blighted. Asta has stood between Alfred and Rita, and Alfred between Asta and Borgheim. Asta, 16 when Eyolf was born, has found some outlet for her fantasies in her mothering of Eyolf, having usurped the role of mother that Rita has not wanted to fill.

The revelation that she is not related by blood to Alfred breaks the deadlock and forces her to decide how she is to relate to him and Rita in the future. When she is freed from the taboo by her discovery, her relationship with Alfred, in particular, becomes subject to the law of change, and she is compelled to choose between staying with Alfred in a ménage-à-trois and leaving the household.

She reaches her decision to leave in three steps. Firstly, she breaks symbolically with the past when she gives Alfred water-lilies as 'a final greeting' from Little Eyolf – 'from us both'. Secondly, recognising that without Eyolf to look after, she has no duties nor obligations in the Allmers' home, she decides that she must go away alone, catching the steamer, whereas Borgheim is to take the train. Thirdly, after a long conversation with Borgheim and a confrontation with Alfred and Rita, she changes her mind, inviting Borgheim to join her on the steamer. He has offered her partnership in a practical, constructive enterprise, in the joy of building new roads. 'Real happiness takes two people', he says, 'sharing with one person alone.'

Alfred and Rita plead with her to stay with them. 'You shall be our Eyolf', Rita pleads, 'as you were before'; and Alfred: 'Stay. And share your life with us, with me your brother.' This represents a return to the past, a past that is no longer accept-able to her though she admits when challenged by Alfred that she is 'running away, from you and from myself'. The delicate balance she had achieved in meeting the conflicting demands made on her tips when the circumstances change, and she has to reassess her responses to them.

When she leaves, Rita and Alfred have to come to terms with each other, and achieve some sort of reconciliation and relief from the pain of real experience in a fantasy scenario of social good works. They will care for the poor children of the parish, in Eyolf's place. Alfred supposes that looking 'upwards towards the mountains. Towards the stars. Towards the vast silence,' they will 'sense the presence of spirits – those we have lost'. 'Our little Eyolf', Rita says, 'and your big Eyolf too.'

They thus try to recreate relationships through fantasies that deny the realities of the past and sustain idealised memories. Such memories, retrospective and absurd, are disabling when the demands of life in the real world have to be faced. Alfred annexes Rita's plan of looking after the poor children and converts it into a romantic mission. She accepts his travesty of her vision because it offers a life shared with him. But his egocentric gaze towards the mountains, the stars and the vast silence amounts to extreme emotional violence, from which the only escape open to her may indeed be death.

DECIDING

Characteristic of an Ibsen play is that at its climax one or more of the characters takes a decision to change direction in life, whereas in a Chekhov play, the characters tend to be passive. Feeling themselves to be at the mercy of forces of fate they little understand, they appear to allow events to take their own comic or tragic course.

In contrast, Dina Dorf in *Pillars of Society* decides to leave her home with Johan Tönnesen. 'Yes, I will be your wife,' she says to him. 'But I will work first and become something myself, just as you are. I won't be just a thing that is taken.' Nora in *A Doll's House* says something similar when she decides to leave her husband and home, giving as her reason that she must get experience and, as part of her duty to herself, 'try to be an individual, and discover who is right, society or me'. She chooses freedom, but at the cost of disengaging from current relationships, with uncertain prospects of re-engaging in any new ones.

Kristine Linde, on the other hand, chooses the shackles of marriage with Nils Krogstad in place of the 'unspeakable emptiness' of her life as a widow – a point sometimes missed by those who see *A Doll's House* as a breakthrough for feminism. She has explained to him that when previously she had broken with him, 'At that time there was no other choice.' But she is now free to choose. She accepts the realities, both Nils and she recognising that they are 'shipwrecked – castaways in need of one another'.

Ellida's liberation falls short, as does Asta's, of the ideal as expressed by Dina Dorf, but is more down-to-earth because Dina and Johan have to escape to America as the promised land. Ellida has to make the best of her life in the real world of Doctor Wangel's home with all its limitations. Ibsen's message in *The Lady from the Sea* is optimistic: 'Once a creature has settled on dry land, there's no going back to the sea'; 'The mermaid when washed up on the shore dies. Men and women can "acclimatise themselves" if they are free and act responsibly.'

That is, freedom to decide is not enough. There has also to be compromise so that people can live together. Having freed themselves from the past – Ellida from her former fiancé, her dead son and her father, and Doctor Wangel from his first wife – likewise, Asta from Alfred, Rita and Eyolf, and Kristine from her dead husband – each is able to re-engage and fit into a new system of relationships, on terms and with expectations appropriate to the current circumstances. With the re-engagement go obligations, but these are welcomed, because, as Ibsen makes clear, each needs to be needed.

Not all the decisions taken in Ibsen's plays are constructive. Hedda Gabler, rejecting the roles prescribed for her, decides to break out of the trap of bourgeois domesticity, Tesmanism and sexual harassment by Brack, to achieve the beautiful autonomy she has urged on Eilert Lövborg, and to shoot herself.

Ibsen was of course well aware of the pressures on the women of his generation, not to decide for themselves but to accept the roles prescribed for them, not least when he wrote for the German stage an alternative ending for A Doll's House in order to forestall an even more outrageous one.[27] In Ibsen's version, Nora is forced by Helmer across to the door of the children's bedroom; here a few words are exchanged, Nora sinks down at the door, and the curtain falls.

Some critics deride what they see as Ellida's capitulation when trapped into accepting a confining domesticity and abandoning hope of a liberated life elsewhere, and refer to Ibsen's juxtaposition of her capitulation with the older daughter's reluctant acceptance of the middle-aged, balding Arnholm as a suitor, with a contractual marriage in prospect. But Ellida, accepting obligations and compromises, does decide for herself and acts accordingly.

The Danish censor in 1889 took another view, putting the blame on Doctor Wangel. He had serious misgivings about the morals of a play that appears to condone the one marriage partner, releasing the other from all responsibilities as soon as some criminal comes along to exercise his fascination upon her.[28] Remember too the fury of the public when Nora walks out of the doll's house.

The conditions and processes in the taking of decisions are of particular interest to psychotherapists, for a decision is the crucial step in bringing an end to a period of instability. Deciding and the freedom of will to choose are given special importance by psychotherapists who are influenced by existentialism. By choosing, people define themselves; by choosing what to do, they choose what they will be. Deciding is a step towards 'self-actualisation'. 'Sow an action', William James remarks,[29] 'and you reap a habit; sow a habit, and you reap a character; sow a character, and you reap a destiny.'

Two stages can be distinguished when reaching what James calls the reasonable type of decision, the first being recognition or diagnosis (or anagnorisis), in the 'quest for the right conception', through exploration and analysis of the situation and each of the options, including the prospects of finding satisfactory roles. Is there, in the jargon of modern social sciences, a basis for meaningful sociality? The therapist helps in the exploration and analysis.

The decision itself, taken in the second stage, does not spring immediately from the recognition. There has also to be acceptance that there is necessity ('anankē'); that is, both freedom to choose and compulsion to do so. Decision and action relieve the tension of doubt and hesitancy – 'the impatience of the deliberative state' – but are held up by the 'dread of the irrevocable'. When does the time for decision become ripe? How much analysis, how much exploration? Should one leap without looking? How long should one look? The decision is taken, with the encouragement of the therapist, when the balance has shifted so that the pros outweigh the cons.[30]

THE LESSONS

What are the conditions that allow a happy outcome in *The Lady from the Sea*, but not in *Ghosts* or *Rosmersholm*? Firstly, solutions are available. Ellida's marriage has been more or less satisfactory until her son's death, and roles are available to her if the impediments can be removed. Secondly and most importantly, help is given from outside by a third party. Husband and wife each gain insight as a result of his help in the first stage of deciding and, as a result of his mediation, are able to talk together about the issues in their marriage. Ellida, dismissing the stranger and her fantasies of rejoining him in death in the sea, decides to accept the offer of a restored marriage and the mothering of her step-daughters. Likewise, Asta breaks away from Alfred and, accepting without romancing the uncertainties, departs with her road-builder for a new life.

The plays have features in common. In each, there is a crisis in a system of relationships, followed by a phase of exploration. Events then move to force a decision. In *Ghosts*, the crisis, prefaced by the son's return home and the mother's recognition of the danger that he will recapitulate his father's behaviour and fate, comes to a head with the burning down of the orphanage and the revelation about Regine's parentage. Exploring what courses are open to him, Oswald finds that all lines are blocked other than those leading to a renewed childlike dependence on his mother. He can longer decide for himself.

Rosmer and Rebecca have no help from a third party. Doctor Kroll adds to their difficulties, and Ulrik Brendel points to a destructive solution. Like Alfred and Asta, they resolve the conflicts facing them by a return to the fantasies of the past, and rejoin Beata in death in the millstream, seeking through death the ménage-à-trois she had proposed. Alfred and Rita, denying the realities of the past, return to fantasies of rejoining Eyolf in the vast silence of death.

The plays raise questions, to be further discussed in the next chapter, about the part played by the outsider who intervenes as a third party or mediator. Arnholm provides the model. If he does nothing else, he reopens and keeps open the channels of communication between husband and wife. The casualties in the plays cut off their relationships with others and enter into a world of fantasy.

SUMMARY

'The future can only be built upon the real past.' Uncovering the past and coming to terms with it, or gaining insight, are the first steps towards recovery. Yet there is consolation in preserving a family myth or keeping the 'life-lie' alive, and there are dangers in revealing the truth. A further step is to take a decision to change direction in life, the first stage in deciding being recognition or diagnosis through exploration in 'the quest for the right conception'. In the second stage, there has to be necessity – namely, both freedom to choose and compulsion to do so. In both, mediation by an outsider may play an important part.

8

RECOVERIES

Canst thou not minister to a mind diseas'd:
Pluck from the memory a rooted sorrow;
Raze out the written troubles of the brain;
And with some sweet oblivious antidote
Cleanse the stuff'd bosom of that perilous stuff
Which weighs upon the heart?

(*Macbeth*, 5.3.40–5)

Macbeth makes on his wife's behalf and his own this most poignant demand on the doctor, who replies: 'Therein the patient/Must minister to himself' (46). 'More needs she the divine than the physician' (5.1.70), because her illness arises out of mortal sin. This advice, although approved by Jaspers,[1] offers too little. Macbeth rejects any sweet antidote: 'Throw physic to the dogs! I'll none of it' (5.3.47), and for both the move to a tragic end is relentless.

PUTTING THE MADNESS INTO ITS CONTEXT

The theatre has been the place to which people have traditionally gone in order to explore the issues affecting their lives. Individuals share there the emotions aroused by the events portrayed, their common predicament is revealed, and they are encouraged to examine the implications and consequences of what they themselves have experienced. They can do so there in the terms of the metaphors, fables and cover stories offered by the play, in the terms too of the formulas on which the relationships of characters with one another are restored, perhaps to bring about a happy ending. Also, their experiences

142

are put into a more general context, in which disasters are transcended and people live on.

BRINGING FEUDS TO AN END

The plays of ancient Greece describe processes which weaken the constraints of the past, and bring relief to distress and recovery from madness. In Homer's *Iliad*, Achilles and Priam give each other effective help and support while working through the grief, guilt, shame and anger aroused by the death of Hector, Priam's son, at the hands of Achilles. In this and other examples in the Homeric epics, mental illness is seen to arise as a result of falling out with the social order and at the same time disrupting the social equilibrium of others. The person afflicted feels that external forces from which the illness results have taken over.

There is recovery when new roles are found in the family, this being composed not only of those alive, but also forebears and posterity. The new roles require several identifications, such as male and female, active and passive, destroyer and destroyed, bereaver and bereaved, and parent and child.[2] Therapy, initiated from outside as a general rule, is made effective not only by the support and intervention of others, but also by the proceses by which the afflicted work through the conflicts within themselves.

THE COUNCIL OF AEROPAGUS

The manifest cause of the madness in every one of the many cases portrayed in the plays of ancient Greece is a divine agency personified, who plays a part too in the processes of recovery. *The Oresteia* tells how the feuds that have affected the house of Atreus over several generations and culminated in the killing of Clytemnestra by her son Orestes are brought to an end by Athena at his trial at the Council of Aeropagus. Her intervention breaks a vicious circle of escalating conflicts, brings them under control and helps to resolve them.

She gives the casting vote in his favour after the jury of ten citizens, their votes having tied, has failed to either condemn him as a criminal or justify his killing of his mother as a duty. She renders 'the final judgment', and clears him of 'the charge of blood'. Persuaded by her, the Furies, the agents of retaliatory justice, who have been hounding him and making him mad, call off their pursuit, and are transformed into gracious spirits (Eumenides), and he recovers. Apollo has declared him to be free of pollution.

The Council in Aeschylus' play has features that fit its function of mediating between perpetrator and victim. The prosecutors are not the victim's kinsmen, but the avenging Erinyes who represent the victim. The tribunal is composed of citizens, not gods, although Athena presides, and the court's decision is that of an independent, impartial authority, not that of the person wronged. The perpetrator submits to the judgment of the court.

Making a judgment is seen as a last resort by the modern therapist, Athena's counterpart. Blame is not apportioned. The information and advice offered are seen as subsidiary, the essential purpose being to create the conditions in which the members of a system can feel safe enough to re-engage with one another, explore the issues in dispute, and then define them in terms that make them amenable to negotiation and compromise. New terms for the future have to be agreed; there can be no return to the old.

Communal action thus brings Orestes' madness under control. The court of justice, by regulating impulsive violence, restores law and order and, as a crucial step forward, justice takes the place of a primitive concept of vengeance or retaliation. The civic state is upheld. With due ceremony the perpetrator is restored to a place in the community. For him the sequence has been confession, expiation and reconciliation with acceptance of the sacraments.

Until the institution of the court there had been no way in which feuds could be brought to an end. Men in ancient Greece had acted to placate the gods, whose will they had had to discover, and to do so they had turned to seers or soothsayers. The court provided the means of achieving public discussion and acceptance of the terms of the reconciliation.

In Aeschylus' version, Athena's intervention plays an essential part in the therapeutic process. Before the trial, Orestes, hounded by the Furies, and excluded and kept apart, has grieved in silence. In Euripides' *Electra*, Castor and Pollux intervene, in his *Orestes*, Apollo. Appearing aloft and speaking *ex machina*, out of the stage machine, the gods uphold the law,

144

and initiate from aloft the processes of reconciliation on the terms they prescribe.[3]

In Aeschylus' plays there is mostly dramatic dialogue, in the course of which conflicts are exhibited. A crucial step forward in dramatic technique was taken by Sophocles when he increased the number of actors to three. Creating the three-actor scene, he shows on the stage how a third person can change the form of a couple's interaction with each other. In place of confrontation he puts mediation, which is the essence of many forms of psychotherapy.

A third party, or intermediary, is shown to play an important part in mediating between two or more people and thus to bring a feud to an end. He is typically an outsider, who serves as a broker or negotiator rather than arbitrator.

In *The Comedy of Errors*, the representative of justice is the Duke. Appealed to separately by Adriana and Antipholus of Ephesus, he calls the quarrellers before him and presides over the uncovering of the sources of the errors at the heart of the quarrels.[4] The quarrellers, thus reconciled, rediscover their identities; order and harmony are restored.

THE THREE PHASES

In the Greek plays can be seen the three phases discussed in Chapter 4, there called crisis (or challenge), exploration and reorganisation. A similar formula is to be found in Dante's *Divine Comedy*. In the first phase, 'Inferno', the sufferer is in a private hell; in the second, 'Purgatorio', there is repentance and penance; in the third, 'Paradiso', reconciliation. In his account in *Inferno* of his own illness, with its themes of suffering and punishment, Strindberg[5] uses Dante's terms. Thus he writes of 'The Fall and Paradise Lost', 'Purgatory', 'Inferno' and 'Pilgrimage and Atonement'. *To Damascus I*, written less than a year later, tells of his conversion, reconciliation and recovery.

This scheme provides a model for the analysis of other plays, as it does too for psychotherapy. The greater part of nearly every play portrays the protagonists as they explore the antecedents of their predicament. Looking for enlightenment, they ask questions, just as Hamlet does, about what has happened, in order to discover the pattern of cause and effect and what went wrong. Understanding comes through retrospection.

They then revise and reinterpret accordingly the myths that have guided them. Hamlet's madness remits when Claudius reveals his guilt in his reaction to the Gonzago play. Pressing questions being answered, Hamlet is guided thereafter by reality rather than fantasy.

DISCUSSION AND RECONCILIATION

Another step forward in the techniques shown in plays is taken when characters discuss their own behaviour and that of others. They are said then to 'meta-communicate'; that is, talk about what they talk about to one another.[6] Bernard Shaw[7] gives as the landmark Nora's request to Helmer (in *A Doll's House*): 'We must sit down and discuss all this that has been happening between us.' Kristine in the same play reinforces the point when she says: 'The two must have the whole thing out between them.'

Another aspect of psychotherapy lies in the reconciliation of the two sides of the person: the outer and the inner self, or the tempter and the tempted. This is done, not by trying to dismiss one side – for example, through the exorcism of evil spirits – but by making whole. This means accepting that there are two or more sides of the whole, the bad as well as the good, and then choosing what kind of person to be.

For Faust no such reconciliation with Mephistopheles is possible, and there can be no healing. Hamlet struggles with the madness he sees as part of himself. Ellida is helped to make a choice between the fantasy of herself as fiancée and the reality of herself as wife and as mother to her two step-daughters, and thus achieves a remarkable recovery, thanks to the astute, impartial mediation of Arnholm.

Kurt in *The Dance of Death, Part 1*, in contrast, is inept and ineffective in mediating in the quarrel between Captain Edgar and Alice, whatever his intentions may be. Uncertainty about his loyalties may even add to their difficulties. Manipulated by husband and wife in turn, he takes sides, first one side and then the other, and is seen by each as weak and unreliable – a 'milksop', the Captain calls him.

THERAPEUTIC PROCESSES[8]

Many plays come to a happy end. Although perhaps no more than a wish-fulfilling fantasy, the end may show how conflicts can be resolved, and relationships restored, not as life always is, but as it might be.

Prometheus Unbound

One of the plays often seen as liberating is Shelley's *Prometheus Unbound*,[9] which shows in an allegory how evil – 'the immedicable plague' – can be expelled. Preoccupied with the tyranny of venereal disease, which for him signified evil, Shelley seeks to show how 'the monster syphilis with all its gorgon terrors can yet be driven from the earth'. Venereal disease was not the only evil Shelley was concerned about. Republican, anti-militarist, atheist and leveller, he was concerned too about the divisions in society and the tyranny to which the working class was subjected by the ruling class. His recipe applied to this struggle too.

The source of evil is represented in the play by Jupiter (Zeus), who is the celestial tyrant; hope is represented by Panthea, passion by Asia, and reason by Prometheus, who is a physician and master of practical arts, with knowledge of the hidden medicinal powers of herbs. Prometheus has provoked Jupiter and is being punished for doing so. Fettered to a rock, he suffers every day the pain of a griffon-vulture tearing at his liver – these are the pangs of disease or evil. He cannot do anything to free himself; nor can Panthea, nor Asia by themselves. Only the mysterious Demogorgon, representing perhaps the power of the people, united and confident, can overthrow Jupiter.

The precondition for the downfall of tyranny is the love of Prometheus and Asia. Prometheus, unbound and recovering physical and sexual vitality, restores health to Earth through physical contact. Offered a cave by Earth, he withdraws to it to make love with Asia. The energy their love-making releases diffuses through the world as joy and creativity. The very processes by which venereal diseases are transmitted have become regenerative. The ingredients of the recipe for liberation are the courage to challenge the authority of tyrants through passive resistance without violence, the union of reason and

147

SCENES OF MADNESS

passion – which Shelley called 'consentaneous love' – and knowledge of natural processes.

ARNHOLM AS MEDIATOR[10]

Serving as a third party or mediator in what amounts to 'conjoint therapy', Arnholm starts husband and wife off separately, later together, on an exploration of their expectations of each other. Ellida Wangel is able to tell him things about her affair with the sailor she has not been able to tell her husband. 'I must talk to someone about it,' she says. 'I admitted to my husband that my affections had once lain elsewhere. He has never asked to know more. And we've never raised the matter since.'

Encouraged by her conversations with Arnholm, she talks more freely with her husband. Arnholm helps him to understand the difficulties she has experienced in their marriage, and creates the conditions in which his attitudes towards her can change. The husband then shows her that although he married her because he could not bear the emptiness of the home after his first wife's 'untimely departure', he now has need of her as a wife. She recognises too that the second daughter Hilde craves to be mothered. Satisfying roles in which she is needed are available to her as wife, mother and housekeeper. With the prospect before her of a partnership with him on new terms, she is ready to decide in favour of Doctor Wangel when the Stranger's return forces her to do so.

A solitary person's tentative relationship with a mediatior provides the conditions in which 'reality testing' can be resumed, and distinctions made again between fantasy and reality. Once she has begun to talk with Arnholm, Ellida, her depression relieved at least partially, is able to re-evaluate her experience of the Stranger. Her preoccupation with the past is reduced, and she can start again to explore future possibilities. Her relationship with Arnholm restores her confidence, confirms her as a person, and prepares her to take a decision, whether to restore her marriage with Doctor Wangel on new terms or leave with the Stranger.

THE COCKTAIL PARTY

Many plays provide a commentary on the processes through which recovery comes about, and anticipate ideas now current

148

in psychotherapy. As several have recognised,[11] T.S. Eliot's *The Cocktail Party*,[12] published in 1940, anticipates by a decade or more ideas that have been crucial in the development of the technique of psychotherapy with couples, now called conjoint therapy. This play rediscovers ideas that are inherent in Arnholm's mediation between Ellida and her husband.

Eliot puts these words into the mouth of the authoritarian and devious doctor, Sir Henry Harcourt-Reilly, whose style is by no means to be imitated, when he addresses the married couple, Edward and Lavinia: 'It is just because you are not free that you have come to me.' He reproves them: 'You have both of you pretended to be consulting me; both tried to impose on me your own diagnosis, and prescribe your own cure.'

He pronounces: 'It is often the case that my patients are only pieces in a total situation, which I have to explore. The single patient who is ill by himself, is rather the exception.' 'I always begin from the immediate situation and then go back as far as I find necessary. You see the memories of your childhood – I mean in your present state of mind – would be largely fictitious.' These were refreshing ideas when psychotherapy was still dominated by ideas that the search for meaning should be retrospective, because they drew attention to the part played by the 'here-and-now' in the persistence and also the genesis of symptoms.

Of his technique he says: 'I learn a good deal by merely observing you, and letting you talk as long as you please, and taking note of what you do not say.' Revelation is the essence of what he offers the couple. The truth can make people free to find not cure but salvation. 'The best of a bad job is all that any of us make of it,' he adds.

Although its emphasis, as in *The Family Reunion*, is on the finding of a personal salvation, rather than reconciliation, *The Cocktail Party* makes the point that change in the relationship of a couple to each other is accompanied by changes in the larger system of which they are a part. A cocktail party is a metaphor for such a system, albeit a loosely organised and impermanent one. Guests at the cocktail party in Act One learn that Edward and Lavinia have separated. In Act Two – exploration – the couple accept treatment, and become reconciled on new terms. In Act Three – reorganisation – two years later, the reconvened cocktail party reveals that there has been kaleidoscopic change in the pattern of the relationships of their friends; there are notable absences.

A DELICATE BALANCE

Edward Albee's *A Delicate Balance*,[13] while portraying in dramatic terms the complex interactions in a family under stress, shows how change takes place in the delicate balance in the system. A middle-aged couple, Tobias and Agnes, estranged from each other, have yet achieved in their marriage a balance that allows them a tolerant and painless coexistence. Claire, Agnes's sister, who has a drink problem, speaks of the expectations that stabilise relationships: 'We have our friends and guests for patterns, don't we – known quantities. The drunks get drunk; the Catholics go to Mass, the bounders bound. We can't have changes – throws the balance off.'

The balance is thrown off in Act One – challenge – by the arrival uninvited of old friends, Edna and Harry, in distress after an experience of emptiness and loneliness. They have gone further down the road of estrangement that Tobias and Agnes too are treading. Also, Julia, Tobias's and Agnes's daughter, returns home after the breakdown of her marriage.

In Act Two, Tobias and Agnes, forced by these events out of their expedient detachment, explore through the night – with the foreshortening of time that is characteristic of plays – the problems in their relationships with each other, and with Edna and Harry, and Claire and Julia. As the sun rises – Act Three – there is promise that they will work through to a new, more satisfying relationship with one another. Breakfast is prepared, order and balance are restored, and the madness of the night is forgotten. Family myths have been abandoned.[14] The formula is the same as in Shakespeare's *A Midsummer Night's Dream*. After the bad dreams of the night, order, sanity and maturity are restored as day breaks.

AN INSPECTOR CALLS

Another play in which the mechanisms of change in family relationships are clearly revealed is J.B. Priestley's *An Inspector Calls*.[15] The curtain rises on a family dinner party being held to celebrate the engagement of the daughter Sheila to Gerald. The conversation in the opening minutes of the play defines the pattern of the relationships within the family and tells of their expectations of one another. A police inspector is then shown in, and tells them that he is making enquiries in connection with a girl's death after drinking disinfectant. This dramatic revelation initiates the exploration of their relationships with one another.

Keeping a distance psychologically, he elicits from each member of the family in turn, in a Socratic dialogue, information previously held secret. This is the challenge because it reveals the falsity of the assumptions they have been making about one another. Each has to abandon them, and the old pattern of relationships is destroyed. In Act Three a new pattern emerges, which promises to free Sheila from subservience to her parents and to Gerald.

Through a *coup de théâtre* Priestley throws doubt on the reality of the inspector. Is he any more than a shared fantasy? The resulting enigma can be interpreted to make the point that at times of transition – for example, when there is an engagement, childbirth or death – members of a family explore their relationships with one another. Uncomfortable questions are asked, and guilt about misdeeds may lead each of them to conjure up in fantasy a policeman or judge to whom they feel they have to account for what they have done.

INTRUDERS AND THERAPISTS

The policeman, whether a real or a fantasy figure, is an intruder into the system of relationships. By challenging assumptions and expectations he brings the system to a crisis. This may not be his intention. Nevertheless the effect of his intrusion is similar to that produced by the intrusion of Arnholm. Other intruders discussed in previous chapters include the ghost of Hamlet's father, the unseen ghost of Chamberlain Alving, Ulrik Brendel, and the Rat-Wife. As to the reality of these characters, other than Arnholm, the playwright has deliberately left them ambiguous.

So important are the intrusions by fantasy figures that some therapists ensure that in the consulting room there is an empty chair as a token for the absentee, who may be a parent or another lover. In some of Munch's drawings of Oswald's family the ghost of his father is seen to occupy a chair.[16] In many plays there are characters who play an important part in the proceedings but who do not appear – Godot, for instance.[17] Sometimes the other person gives a degree of stability to a stormy relationship by creating a deadlock in the resolution of conflicts. Arbitrary distinctions can be made between an intruder and a therapist. Intervention by a therapist is invited, or at least accepted. He is impartial, and his agreed intention is to mediate; that is, to bring about change in a system of relationships and reconciliation. Some would require that he should have a degree of expertise. On all but the last criterion, Arnholm's intervention is therapeutic, as is Athena's and Sir Henry's. The others are intruders, whether the effect of their intervention is beneficial or otherwise.

MUCH ADO ABOUT NOTHING

There are many expedients by which intervention can bring about change. In Shakespeare's *Much Ado about Nothing*, Benedick and Beatrice are hung up in an awkward, teasing and unhappy relationship; they vie with each other in their teasing insults. Don Pedro intervenes with a therapeutic intention, and conveys by subtle although not wholly honest means that each is pining for the other and is deserving of love. Each thus confirmed as a person is given the impetus to explore attitudes towards courtship and marriage. Released from the games which they had been playing with each other, and which have become deadlocked, they are reconciled in a trusting partnership and decide to marry, thus bringing the play to a happy end.

DESTRUCTIVE INTERVENTIONS

Mildred

Even a brief encounter may cause a critical change in the way in which a person sees himself. In O'Neill's *The Hairy Ape*,[18] Yank, a stoker in an enormous ocean liner, sees himself as the force that moves the world until Mildred, the languid, doll-like heiress and social worker, descends out of curiosity into the hot, smoky, dusty bowels of the ship, and screams with horror when she meets 'the filthy brute'. The sight of his image in her eyes destroys his sense of self. No longer the moving force, he has become the 'hairy ape'. Blanche in *A Streetcar Named Desire*, in talking about Stanley as 'sub-human' has a similar effect on him. Her self-esteem, on the other hand, is quickly restored by the doctor's courteous behaviour towards her.

The matchseller

There are lessons to be learnt from encounters that prove destructive, whether intentionally or not. In Pinter's *A Slight Ache*,[19] Edward and Flora, whose marriage has long been in difficulties, invite into the house an elderly matchseller standing at the garden gate. He is a third party, more remote and passive than any psychoanalyst has ever been. In the radio version he remains silent. On the stage he does no more than drop his tray of matches on one occasion. He may be seen as a shared construct of their imaginations.

Edward alone with him embarks on a nervous monologue, which becomes a mixture of boasting and confession, and in the course of which he gets more and more anxious and incoherent. The slight ache he has been suffering from grows into a general loss of vitality, and progresses to the point of collapse, when he feels that he might be going blind. Flora in her turn revives sexual fantasies from her childhood about being set upon by wild men. Handing the tray of matches to Edward she leaves with the matchseller, whose intrusion has split the couple. Edward has suffered expulsion, the symbolism of which means that he dies. Flora, liberated from an impotent, despised husband, and experiencing a revival of sexual desire, embarks on a new life.

Martin Dysart

Therapy may prove disastrous even when well-intentioned. In Peter Shaffer's *Equus*,[20] 17–year-old Alan has been struggling to resolve the conflicts aroused by his upbringing by an atheist father and religious mother, each with double standards. Because of his fragile sense of identity he has developed an acute psychosis after failing in love-making with Jill, who works in a stable, and then blinding the horses who have observed them. Intervention by Martin Dysart, the psychiatrist to whom he is brought for in-patient treatment, proves destructive, although intended to be therapeutic, because it pre-empts any chance of restoring his relationship with Jill, who has her nervous breakdown off-stage. Also, it blocks his parents' attempts at reconciliation with him.

Dysart does get Alan to tell him of the love-making, and to abreact the emotion that went with it. He then gives this angry prognosis:

> Do you think feelings like this can be simply re-attached like plasters? . . . My desire might be to make this boy an ardent husband − a caring citizen . . . My achievement . . . is more likely to make a ghost! . . . With any luck his private parts will come to feel as plastic to him as the products of the factory to which he will almost certainly be sent. Who knows? He may even come to find sex funny. . . . Trampled and furtive and entirely in control. . . . Passion, you see, can be destroyed by a doctor. It cannot be created. . . . [But he] will be without pain.
>
> (299–300)

The outcome Dysart expects is akin to the defect state following a schizophrenic illness, that is characterised by blunting of emotional responses, indifference and impoverishment of thought. His patient has been disabled, not liberated.[21] This is a terrible warning of what may happen when a therapist prevents the patient from restoring his relationships with significant others. Dysart does so, it seems, for the sake of a close relationship with his patient, which he cherishes because it does something to meet his own need for self-definition. The proper purpose of a therapist is to create conditions in which the patient becomes free to resume interaction with others.

Equus provides a rich exploration of the symbols and metaphors with which a disturbed adolescent expresses unresolved conflicts in his relationships with parents and peers. It has been praised by some psychotherapists and heavily criticised by others.[22]

Dysart's objective is to convert neurotic misery into ordinary unhappiness.[23] He has not learnt from the penetrating criticisms, made by Virginia Woolf, amongst others, of the attempts of psychiatrists to restore ordinariness, conformity and conventional sex roles. In her novel *Mrs Dalloway*, she describes some aspects of her own experience of treatment by telling of what happens to Septimus Smith, who kills himself. What was lacking in his case, and in her own, was any encouragement towards self-realisation.[24]

Bishop Nikolas

A third person may unwittingly or deliberately make reconciliation more difficult. Kurt in *The Dance of Death* has already been mentioned as one example. Bishop Nikolas in Ibsen's *The Pretenders* deliberately maintains the rivalry between Earl Skule and Haakon, the king elect, by refusing to confirm or deny that Haakon is king by birth. 'Doubt is my best weapon,' he remarks. Uncertainty is often destructive, and the therapist's dilemma may be whether to keep a life-lie going or to relieve doubt by allowing more or less ambiguous facts to be disclosed.

Iago

One of the most astute destroyers in literature is Iago in *Othello*. He knows well how destructive is uncertainty:

[T]hat cuckold lives in bliss
Who, certain of his fate, loves not his wronger;
But, O, what damnèd minutes tells he o'er
Who dotes, yet doubts, suspects, yet strongly loves!
(3.3.165–8)

He is confident in his ability to wreck the relationship between Othello and Desdemona and bring them to disaster. Remember his claim – no idle boast – for his power to bring 'farewell to the tranquil mind':

Not poppy, nor mandragora,
Nor all the drowsy syrups of the world,
Shall ever medicine thee to that sweet sleep
Which thou ow'dst yesterday.
(3.3.327–30)

The roots of his destructiveness lie partly in racial prejudice and sexual jealousy, to which no one is immune – 'Even now, now, very now, an old black ram/Is tupping your white ewe' (1.1.89–90). Every therapist has to recognise and keep control over the Iago in him. Iago for his own reasons exploits Othello's suspicions. The black partner of a white woman, as clinical experience teaches, is liable to become jealous or paranoid towards her – a reaction that has been called the 'Othello syndrome'.[25] Iago knows how to fan the flames, and serves as a model for Laura in *The Father* when she sets out to destroy her husband's sanity.

Iago is encouraged to break Desdemona's marriage by her father, who warns Othello that she may deceive him. As his doubts grow, and are played on by Iago, Othello feels that his world is threatened, so that 'Chaos is come again' (3.3.90)

Gregers Werle

The reasons why Gregers proves so destructive of the Ekdal family are discussed in Chapter 7. He imposes himself on them without their invitation, insists that they face the truth, and presses on them ideals they are hardly ready to subscribe to.

TRIANGULATION[26]

A third person, whether a fantasy figure or real, may give a degree of stability to a relationship, such as a marriage, and hold two people together. One example is the fantasy son in *Who's Afraid of Virginia Woolf?*;[27] another is the real Cliff in Osborne's *Look Back in Anger*.[28] Of his part in holding Jimmy and Alison's marriage together he says:

> This has always been a battlefield. If I hadn't been here, everything would have been over between them long ago. I've been a no-man's-land between them. Most of the time it is simply a narrow strip of plain hell. I love these two people very much. And I pity all of us.

Once incorporated into the system, as Cliff is, the third person loses the capacity to promote change, except by breaking away. It is all too easy for a therapist to become incorporated, take on a role like Cliff's, and likewise lose the capacity to promote change. Providing a neutralised no-man's-land between them serves to perpetuate a deadlock in the development of a couple's relationship, and makes it not easier but more difficult for either to take decisions.

The incorporation of a third person to make a ménage-à-trois[29] is seen sometimes as a way of preserving a marriage. In *Rosmersholm*, Beata proposes it as a means of stabilising the relationships of her husband, Rebecca and herself. Rita and Alfred made a similar proposal to Asta in *Little Eyolf*. At the end of *Rosmersholm* the suicide of Rosmer and Rebecca serves to reunite them in fantasy with Beata.

A third person, such as a parent, family friend or child, may give stability to a marriage. For the therapist there is a dilemma, whether to be a healer, who like Cliff preserves a system of relationships, or to be an agent of change. To formulate it thus is to present too stark a choice. A therapist is brought in or intervenes because the rules governing the relationships are being questioned, and in that sense the system has already become unstable. Minor adjustments may be sufficient to restore its stability. On the other hand, opening up discussion of the issues may be followed by a period of instability while they are explored. The outcome may then be a more drastic reorganisation of the system than was envisaged or its disintegration.

Another condition in which a system is brought to a crisis is when a member drops out by reason of death or moving away. This may happen when, in the case of a fantasy figure, the myth is destroyed, as in Albee's *Who's Afraid of Virginia Woolf?*, when George announces with malice that the son who has only existed in the elaborate myth they have shared has been killed. The myth destroyed, they can settle down to negotiate new terms on which to relate to each other.

COMPANIONS AND CONFIDANT(E)S

There are others who bring about change in a character's behaviour and attitudes, not as third parties, but as companions or confidant(e)s. These, entrusted with private matters, encourage talk about attitudes and intentions and the ventilation of worries and concerns, and comment, giving advice and perhaps representing conscience or other self. Evidence in the psychiatric literature shows that the lack of an intimate, confiding relationship makes a person vulnerable and predisposed to depressive or other mental illness when there are provoking factors.[30]

Horatio

Notable among confidants is Horatio. A fellow student at Wittenberg and good friend, respected as a scholar by the gentlemen of the guard on the battlements, and sceptic, Horatio serves as Hamlet's confidant. Hamlet confides in him: 'I, perchance, hereafter shall think meet/To put an antic disposition on' (1.5.171–2). Seen by Hamlet as 'not passion's slave', 'A man that Fortune's buffets and rewards/Hast ta'en with equal thanks', and among the 'blest' 'Whose blood and judgement are so well comingled' (3.2.65–70), he is a steadying influence on him, the voice of sanity in a threatening world. When he has got away from Rosencrantz and Guildenstern, Hamlet sends for him as a confidant, saying in his letter, 'I have words to speak in thine ear . . . I have much to tell thee' (4.6.13–30).

Horatio's speeches are modest, practical and to the point. He does not 'unpack his heart with words'. A listener rather than a talker, and the audience for Hamlet's comments on life and people, he has been said to have 'no very marked individuality'. He is sparing of advice, but offers it on two occasions, on the first, telling Hamlet not to go with the ghost, and on the second, to give up the fencing match with Laertes. 'On all other occasions he merely says ditto to his friend.'[31] But he earns and retains Hamlet's trust. Above all he treats him as sane.

The Fool

The Fool in *King Lear* appears after he has been sent for by the king (1.4). He is said to have 'much pined away' since Cordelia's going to France, showing the grief that the king might have been expected to show. The king has been annoyed by the neglect and discourtesy shown in his reception in Goneril's household, and the Fool chides him with his foolishness in his treatment of his daughters, abdicating his responsibilities and giving away his land. Then as later he comments in jests and riddles, labouring to 'out-jest his [the king's] heart-strook injuries', and putting interpretations on his errors. At one point the king appoints him and Poor Tom (Edgar) to act as judges in a mock trial of Goneril and Regan.

His role is as a commentator, an all-licensed critic, who sees and speaks the real truth with the wisdom of folly, albeit in cryptic terms.[32] He sees clearly where others do not, but nothing is serious, nothing is solid, nothing has abiding consequences.

He insists that the king takes him with him when, after his quarrel with Goneril, he leaves her household. He remains at the king's side while his madness develops and that and the storm reach their height, except that he stays briefly on the stage to utter a paradoxical prophecy when the king exits to enter the hovel. But he does not reappear after he, Kent and Gloucester bear off the king on a litter (at the end of 3.6).

He plays little or no part in the development of the action of the play, and hardly exists as a person independent of the king, whom he addresses as 'nuncle' (that is, 'mine uncle'), as is the habit of fools. Poor Tom (Edgar), on the other hand, who like the Fool enters into the king's playing out of fantasies, does have an independent existence. The Fool's closeness to the king and his sympathy for him and Cordelia suggest that he should be regarded as the king's other self and as a mark of his madness, and he has been so played in a recent stage production.[33]

He represents sanity, insight and self-criticism – the antithesis of the king's madness. A man with obvious defects, but not devoid of common sense, he gets slapped, but is none the worse for the slapping; he is morally and spiritually resilient. His is the cause of the stupid against the clever, the weak against the strong.

Among other confidants in Shakespeare's plays are Kent for King Lear, Paulina for Leontes, and 'the nurse, her foster-mother' for Juliet in *Romeo and Juliet*. Among those lacking a confidante are Ophelia, Lady Macbeth, Portia and Constance.

In many of Racine's plays there is a confidante or tutor associated with each of the main characters. Oenone, 'nurse and confidante', has an intimate relationship with Phèdre, having been present at her birth. She counsels her, and stops her from killing herself. Having intervened in her relationships with others, she is driven away and drowns herself. In *Andromache*,[34] the confidantes are debating partners, who play no part in the main action. They are dispassionate, or offer alternatives, or condone; thus Cephisa, echoing Phèdre's nurse, advises Andromache: 'One can be overfaithful to one's husband; excessive virtue may become a vice.'

COMMENTATORS

A commentary is often provided by one or more characters who are not confidants. They may participate in the action while remaining more or less peripheral to it; for example, Doctor Relling and Molvik in *The Wild Duck* and Ulrik Brendel in *Rosmersholm*. Less often there is a narrator who stands outside the events as an interested spectator.

In the tragedies of ancient Greece the chorus, bridging the gap between the actors and the audience, refers to the moral and religious principles at issue and hence the significance of what has been enacted or what is to happen. They narrate, inform, comment, interpret and mediate. They may supply background information and, reporting from a different perspective, show how others, who are outside the action, are affected. Although taking part in the events of the drama, the chorus is more or less detached from them and does not influence directly what the characters do. The audience's emotional response to the events depicted is modified also by music and dance.

The prologue and epilogue in some of Shakespeare's plays may do something similar to what the chorus does in the Greek plays. But the commentary is provided more often by another character. In *The Family Reunion* there is, unusually in a modern play, a chorus, formed by several of the minor characters, who provide a commentary. Eliot uses a similar device in *The Cocktail Party*. In *Murder in the Cathedral* there is a chorus more like that in the Greek plays.

SUMMARY

Examples are given of the restoration of relationships and recovery from madness as a result of intervention by an outsider or 'third party', whose intention is to mediate – that is, to bring about reconciliation. Athena brings an end to the feuds in the Atreus family. Arnholm, who shows remarkable skill in 'conjoint therapy', helps to restore Ellida's relationships with her husband and step-daughters. The processes in mediation are illustrated by reference to the part played by Arnholm in the affairs of the Wangel family. Another mediator is the clumsy Sir Henry Harcourt-Reilly. Intervention, whether by a therapist or an 'intruder', may upset the delicate balance in a system of relationships, the result being not reconciliation, but disruption, estrangement and tragedy. The arch-destroyers, although differing in their intentions, are Iago and Gregers. The contribution made to recovery by companions and confidants is briefly discussed, with reference to Horatio (in *Hamlet*), the Fool (in *King Lear*) and the nurse (in *Phèdre*).

9

CONCLUSIONS

> The artist always arrives first, ahead of the scientist and the
> crowd – and he sounds the alarm.[1]

So said Karl Kraus, the Viennese satirist and contemporary
'unmasker' of Freud. He objected with a 'suave savagery' to the
jargon and reductionism he saw as characteristic of psychoanalysis, and was convinced that it is the poet who knows the
secrets of the human soul; the psychoanalyst steals them, and
claims to have discovered them through research.

There are no ownership rights in such secrets, but there is
justification for the claim of priority for the artist. It is Sophocles
who in *King Oedipus* sounds the alarm to warn of the dangers in
searching out the truth when doing so is against the wishes of
the gods.

Euripides sounds the alarm in both *The Bacchae* and *Hippolytus*
to warn of the consequences of denying expression to Dionysian
impulses and so failing to honour the god. Young and old must
dance in his honour, Teiresias advises (ll.206–9).[2] If he is to
recover, Pentheus, 'grievously mad – beyond the cure of drugs'
(326–7) must 'Receive the god into this land, and pour offerings,
and be a bacchant, and garland your head' (ll.312–3). Aphrodite
wreaks vengeance on Hippolytus because of his honouring of
Artemis and so failing to strike a balance between hunting and
passion. Ibsen in *Hedda Gabler* shows what happens if Teiresias'
advice is not heeded; it is not enough to watch from the side-
lines.

Artists are the explorers, scientists the map-makers. To know
the secrets of the soul is one thing, another, to express that
knowledge in terms that make it useful as a guide to the public
in the practical affairs of living and, especially, to mental health

workers in their professional work. The scientist has a key part to play in translating the insights of artists into such terms. Often the first step is to test how far what has been learnt in one case can be generalised to cover other cases. What has the artist discovered about madness? One discovery going back to the ancient Greeks is that it arises out of crises in relationships, or falling out with the social order. A second is that recovery reflects reconciliation. Thus in the plays of ancient Greece, madness is seen as a more or less direct consequence of the anger of the gods, who tend to act capriciously and not in accordance with discoverable principles. It is inflicted as punishment when there is unruly behaviour on the part of the victim, as in the case of Heracles, who is driven mad by the goddess Hera when, jealous of him, she is determined to fasten on him the guilt of kindred blood.

The second discovery directs attention to the procedures of reconciliation through which an end is brought to family feuds. The obstacles to reconciliation have first to be identified and overcome. Intervention from outside by a mediator appears necessary. Notable as mediators are Athena in the case of Orestes, the Duke in the case of Antipholus of Ephesus, Arnholm in the case of Ellida, and Sir Henry in the case of Edward and Lavinia. Reconciliation depends also on the estranged being able to assume suitable roles within a system of relationships.

FORMS OF EXPLANATION

Plays offer 'contextual' explanations by putting behaviour into a context of events, circumstances and their connections. The despair and the 'utter weariness' of Hamlet's 'To be or not to be' speech (3.1.56), his 'antic disposition' and his anger towards and abuse of Ophelia are explained when the playwright shows the place they hold in relation to the complex changes going on in the patterns of interaction in the court at Elsinore after his father's death, his uncle's assumption of power, his mother's remarriage, and the doubts cast on Ophelia's chastity.

There are other related forms of explanation. The understanding is 'subjective', in Jaspers' sense,[3] or 'intuitive', when the playgoer sees the meaning in the behaviour through empathy with the person afflicted, as readily happens in the first few

163

scenes of *Hamlet*. As it develops, it becomes 'causal', the behaviour then being attributed to a particular event or events. Strindberg's warning should then be heeded: 'An incident in real life is usually the outcome of a whole series of deep-buried motives, but the spectator commonly settles for the one that he finds easier to understand, or that he finds most flattering to his powers of judgement.'[4] This criticism can be made of Polonius when, obsessed by Hamlet's courting of Ophelia, he insists that the cause of his madness lies in 'the very ecstasy of love'.

Causal explanations are 'reductionist' when they identify a specific intrapsychic tendency, such as the Oedipus complex, or when the person is seen as the victim of the gods or an external force, such as the Furies, but not when they show how the development of the behaviour is caused by, or is part of, a sequence of interrelated changes in a system of relationships. There is then little difference, other than emphasis, between a causal and a contextual explanation.

The explanation is 'interpretative' when the behaviour is seen to express a general tendency, such as a son's Oedipal hostility to his father, or to be part of a coping strategy – for example, as the means by which Hamlet conceals his true feelings and thus misleads, and protects himself from, those he regards as hostile. Hamlet offers Gertrude an interpretation of her belief in his madness when he says to her: 'Lay not that flattering unction to your soul,/That not your trespass, but my madness speaks' (3.4.145–6). His use of the word 'unction' indicates the intrapsychic mechanism, without specifying it as a psychoanalytic interpretation would tend to do;[5] this mechanism might be specified as projection.

It is seldom that plays offer a 'biological' explanation, although references may be made to biological processes; for example, Banquo, commenting on the apparitions Macbeth and he have seen, asks, 'have we eaten on the insane root/That takes the reason prisoner?' (1.3.84–5), thus supposing that madness can be the result of a chemical process. Brabantio accuses Othello of abusing Desdemona's 'delicate youth with drugs or minerals/ That weaken motion' (1.2.74–5). There are many references in plays to both the beneficial and the harmful effects of wine and drugs.

Only in the latter part of this century could the suggestion be made about Hamlet, satirically by Arthur Miller[6] through a character: 'With the right pill his anxiety would dissolve; correctly medicated he could have made a deal with the king and married Ophelia.' Certainly, there could have been reconciliation if there had been someone in a position to mediate. That medication by itself would be sufficient is questionable. Note the bias in these remarks towards Hamlet coming to terms with the king rather than Ophelia.

In *As You Like It* there is a reference to the 'humoral' theory of mental illness when Le Beau warns Orlando:

> Yet such is now the duke's condition,
> That he misconstrues all that you have done.
> The duke is humorous.
>
> (1.2.253–5)

That is, Duke Frederick misconstrues because of imbalance in the four humours, which have to be in balance if a man is to be normal.

In the sixteenth and seventeenth centuries especially, madness tended to be attributed to imbalance in the humours, but the playwrights of the time – for example, Middleton and Rowley in *The Changeling* – still portray madness as the reflection of mental processes related to changes in social and sexual relationships, with no more than passing references to the humoral theory.

There are occasional references to physical processes in the brain. Regan points to King Lear's 'infirmity of ... age' (1.1.292), and Goneril to 'not alone the imperfections of long-engraffed condition, but therewithal the unruly waywardness that infirm and choleric years bring with them' (295–8). Also mentioned in King Lear's case is his loss of the sleep that might have 'balm'd' his 'broken sinews', and Cordelia sees sleep as the means to 'Cure this great breach in his abused nature!' (4.7.15).[7]

Shakespeare gives an excellent description of the dementia of the elderly in *The Winter's Tale*. Polixenes asks his son:

> Is not your father grown incapable
> Of reasonable affairs? is he not stupid
> With age and altering rheums? can he speak? hear?
> Know man from man? dispute his own estate?
> Lies he not bed-rid? and again does nothing
> But what he did being childish?
>
> (4.4.394–9)

'Genetical' explanations are absent from Shakespeare's plays, there being no suggestions that madness is inherited, whether through genes or physical damage. 'Treason is not inherited', Rosalind tells Duke Frederick (*As You Like It*, 1.3.59). In the plays of ancient Greece, family feuds are continued from one generation to another, but without there being any suggestion that the causes of madness lie in the physical constitution.

This is in contrast to some of the plays written in the last quarter of the nineteenth century when physical inheritance in some way, if not through genes, which were not then known of, is commonly invoked as a cause of illness or degeneracy. This theme in *Ghosts* and also in Gerhart Hauptmann's play *Before Sunrise*, written in 1889, is in keeping with such topics of the time as hereditary alcoholism and constitutional degeneracy,[8] with which genius has sometimes been supposed to be associated.

Hauptmann said that what he portrays in his plays are human encounters, and how people express themselves when they meet, clash and circle round one another, referring in these terms to changes in their relationships. But as a member of the German Naturalist Movement, with its slice-of-life approach, he supposed that how they express themselves is determined as much by what they are as by their circumstances, and that what they inherit physically contributes importantly to what they are.[9] But *Before Sunrise*, like *Ghosts*, still makes sense when no weight is given to physical inheritance, and this is of no relevance in Hauptmann's more famous play, *The Weavers*, which tells of the Silesian weavers' struggle against oppression.

O'Neill's *Strange Interlude*,[b0] written in 1926, comments ironically on the role of physical inheritance. Her rivalrous mother-in-law tells Nina that her husband Sam's great-grandfather, grandmother, father and aunt, all on his father's side, have been insane, and thus creates the expectation that her unborn child, and perhaps also Sam, will be similarly affected. Her pregnancy is terminated as a result. As the story develops, Sam turns out to be the most stable and mentally robust of any of the characters. Nina's son, by another father, is shown to develop mentally in accordance not with any inherited tendencies, but with the expectations of those he wrongly supposes to be his natural parents, and with whom he identifies.

There are a few 'nosological' explanations, albeit primitive ones, to be found in the plays of Shakespeare's time, when distinctions between fools and madmen were usual. Modern critics have been prone to discuss how illnesses like those of Hamlet and Ophelia may be classified, and this may be seen as a step towards explaining them, though not down a path of any promise. Othello has been said to suffer from 'pathological jealousy'.

Lollio in *The Changeling* tells us that in Doctor Alibius's madhouse there are 'but two sorts of people, that's fools and madmen' (1.2.45–8).[11] Locke made the distinction in 1690: 'The difference between Idiots and mad Men is that mad Men put wrong Ideas together, and so make wrong Propositions, but argue right from them. But Idiots make very few or no Propositions, and reason scarce at all.'[12] More detailed classification had not yet been developed, and it was not until the nineteenth century that the third category, 'moral insanity', was added by Prichard.[13]

THE NATURE OF MADNESS

While busy putting examples of mad behaviour into their contexts, I have been risking readers' discontent because I have not laid down any limits on what is to be meant by madness. One reason is that, being a colloquial term, it cannot be defined neatly. Another is that it can be dispensed with, except as a convenient rubric, if the social and psychological processes are sufficiently identified.

The approach to definition I have adopted is to assemble a sample of characters deemed to be mad, and then to ask: what do they have in common? I prefer the term 'madness' to 'insanity' or 'mental illness' because it is the least pretentious.

For J.C. Bucknill in 1854, the essence of 'insanity, mental alienation, unsoundness, derangement' is 'loss of coordinate action of the faculties' due to 'deprivation of the power of the will', his definition being 'A condition of the mind in which a false action of conception or judgement, a defective power of the will, or an uncontrollable violence of the emotions and instincts, have separately or conjointly been produced by disease'.[14]

The modern term 'mental illness' has defied precise definition. In the Mental Health Act 1983 (as in its 1959 predecessor) it replaces the former 'unsoundness of mind', and is one of the categories of 'mental disorder' that in certain circumstances permits the exercise of the powers of the Act to override personal rights, but it is not defined.

In clinical work there are no agreed limits to what mental illness covers. It tends to be diagnosed when there is evidence of either impairment in such key mental functions as perceiving, thinking or remembering or more than temporary alterations of mood or emotional response to a degree to vitiate the person's appraisal of his own situation, past, present or future, or that of others. Delusions – that is, 'wrong propositions' – and hallucinations are seen as cardinal symptoms.[15]

The concept of madness has been illuminated more or less directly in plays but without limits being put on it. In *King Lear*, for instance, the suffering Gloucester compares himself with the king:

> The king is mad. How stiff is my vile sense,
> That I stand up, and have ingenious feeling
> Of my huge sorrows! Better I were distract.
> So should my thoughts be sever'd from my griefs,
> And woes by wrong imaginations lose
> The knowledge of themselves.

> (4.6.278–83)

He, but not the king, remains conscious of his huge sorrows, and his response to them is inflexible. How much better it would be to be mad, and to lose knowledge of his woes by entering into wrong imaginations.[16]

BEATRICE

In *The Changeling* the folly and madness of those in the sub-plot who are confined in Doctor Alibius's madhouse provide standards for subtle comparisons with the behaviour of Beatrice, De Flores and the others in the main plot who are outside the madhouse. The regular inmates, dressed as birds and beasts, are confined because of their lack of control over their passions (or 'emotions and instincts'). With them in the madhouse are Isabella, who is sane, but confined because of her husband's irrational suspicions of her faithfulness, Antonio feigning foolishness in order to hide that he is in love with Isabella, and Franciscus masquerading as a poet mad from love sickness.

Whereas Isabella is sane, Beatrice is insane. She is in love with

Alsamero, whom she wishes to marry, although he entertains irrational suspicions of her. She forms an alliance with De Flores, her father's servant, whom she hates, and persuades him to kill Alonzo in order to break the shackles put on her freedom by her father's insistence that she marries Alonzo. Put into De Flore' power by her complicity in the killing, she submits to sexual intercourse with him. She marries Alsemero nevertheless, but has to resort to devices to hide from him that she is not a virgin. The end is disaster. Their wicked deeds being discovered, she is wounded by De Flores while they are having sexual intercourse and dies. De Flores kills himself.

Beatrice's madness lies in her blind disregard for moral, social and legal restraints, although such disregard is more characteristic of psychopathic disorder than mental illness. Also, she acts in ways that prove destructive both to herself and others, far more destructive than the uncontrolled behaviour of the inmates of the madhouse. Moreover, her appraisal of reality, like Doctor Alibius's and Alsemero's, is faulty to a delusional degree, as the critics[17] have pointed out. 'In a sleep-walking delirium of love', as one critic has described her,[18] she is 'without sense of the reality about her or within her.' Much of her behaviour reflects misjudgements due to her mistaking fantasy for fact. Blind hitherto to the consequences of her actions, she is deeply shocked when De Flores shows her Alonzo's severed finger with her ring on it as evidence of his murder.

She fails to recognise, or lacks insight into, her sexual interest in De Flores and his in her, and acts in ways that arouse him further, without seeing the significance of what she is doing. After intercourse with him, she projects on to Diaphanta, her waiting maid, faults she denies in herself, accusing Diaphanta of being a 'strumpet' and having a greedy sexual appetite.

There is no suggestion in *The Changeling* that sexual impulses are harmful in themselves. The harm lies in the failure to recognise and acknowledge them, anticipate their consequences, and especially to strike a balance between reason and passion. Beatrice's reason fails to regulate the expression of passion, in contrast to Pentheus, Hippolytus and Hedda Gabler, in whose cases reason prevents sufficient expression. Her madness arises too out of her failure to free herself from her father's influence, and to make her own choice of husband, without resort to criminal action.

The medical concept of illness (or disease), whether mental or physical, implies a change from a previous normal state or normal function. Changes in behaviour are going on all the time, and a change is taken to indicate illness only when it is for the worse in some way;[19] a change due to natural decay is usually excluded.

In every one of the cases of madness reviewed in previous chapters, the changes for the worse arise out of a crisis in a system of relationships as a result of a challenge from outside of such an intensity or kind that the homeostatic mechanisms fail to restore the system, which is disrupted. Each member, in order to adapt to the new circumstances, tries to restore not the status quo, but the relationships on new terms.

Beatrice's attachment to Alsamero, her rejection and killing of Alonzo, and her seduction by De Flores all challenge an already unstable system. Alonzo is killed. Her relationships with her father and Alsamero cannot be restored, and the only possible outcome is that both she and De Flores, already an outsider, are excluded.

Some of the elements of the behaviour portrayed in *The Changeling*, seen by playgoer and critic as madness, invite attempts to formulate hypotheses about madness. In other plays, such as Pirandello's *Henry IV*,[20] the behaviour portrayed is contrived in order to fit into and illustrate the playwright's thesis about the nature of madness, amongst the characters being a doctor who expounds on 'the special psychology of the mad'. For this reason his observations are not reliable as a basis for hypotheses.

THE CHARACTERISTICS OF THE MAD

What changes for the worse are shown by those who are seen as mad? There are several. When there is no reconciliation, they become estranged and withdraw from family or other social group, or are excluded or extruded. With the consequent reduction in interaction with others, there tends to go some confusion or distortion in roles as well. One aspect of estrangement is egocentricity, this being akin to the self-sufficiency that, as Peer Gynt is told, distinguishes trolls from humankind.

There are changes for the worse in the character of communication, which, becoming less spontaneous and less frank, disguises feelings and intentions. In response, those interacting with the estranged become defensive and reticent. Misinformed about each other, Hamlet and Ophelia, in their mad encounters in Ophelia's closet (2.1.74–97) and again in the lobby of the audience chamber (3.1.56–162 – the 'nunnery' scene), fail to convey their true feelings. Hamlet, misunderstood, is seen as mad and therefore to be feared. Ophelia on her own, and without a confidante, becomes 'distract', and her 'unshapèd' use of speech leaves her hearers unsure of what she is saying, which carries 'but half sense' (4.5.7).

Shakespeare provides other examples of the disordered speech of the estranged; for instance, Lady Macbeth's 'thick-coming fancies', that trouble her, and keep her from her rest (5.1, 5.3), and the rambling and obscure metaphors of Titus Andronicus' speech when 'distract' (4.3.1–27). Again, Desdemona, recognising Othello's suspicion and anger, comments:

> what doth your speech import?
> I understand a fury in your words,
> But not the words.
>
> (4.2.30–2)

The estranged tend to disengage from the world of reality, as Ellida does. She becomes preoccupied by nostalgic fantasies, which, taking on the character of real experience, become the salient features of her current life, with failure first to distinguish fantasy from fact and then test the reality of what is experienced. The failure to test is a cardinal feature of madness, even when the failure is no more than the lack of a critical attitude. Ellida accepts for a while that the Stranger is a real person, but starts to question his reality after she has told Arnholm about him.

Another example of disengagement is Old Ekdal (in *The Wild Duck*). Playing little or no part in the life in the home, and largely estranged from the real world, he makes a life for himself in the fantasy world of the loft, in which, his wishes being fulfilled, he is free again to be the huntsman he had been in his good days. His drinking contributes to his disengagement and harmless eccentricity.

The disengagement may be short-lived, as it is in the cases of Richard III, Brutus and Macbeth, when they hallucinate their victims in particular circumstances. Yet the effects on

171

subsequent attitudes and behaviour may be lasting and profound, as it is in the case of Hamlet as a result of the appearance
of his father's ghost, and in the case of Macbeth as a result of his
meetings with the witches, who impart ideas that he is to be
'king herafter' and invulnerable.

Another effect of estrangement is that the past exerts more of
an influence. Both Rosmer and Rebecca stop planning for the
future after their estrangement from Doctor Kroll and from each
other, and feel constrained by their pasts. Ellida recalls her
earlier life and the fiancé she has lost. Hamlet is tied by the past;
otherwise he might have left Elsinore and returned to student
life in Wittenberg.

In many cases there is a vicious circle because the crisis evokes
behaviour that intensifies the crisis. Tasso's inept behaviour
evokes further hostility. Almost everything Macbeth does
increases his estrangement. The tragic paradox is that the
actions he takes to dispel his fears that 'To be thus is nothing'
(3.1.47) disrupt any system of relationships that could have
made him something, and he sets off on a course from which
there is no turning back, as he recognises:

> I am in blood
> Steptd in so far that, should I wade no more,
> Returning were as tedious as go o'er.
>
> (3.4.135–7)

A vicious circle like that affecting Macbeth tends to bring with it
a progressive disorganisation, or disintegration, of behaviour,
which becomes more impulsive, less restrained and less effective, although it may still reflect efforts to cope with a threatening
situation. With disorganisation tends to go aggression directed
against those who appear to stand in the way, as in the case of
Macbeth. Claudius' resolve to kill Hamlet strengthens as his
fears grow. Heracles, threatened by Lycus, becomes frenzied in
his killing. The afflicted person, as he loses control, may feel
that he has been taken over or possessed by the devil, this
reflecting the giving over of control by the one to the other self.

These several changes for the worse are not distinct from one
another, but are interrelated parts of a complex sequence. They
are presented here as the constituents of madness. It could be
argued that they are but the effects of some other, underlying,
process, as yet unidentified. If that is so, any therapeutic

intervention along psychological lines might be said to do no more than mitigate the effects, without affecting the underlying process. No matter, every intervention should be judged on what it achieves, the question being put in the form: suitable criteria being agreed, what benefit does Orestes derive from Athena's intervention? The answer arrived at is the same whether his madness is caused by a biochemical disorder or arises out of a crisis in the relationships in his family.

HAMLET'S MADNESS

Should Hamlet be regarded as mad? Several points can be made in support of the view that he is. He cuts himself off from Gertrude and Claudius, although not from Horatio, and keeps his thoughts and feelings so hidden that he is not understood by them. His behaviour towards Ophelia is extravagant and disruptive and lacks restraint. He is emotionally unstable and at times inappropriate in his emotional responses, and entertains suicidal ideas. He is preocccupied with fantasies. There is no place for him in the new order in Elsinore, with little prospect of finding one, but he shows no inclination to return to Wittenberg and resume his studies.

On the other hand, his appraisal of his situation is empirical and reasonable, and he takes steps, with the help of the Gonzago players, to corroborate it. After Claudius has given himself away, a change comes over Hamlet's attitudes and behaviour. Is it for the worse? He holds back from killing Claudius, for reasons that are more indicative of sanity than insanity, as I have argued in Chapter 6. His conversation with his mother in the closet scene (3.4), although it expresses strong feelings, has nothing in it to suggest madness, except for the appearance of his father's ghost. But he kills Polonius, and talks about his corpse with a macabre wit which is inappropriate.

His resolution – 'O, from this time forth,/My thoughts be bloody, or be nothing worth!' (4.4.65–6) – means that he has become more dangerous to Claudius. Is this because of a morbid change within him, as the medical concept of disease requires, or is it that his situation has become more threatening, because of the actions being taken against him by Claudius? There is nothing to indicate madness in his review of his situation in his soliloquy (4.4.31–66) in which he reasserts his capacity to act:

This thing's to do,
Sith I have cause, and will, and strength, and means,
To do't.

Also, he shows himself to be keenly aware of the implications of the courses open to him.
Of special interest is his recognition subsequently that he is 'punish'd with sore distraction' (5.2.227). Asking pardon of Laertes, he proclaims that what he has done 'was madness' (230), but denies his part in it:

If Hamlet from himself be ta'en away,
And when he's not himself does wrong Laertes,
Then Hamlet does it not, Hamlet denies it.
Who does it, then? His madness: if't be so,
Hamlet is of the faction that is wrong'd,
His madness is poor Hamlet's enemy.

(232–7)

He draws thus a line between himself and his madness, as Dover Wilson[21] points out. He disowns the madness. Shakespeare is 'artful' in not allowing us to perceive exactly where the line falls, or which of his actions reflects madness, and which not.

He shows insight, in the sense in which this term is often used by psychiatrists, in that he sees his behaviour as having been abnormal or due to illness or 'madness', but the insight is faulty in that he still denies his part in the wrong done. He is at a stage reached, usually after a few years, by patients who have killed, but this is no more than the first stage in coming to terms with what they have done. He has yet to accept that it is he himself who has killed Polonius. Heracles, in Euripides' play (see pages 31–2), has gone much further towards gaining true insight in that he acknowledges that he is guilty – 'I am ashamed of my deep guilt' (l.1159) – and that he must 'live and suffer', without attributing his offence to madness, his other self, or anyone else.

It would not be safe to say that Hamlet is mad when he kills Polonius. Certainly, in Act Five, he has not yet worked through the implications and consequences of having done so. However, to say that he is or has been mad contributes nothing to understanding. Indeed, to do so embarrasses the study of the mental processes by which he is 'ta'en away' from himself. The important questions lie not in what it is called, but in how his behaviour relates to the circumstances.

MADNESS MISTAKEN

Reference has been made in previous chapters to the warnings to be found in plays about the mistakes that can be made when supposing someone to be mad. Hamlet reproves his mother for supposing that it is 'not your trespass, but my madness' that speaks. Rosmer comes to recognise the mistake he made when supposing Beata to be mad. To see someone as mad obscures the real issues and offends against the truth.

In *The Comedy of Errors* Shakespeare makes comedy out of the treatment of Antipholus of Ephesus who, when thought mistakenly to be mad, is given over to Dr Pinch, who tries to exorcise the spirits of madness, and then locks him away in a cellar.

Hamlet warns Guildenstern when he teases him for his inability to play the recorder:

How unworthy a thing you make of me! You would play upon me; you would seem to know my stops; you would pluck out the heart of my mystery; . . . do you think that I am easier to be played on than a pipe? Call me what instrument you will, though you can fret me you cannot play upon me.

(3.2.366–74)

Ivanov issues a similar warning, with a different metaphor: 'No, Doctor, we all have too many wheels, screws and valves to judge each other on first impressions or one or two pointers.'

Malvolio

In *Twelfth Night* Sir Toby Belch and his associates deceive the vain, socially inept, unpopular Malvolio so that he behaves in such a strange, extravagant and ridiculous way, while expressing incoherent fragments of wisdom, that he seems to Olivia and others to be suffering from midsummer madness, especially so when he wholly misjudges the occasion by smiling when others are sad. Charged by her to take 'a special care of him', they are able to tease him and confine him by putting him into a dark room. So provoked, he behaves in ways that confirm the view that he is mad. Kraus comments: 'The psychiatrist unfailingly recognises the madman by his excited behaviour on being incarcerated.'[22]

Olivia comes to disbelieve Feste's assertions that Malvolio is mad, and recognises, after she has had read to her the moving letter of complaint in which he gives her the reasons for his behaviour, that 'This savours not much of distraction' (5.1.311). She can then say to Malvolio, 'Alas, poor fool! How they have baffled thee!' (367) and recognise that 'He hath been most notoriously abus'd' (376). The suspicion that he has been mad is removed as soon as the plot against him by Toby, Fabian and Maria is uncovered, and a new light is thrown on his behaviour.

If there are sometimes grounds for supposing a person to be mad, there are sometimes positive grounds, other than lack of symptoms, for dismissing the idea. These are the grounds on which Sebastian in *Twelfth Night* dismisses the idea that Olivia is mad:

> Or else the lady's mad; yet if 't were so,
> She could not sway her house, command her followers,
> Take and give back affairs and their despatch
> With such a smooth, discreet, and subtle bearing
> As I perceive she does.
>
> (4.3.16–20)

This passage gives as good a short definition of mental health as any I know of. The qualities attributed to Olivia are the opposites of the elements that make up a picture of madness.

HAPPY ENDINGS

The therapist tries on behalf of those seeking his help to avert disaster and contrive a happy ending. About a tragedy one may ponder how intervention might change the outcome. Would medication help Hamlet to come to terms with Claudius? Or suppose that Doctor Rosencrantz and Mr Guildenstern at the beginning of 3.1. are a crisis-intervention team, psychiatrist and approved social worker, sent for by a step-father who is afraid of a step-son affected by 'confusion' and 'turbulent and dangerous lunacy' (3.1.2–4); this was before the killing of Polonius.

They may well have had previous experience of just such a

case, and might decide as a professional judgement that Hamlet ought to be detained in a hospital for a limited period for 'assessment'.[23] There would then be opportunities for casework with the family, especially for a therapist (or two therapists) to help Hamlet and Ophelia to work through their misunderstandings and doubts of each other and restore a loving, trusting relationship. In the play he is not detained until 4.4, after the killing of Polonius, then not for medical treatment.

A consequence of Freud's emphasis on the oedipal conflicts is that attention tends to be focused on the 'vertical' relationships between son and parents. Yet in a case like Hamlet's, or for that matter like Alan Strang's (in *Equus*), it is often better for efforts to be directed in the first instance to help the patient to re-engage in 'horizontal' relationhips with peers. Hamlet and Ophelia, had they not quarrelled, or had they been reconciled, might have been able to break free, with each other's support, from their parents and family and to move away, as many young couples do at that stage in their lives, and as Cordelia and the King of France do, as well as Desdemona and Othello.

Several of the endings of Ibsen's plays invite therapists to indulge in intriguing speculations on what intervention might achieve. Suppose that after the curtain falls Oswald is admitted to a psychiatric unit. Suppose that Ulrik Brendel (although unkempt) is a psychotherapist. Suppose that once again everything that Hedda touches 'is destined to turn into something mean and farcical', and that the gunshot does no more than stun her and inflict a nasty face and scalp wound. The clinical problems so arising would be challenging.

There are lessons to be learnt from comedies as well as tragedies about what are seen as the elements of a happy ending. After the madness or the bad dreams of the night, as day breaks, order, sanity and maturity are restored, as in, amongst other plays, *A Midsummer Night's Dream*. Madness has been induced in this play by Oberon or Puck squeezing the 'love juice' of a little western flower on sleeping eyedids. There has been recovery after a similar instillation of the juice of another herb. Misunderstandings are cleared up. Lovers, reunited, are again as they are 'wont to be' and see as they are 'wont to see' (4.1.70–1). The past is forgotten, and they are free to make their own choices and plans for the future.

In *The Tempest* there are other elements in the happy ending, which is presided over by Prospero. He may be seen as a therapist, although he has powers therapists do not have. Thus in the dream world of the island, but not outside it, he can control the wild waters, raise winds, darken the sun and command spirits, and he can exercise spells over people that bind up their senses. But he cannot alter their inclinations and ideas, although he can create the conditions in which these can be modified through learning, and in which there can be reconciliation.

In the happy ending that is typical of a romance, the parted are restored to one another, the wrongs of the past are repented and forgiven, misunderstandings are unravelled, and for a while people speak and feel as one. Ferdinand and Miranda, both freed, though in different ways, from their fathers, come together as a loving couple. Alonso, resigning his dukedom in favour of Prospero, repents and is forgiven. Sebastian and Antonio, their normal world dislocated by the shipwreck, and their wicked plans frustrated, stay silent. Caliban, recognising his foolishness in worshipping the drunkard Stephano as a god, resolves, without any real change of heart, to be 'wise hereafter, and seek for grace'. Prospects for the future are bright, but there is unfinished business, and Caliban and others continue their wicked ways as before. Prospero breaks his staff and his 'charms are all o'erthrown'.

'Of happiness the crown and chiefest part is wisdom,' the Chorus in Sophocles' *Antigone* (ll.1406–8) advises.[24] Yet the epithet 'happy' hardly fits another element in the endings of plays that deserves a final comment. This is self-discovery, which in the cases of King Oedipus and Heracles, if it brings wisdom, also brings pain and distress.

After the madness and the bad dreams of the night, and the searching, there is gain in self-knowledge at the end, with recognition of the errors, deceptions and misunderstandings of the past. Peer Gynt, recognising that self-sufficiency is not enough, learns from Solveig that the answer to the riddle of where he has been is that he has lived in her faith, her hope and her love. The playgoer shares in the self-discovery.

NOTES AND SOURCES

1 INTRODUCTION

1 Stevie Smith, *Selected Poems*, London, Longman, 1962, p. 18.
2 Claude Bernard's classic work, called in its English translation *An Introduction to the Study of Experimental Medicine*, was first published in 1865. A convenient source is the Dover Publications' edition, 1957.
3 This formulation is attributed to Fredericq in 1887.
4 S. Freud, *Beyond the Pleasure Principle*, The Pelican Freud Library, vol. 11, London, Penguin Books, 1977, p. 277.
5 S. Freud, *The Interpretation of Dreams*, The Pelican Freud Library, vol. 4, London, Penguin Books, 1975, p. 263 and elsewhere.
6 D.R. Davis, 'A reappraisal of Ibsen's *Ghosts*', *Family Process*, 1963, vol. 2, pp. 81–94.
7 D.R. Davis, 'Intervention into family affairs', *British Journal of Medical Psychology*, 1968, vol. 41, pp. 43–9.
8 D.R. Davis, 'Hurt minds', in: *Focus on Macbeth*. J.R. Brown (ed.), London, Routledge & Kegan Paul, 1982, pp. 210–28.
9 S. Freud, *The Interpretation of Dreams* – see note 5 – pp. 362–3.
10 S. Freud, 'Some character-types met with in psychoanalytic work: those wrecked by success', in: *Art and Literature*, The Pelican Freud Library, vol. 14, London, Penguin Books, 1985, p. 315.
11 G.B. Shaw, *The Quintessence of Ibsenism*, 3rd edn, London, Constable, 1926; the first edition was published in 1891.
12 Freud is reported to have interpreted a dream of C.G. Jung's as showing that Jung wished to dethrone him and take his place – see: P. Roazen, *Freud and his Followers*. London, Allen Lane, 1976, pp. 254–5. Ibsen expressed his fear of the younger generation in, notably, *The Master Builder*.
13 Various versions have been given of the Oedipus legend, the most comprehensive being that of J. Lemprière, *Classical Dictionary*, London, T. & J. Allman, 1829. See also the versions given by Robert Graves in *Greek Myths*, London, Penguin Books, 1984, pp. 111–16, and G. Devereux, 'Why Oedipus killed Laius', *International Journal of Psychoanalysis*, 1953, vol. 34, pp. 132–41.
14 In Alan Ayckbourn's *Woman in Mind* (London, Faber & Faber, 1986),

for instance, the stage instructions say: 'Throughout the play, we shall hear what she hears; see what she sees – a subjective viewpoint. ...'

15 T. Lidz, S. Fleck, A.R. Cornelison, *Schizophrenia and the Family*, New York, International Universities Press, 1965. See also: S. Fleck, 'Family dynamics and origin of schizophrenia', *Psychosomatic Medicine*, 1960, vol. 22, pp. 333–44.

16 R.D. Laing, *Sanity, Madness and the Family: Families of Schizophrenics*, London, Penguin Books, 1970.

17 Gregory Bateson, *Steps to an Ecology of Mind*, St Albans, Herts, Paladin, 1973. Of particular interest as a study of plays in the terms of systems theory is: P. Watzlawick, J.H. Beavin, D.D. Jackson, *The Pragmatics of Human Communication*, London, Faber & Faber, 1968.

18 Lillian Feder, *Madness in Literature*, Princeton, NJ, Princeton University Press, 1980.

19 Bennett Simon, *Mind and Madness in Ancient Greece: The Classical Roots of Modern Psychiatry*, London, Cornell University Press, 1978.

2 LESSONS AT THE THEATRE

1 P.B. Shelley, *Poetical Works*, Oxford, Oxford University Press, 1986, p. 276.

2 G.B. Shaw, *The Quintessence of Ibsenism*, London, Constable, 1926, pp. 87–8.

3 *Hedda Gabler* provoked a similar reaction from *The Times* critic, who wrote of it: 'a demonstration of the pathology of mind, such as may be found in the pages of the *Journal of Mental Science* or in the reports of the medical superintendents of lunatic asylums'. (cited by Elaine Showalter, *The Female Malady*, London, Virago, 1987, p. 146).

4 Sexual rivalries between a man and woman for the affection of another woman is a theme in Pinter's *Old Times*. Recently played in big theatres in Germany, but not in England, has been John Hopkins' *Verlorene Zeit* (*Losing Time*), a contemporary study of the sexual rivalries within a similar triangle of a man and two women, with the rejection of the man because of the preference of the women for a relationship with each other. The Jacobean John Ford's play about the incestuous relationship of a brother and sister, *'Tis Pity She's a Whore*, has recently been revived at the National Theatre.

5 E.g., Arthur Miller writes in *Timebends: A Life* (London, Methuen, 1987) about the pressures put on him by producers and others to make changes in his picture in *Death of a Salesman* of the American travelling salesman.

6 *Bent* by Martin Sherman was first produced at the Royal Court Theatre in 1979.

7 See my study of *Macbeth* for an example: 'Hurt minds', in: *Focus on Macbeth*, J.R. Brown (ed.), London, Routledge & Kegan Paul, 1982. Among modern plays, David Hare's *The Secret Rapture* (London, Faber & Faber, 1988) is notable for its account of the circumstances

and the psychological processes through which a man comes to kill the woman he is in love with.

8 See: D.R. Davis, 'Virginia Woolf on the experience of being insane', *Southampton Medical Journal*, 1984, vol. 1, pp. 141–4.

9 According to George Steiner (in *Antigone*, Oxford, Clarendon Press, 1984) there are a hundred or more versions of the Antigone myth in Western literature, art and thought. Oscar Mandel has located six modern versions of *Philoctetes* in *Philoctetes and the Fall of Troy*, London, University of Nebraska Press, 1981, p. 155.

10 Attributed to Euripides.

11 *Hamlet*, 2.2.206.

12 *Macbeth*, 4.3.209. The passage goes on:

the grief that does not speak
Whispers the o'er-fraught heart, and bids it break.

There is wise advice to be found in plays on the expression of grief; e.g. in Sophocles, *Antigone* (*The Theban Plays*, E.F. Watling, trans., London, Penguin, 1974, p. 159), the Chorus comments with reference to Eurydice who has just heard of the suicide of her son Haemon:

Yet there is danger in unnatural silence
No less than in excess of lamentation.

13 *A Midsummer Night's Dream*, 1.1.14.

14 This point is made well by Leonhard Fiedler in 'Reinhardt, Shakespeare and the "Dreams"', *Max Reinhardt: The Oxford Symposium*, M. Jacobs and J. Warren (eds), Oxford, Oxford Polytechnic, 1986, when discussing the relevance to one another of Freud's *The Interpretation of Dreams*, published in 1900, and Reinhardt's first production of *A Midsummer Night's Dream* in 1905.

15 In *A Midsummer Night's Dream* (4.1.203–5), Bottom says: 'I have had a dream – past the wit of man to say what dream it was. – Man is an ass if he go about to expound this dream.' Yet for the audience in the know about the spell put on him, his dream makes comic sense.

16 Roy Porter makes this point in *A Social History of Madness*, London, Weidenfeld & Nicolson, 1987.

17 T.S. Eliot, *The Cocktail Party*, London, Faber & Faber, 1958, p. 115.

18 T. Szasz, *Karl Kraus and the Soul Doctors*, London, Routledge & Kegan Paul, 1977, p. 154.

19 E.g., D. Enoch and W.H. Trethowan, 'The Othello syndrome', in: *Uncommon Psychiatric Syndromes*, Bristol, John Wright & Sons, 1979.

20 Tennessee Williams, *The Glass Menagerie*, London, Penguin Books, 1965, pp. 229, 233. See also his *Memoirs*, London, W.H. Allen, 1976, p. 120; and D. Spoto, *The Kindness of Strangers: The Life of Tennessee Williams*, London, Bodley Head, 1985. He described a later play *Vieux Carré*, written in 1977, and looking back to the years 1938–9, as 'his memory play'.

21 S. Freud, *The Interpretation of Dreams*. The Pelican Freud Library, vol. 4, London, Penguin Books, 1958, p. 723. Of Freud's many references

SCENES OF MADNESS

to the relationship between dreams and mental disorder, the most important are in *The Interpretation of Dreams* and Lecture 29, 'Revision of the theory of dreams' in *New Introductory Lectures on Psychoanalysis*, The Pelican Freud Library, vol. 2.

22 I have discussed the issues in an article with this title in *Bulletin of the Royal College of Psychiatrists*, 1981, vol. 5, pp. 82–5.
23 Francis Schiller, *A Möbius Strip: Fin de Siècle Neuropychiatry and Paul Möbius*, London, University of California Press, 1982.
24 Karl Jaspers, *Strindberg und Van Gogh*, Munich, Piper, 1949.
25 S. Freud, Preface to Marie Bonaparte's 'The life and work of Edgar Allan Poe', in: *Standard Edition of the Complete Psychological Works of Sigmund Freud*, J. Strachey (trans.), London, Hogarth, 1933, vol. 12, p. 254.
26 Freud's papers on literature are conveniently brought together in *Art and Literature*, The Pelican Freud Library, 1985, vol. 14. Lady Macbeth and Rebecca West are discussed in the essay 'Psychopathic characters on the stage'. Among other pioneering works by psychoanalysts are: Otto Rank, *Das Inzest-motiv in Dictung und Sage*, Leipzig, Deuticke, 1926; and Ernest Jones, *Hamlet and Oedipus*, London, Gollancz, 1949.
27 E.g., M.A. Skura, *The Literary Use of the Psychoanalytic Process*, London, Yale University Press, 1981.
28 E.g., W.R. Brain, 'Authors and psychopaths', *British Medical Journal*, 1949, vol. ii, pp. 1427–32.
29 K. Jaspers, *General Psychopathology*, J. Hoenig, M.W. Hamilton (trans.), Manchester University Press, 1963.
30 Eliot Slater, 'The problems of pathography', *Acta Psychiatrica Scandinavica*, 1971, Supplement 219, pp. 209–15.
31 This was the question on which I was asked for advice by P. Spencer, *Flaubert: A Biography*, London, Faber & Faber, 1953.
32 Controversies have raged over the class of the mental illness Strindberg suffered from during the 'inferno' period, the main contributors being: Jaspers, *General Psychopathology*, note 24; S. Hedenberg, *Strindberg i Skärselden*, Göteborg, Akademieforlaget-Gumperts, 1961; E.W. Anderson, 'Strindberg's illness', *Psychological Medicine*, 1971, vol. 1, pp. 104–17; M. Sandbach, Introduction to Strindberg's *Inferno and From an Occult Diary*, London, Penguin, 1979; and M. Meyer, *Strindberg: A Biography*, London, Secker & Warburg, 1985.
33 Cited by Elaine Showalter in *The Female Malady* – see note 3 – in a discussion of Ophelia as a prototype of a deranged woman. John Connolly, like Bucknill, one of the leading psychiatrists in the middle of the nineteenth century, wrote *A Study of Hamlet* (1874). See also: J.C. Bucknill, *The Psychology of Shakespeare*, London, Longman, 1859, or *The Mad Folk of Shakespeare*, 2nd edn, London, Macmillan, 1867; and A. Brigham, 'Shakespeare's illustrations of insanity', *American Journal of Insanity*, 1894, vol. 1.
34 L. Woods, 'Garrick's King Lear and the English malady', *Theater Survey*, 1986, vol. 27, pp. 17–35.

35 This interpretation is noted, but not approved, by J. Miller, *Subsequent Performances*, London, Faber & Faber, 1986.

36 Cited by Skura, *The Literary Use of the Psychoanalytic Process* – see note 27, p. 65.

37 Anton Chekhov, *The Seagull*, E. Fen, trans., London, Penguin Books, 1954, p. 126.

38 S. Freud, in: 'Psychopathic characters on the stage', in *Art and Literature*, note 26, p. 121.

39 For a discussion of catharsis in Greek plays, see: E.R. Dodds, *The Greeks and the Irrational*, Boston, Beacon Press, 1957.

40 This advice is given in, e.g., Jean Racine's First Preface to *Andromache*, in: *Jean Racine: Five Plays*, K. Muir (trans.), London, Macgibbon & Kee, 1960, p. 3.

41 See: M. Esslin, *Brecht: A Choice of Evils*, London, Heinemann, 1959, p. 42.

42 See Chapter 7 for further discussion of *Long Day's Journey into Night*.

43 S. Freud, 'Inhibitions, symptoms and anxiety', *On Psychopathology*, The Pelican Freud Library, vol. 10, London, Penguin Books, 1979, p. 327.

44 S. Freud, *Art and Literature*, note 26, p. 132.

45 Glynne Wickham, *A History of the Theatre*, Oxford, Phaidon, 1985, p. 17.

46 *The Flies* (*Les Mouches*), written in 1943, is contained in: Jean-Paul Sartre, *Three Plays*, S. Gilbert (trans.), London, Penguin Books, 1962.

47 Georg Büchner, *Leonce and Lena, Lenz, Woyzeck*, Michael Hamburger (trans.), London, University of Chicago Press, 1972.

48 From a version by Alan Brownjohn, *Torquato Tasso*, London, Angel Books, 1985, ll.3430–3. Ibsen makes a similar point in *The Vikings at Helgeland* (*The Oxford Ibsen*, vol.2, pp.85–6). The bereaved Ørnulf has still in his possession 'the gift of poetry':

> Yet the arts of language
> still are mine, by which to
> voice my grief in singing.
> To my speech she granted
> gifts of lyric power.

49 In a letter about his writing of *Peer Gynt*, *The Oxford Ibsen*, vol. 3, J.W. McFarlane (ed.), Oxford, Oxford University Press, 1972, pp. 492–3.

3 MODELS OF MADNESS

1 Polonius is telling the king that Hamlet is mad.

2 Aeschylus, 'The Libation Bearers', *The Oresteia*, R. Fagle (trans.), London, Penguin Books, 1966.

3 Euripides, *Orestes*, *Euripides IV*, W. Arrowsmith (trans.), London, University of Chicago Press, 1958. Another account of Orestes'

illness is given by Euripides in *Iphigenia in Tauris*, P. Vellacott (trans.), London, Penguin Books, 1974.

4 Among other plays about Orestes' family and their engagement in the Trojan wars are: Sophocles' *Electra*; Euripides' *Helen*, *Electra*, *Iphigenia in Aulis* and *The Trojan Women*. Another incident in his life is told of in Euripides' *Andromache*.

5 *Ajax* in: *Sophocles: Electra and Other Plays*, E.F. Watling (trans.), London, Penguin Books, 1984.

6 Euripides, *Heracles*, in *Medea and Other Plays*, P. Vellacott (trans.), London, Penguin Books, 1963.

7 The reasons for the differences in outcome between Ajax and Heracles are discussed by Bennett Simon, *Mind and Madness in Ancient Greece*, London, Cornell University Press, 1978, pp. 130–9 especially.

8 *The Comedy of Errors*, R.A Foakes (ed.), London, Methuen (The Arden Shakespeare), 1980.

9 *Hamlet*, J.D. Wilson (ed.), Cambridge, Cambridge University Press, 1936.

10 C.M. Parkes, *Bereavement: Studies of Grief in Adult Life*, London, Tavistock, 1972, ch. 4.

11 R.D. Laing in *The Divided Self* (London, Penguin Books, 1969, p. 163) discusses the deliberate use by patients of obscurity and complexity as a smoke-screen in order to preserve secrecy.

12 For a discussion of 'looses' and the 'nunnery' scene, see: J.D. Wilson, *What Happens in Hamlet*, Cambridge, Cambridge University Press, 1959.

13 Othello's reason for delay before he kills Desdemona is that he would not 'kill thy unprepared spirit; . . . I would not kill thy soul' (5.2.31–2).

14 E.g., Wilson, *What Happens in Hamlet*, note 12.

15 S. Freud, *The Interpretation of Dreams*. The Pelican Freud Library, vol. 4, pp. 366–8.

16 The reason for Lady Macbeth's restraint is: 'Had he not resembled my father as he slept, I had done't' (2.2.12–13).

17 This contradicts R.D. Laing, when he writes, 'In her madness, there is no one there. She is not a person. There is no integral selfhood expressed through her actions or utterances', in *The Divided Self*, London, Penguin Books, 1965, p. 195n.

18 *Julius Caesar*, N. Sanders (ed.), London, Penguin Books, 1967.

19 *Macbeth*, J.D. Wilson (ed.), Cambridge, Cambridge University Press, 1947.

20 They have gradually become estranged from each other, with a turn for the worse at the end of the banquet scene (3.4), as I have argued in 'Hurt minds', *Focus on Macbeth*, J.R. Brown (ed.), Routledge & Kegan Paul, 1982.

21 S. Freud, 'Some character-types met with in psychoanalytic work', The Pelican Freud Library, vol. 14, pp. 301–7.

22 *King John*, E.A.J. Honigmann (ed.), The Arden Shakespeare, London, Methuen, 1967.

23 *Titus Andronicus*, J.C. Maxwell (ed.), The Arden Shakespeare, London, Methuen, 1953.

24 *King Lear*, K. Muir (ed.), The Arden Shakespeare, London, Methuen, 1952.

25 The tendencies described in King Lear, the demands for love, the denial of dependency and loneliness, the tyrannical control over others, and the resistance to change, are commonly observed in the disturbed elderly. See: N. Hess, 'King Lear and some anxieties of old age', *British Journal of Medical Psychology*, 1987, vol. 60, pp. 209–15; and C. Hanly, 'Lear and his daughters', *International Review of Psychoanalysis*, 1986, vol. 13, pp. 210–20.

26 K. Muir, 'Madness in King Lear', in: *Aspects of King Lear*, K. Muir and S. Wells (eds), Cambridge, Cambridge University Press, 1982.

27 The quotations are from *The Winter's Tale*, E. Schanzer (ed.), London, Penguin Books, 1969.

28 Goethe started writing *Torquato Tasso* in 1780, completing it in 1790. The quotations are taken from J.W. von Goethe, *Torquato Tasso*, a version by A. Brownjohn, London, Angel Books, 1985. My account owes much to E.M. Wilkinson and L.A. Willoughby, 'Goethe's *Torquato Tasso*: The Tragedy of the Poet', *Goethe: Poet and Thinker*, London, Edward Arnold, 1962; R. Peacock, *Goethe's Major Plays*, Manchester, Manchester University Press, 1959; and especially M. Patterson, *Peter Stein*, Cambridge, Cambridge University Press, 1981.

29 *Ghosts*, J.W. McFarlane (trans.), *The Oxford Ibsen*, vol. 5, Oxford: Oxford University Press, 1961.

30 I have discussed the diagnosis of Oswald's illness in: 'A reappraisal of Ibsen's *Ghosts*', *Family Process*, 1963, vol. 2, pp. 81–94.

31 Notably Georg Brandes in: *Correspondance der Georg Brandes. Lettres choisis et annotées par Paul Kruger. II. L'Angleterre et la Russie*, Copenhagen: Rosenkilde & Bagger, 1956.

32 The contemporary arguments against a psychological explanation of Oswald's illness are summarised by R. Young, *Time's Disinherited Children*, Norwich, Norvic Press, 1989.

33 Some of Munch's sketches of *Ghosts* portray the ghost of Oswald's father.

34 Munch painted this picture between 1887 and 1889.

35 From Ibsen's preliminary notes for *Ghosts*, *The Oxford Ibsen*, vol. 5, p. 467.

36 I discuss the autobiographical aspects of *Ghosts* in: 'Death of the artist's father: Henrik Ibsen', *British Journal of Medical Psychology*, 1973, vol. 46, pp. 135–41.

37 The points below are discussed by D.R. Davis and D.B. Thomas, 'Rosmersholm: existentialist tragedy or escapist fantasy? A dialogue', *Contemporary Approaches to Ibsen*, vol. 4, Oslo, Universitetsforlag, 1979, pp. 83–100, from which the quotations are taken. See also: D.B. Thomas, 'Patterns of interaction in Ibsen's *Ghosts*', *Ibsenaarbok*, Oslo, Universitetsforlag, 1974, pp. 89–117.

38 'Double-bind messages' offer alternatives both of which have unpleasant connotations or present unresolvable paradoxes. They

are said to be a form of communication characteristic of the families of schizophrenic patients. See: Gregory Bateson, *Steps to an Ecology of Mind*, London, Picador, 1973, pp. 173–98.

39 *Ivanov* was written from 1887 to 1889. This account is based on the fourth version. In the first, Ivanov dies from heart failure – an ending that lacks credibility. See: D. Magarshack, *Chekhov: The Dramatist*, London, Eyre Methuen, 1980. The quotations are from *The Oxford Chekhov*, vol. 2, Ronald Hingley (trans.), Oxford: Oxford University Press, 1967.

40 Chekhov, who had trained as a doctor, 'cherished the daring dream of summing up all that has been written up to now about whining and melancholy people'. 'In conception', he added, 'I more or less got it right, but the execution is worthless' – quoted by R. Peace, *Chekhov: A Study of Four Major Plays*, London, Yale University Press, 1983, p. 12.

41 Chekhov gives an account of Ivanov as a character in a letter in 1888 to Alexei Suvorin, in: *The Selected Letters of Anton Chekhov*, Lillian Hellman (ed.), London, Picador, 1984, pp. 69–77. He emphasises Ivanov's solitude and the lack of outlet for his energies, in a diagnosis reminiscent of Helene Alving's in *Ghosts* of her dissolute husband.

42 Ivanov's illness has many of the features of Chekhov's own, as revealed in the letters he wrote at the time. He had been greatly affected by his brother's death and lapsed after some years into what has been regarded as a depressive illness – see: S. Behrman, *Journal of the Royal Society of Medicine*, 1989, vol.82, pp. 163–4. He is said to have written the play in an effort to clarify his own mental state.

43 See the discussion in Chapter 9 of mistakes in diagnosis.

44 Peter Watts (trans.), *Three Plays by August Strindberg*, London, Penguin Books, 1958.

45 Strindberg said of *The Father*, written in 1887, which describes a marriage like his might have been: 'I don't know if *The Father* is a work of the imagination, or if my life has been.' See: *August Strindberg's brev*, Torsten Eklund (ed.), vol. 6, p. 298. That the theme of *The Father*, the quarrel of parents over a daughter, is similar to that of the tragedy of Clytemnestra and Agamemnon is pointed out by B. Mortensen and B. Downs, *Strindberg: An Introduction to his Life and Work*, Cambridge, Cambridge University Press, 1965, p. 108.

46 Tennessee Williams, *A Streetcar Named Desire*, London, Penguin Books, 1948. The author writes about the play in *Memoirs*, London, W.H. Allen, 1976. See also: R. Boxill, *Tennessee Williams*, London, Macmillan, 1987.

47 The effect on Stanley of being regarded by Blanche as ape-like is similar to that on Yank, the stoker in Eugene O'Neill's *The Hairy Ape*, when he sees how Mildred recoils from him – see Chapter 8.

4 THE STORIES PLAYS TELL

1 Aase is telling Solveig about her son Peer in Ibsen's *Peer Gynt*. *The Oxford Ibsen*, vol. 3, p. 286.
2 Peter Brook, 'Foreword' to *The Mahabharata*, London, Methuen, 1987, p. xv.
3 E.g., H.S. Sullivan, *The Interpersonal Theory of Psychiatry*, London, Tavistock, 1953.
4 There are many accounts of the difficulties met by playwrights in getting actors to follow their intentions, especially when little time was spent in rehearsal. Chekhov's in the first productions of *Ivanov* are described by D. Magarshack, *Chekhov the Dramatist*, London, Eyre Methuen, 1980; also Lillian Hellman (ed.), *The Selected Letters of Anton Chekhov*, London, Picador, 1984, p. 40. For a discussion of Ibsen in production, see D. B. Thomas, *Ibsen*, London, Macmillan, 1983, ch. 6.
5 Ensemble acting was introduced at the private theatre at the court of Meiningen in 1870.
6 Martin Esslin took this example from *The Cherry Orchard* to introduce a discussion of Harold Pinter's linguistic techniques, in *Pinter: A Study of his Plays*, London, Eyre Methuen, 1977, p. 46. See also, on Chekhov: M. Hollington, 'Svevo, Joyce and modernist time', in M. Bradbury and J.W. McFarlane (eds), *Modernism 1890–1930*, London, Penguin Books, 1976, p. 430; and R. Peace, *Chekhov: A Study of the Four Major Plays*, New Haven, CT, Yale University Press, 1983.
7 This example is taken from D.B. Thomas, *Ibsen*, note 4, pp. 151–2.
8 H. Pinter, *The Caretaker*, London, Methuen, 1960.
9 See Esslin, *Pinter: A Study of his Plays*, note 6.
10 Martin Esslin, *The Theatre of the Absurd*, London, Penguin Books, 1968.
11 C.G. Jung, *The Integration of the Personality*, London, Kegan Paul, 1940, p. 107. See also: A. Storr, *Jung*, London, Fontana/Collins, 1973, p. 13.
12 See: R. Rogers, *The Double in Literature*, Detroit, Wayne University Press, 1970, for a discussion of decomposition; also Ernest Jones, *Hamlet and Oedipus*, New York, Doubleday, 1949, pp. 149–51. The concept of decomposition is foreshadowed in Freud's *The Interpretation of Dreams* (The Pelican Freud Library, vol. 4.), in which there is also a section on condensation (pp. 383–413).
13 J.W. McFarlane, *The Oxford Ibsen*, vol. 7, p. 438.
14 A. Miller, *Timebends*, London, Methuen, 1987, p. 522. Hugh MacLennan in his novel *Two Solitudes* (Toronto, Macmillan of Canada, 1987) says of a writer: 'He heard the voices of his characters talking to one another.'
15 Cited by Karl Miller in *Doubles*, Oxford, Clarendon Press, 1985, p. 418.
16 Esslin discusses these features of drama in *The Field of Drama*, London, Methuen, 1987.
17 G. Wickham, *A History of the Theatre*, Oxford, Phaidon, 1985.

18 Among recent writers on duality in literature, Otto Rank, Ralph Tymms, Robert Rogers, Wilhelmine Krauss and Karl Miller have written about 'doubles', Keppler about the 'second self', Jeremy Hawthorn about 'multiple personality', R.D. Laing and Masao Myoshi about the 'divided self' or the 'embodied' and 'unembodied' self. I have discussed 'multiples' in literature and drama in a critical review of Karl Miller's *Doubles* (note 15) in *Essays in Criticism*, 1986, vol. 36, pp. 89–94.

19 Joseph Conrad, 'The Secret Sharer', in: *Twixt Land and Sea*, London, Dent, 1966.

20 C. F. Keppler, *The Literature of the Second Self*, Tucson, Arizona, University of Arizona Press, 1972, p. 25.

21 Ernest Jones, *Hamlet and Oedipus*, p. 140, note 12, discusses Hamlet and Claudius, and Hamlet and Laertes, as self and other self.

22 For a discussion of the relationship of King Lear to the Fool and Kent, see: K. Muir, 'Madness in King Lear', *Aspects of King Lear*, K. Muir and S. Wells (eds), Cambridge, Cambridge University Press, 1982; and J. Miller, *Subsequent Performances*, London, Faber & Faber, 1986, p. 133.

23 'To yourself be self-sufficient' is a recurrent theme in Ibsen's *Peer Gynt* – see Chapter 5, pp. 83–4.

24 See: Keppler, *Literature of the Second Self*, pp. 14–26, note 20.

25 The story of Phaedra and Hippolytus is told in Chapter 6, pp. 111–13.

26 Cited by Rogers, *The Double in Literature*, note 12, p. 79, the former being from F.R. Leavis, and the latter, James Joyce.

27 S. Freud, 'Some character types met with in psychoanalytic work' in *Art and Literature*, The Pelican Freud Library, vol. 14, pp. 307–8.

28 In Emilie Bardach's album, Ibsen wrote on 20 September 1889, quoting Faust: 'Hohes, schmerzliches Glück – um das Unerreichbare zu ringen!' (High, painful fortune – to struggle for the unattainable), referred to by Else Høst, *Hedda Gabler*, Oslo, Aschehoug, 1958, p. 28.

29 E. Høst, *Hedda Gabler*, note 28, pp. 177–92.

30 Ibsen used the expression 'det demoniske underlag' in a letter written in 1890 (*Samlede Verker*, vol. 18, p. 270), referred to by J. Northam, *Ibsen's Dramatic Method*, London, Faber & Faber, 1953, p. 170.

31 Karl Miller, *Doubles*, p. 328, note 15.

32 In a letter to Edmund Gosse, Ibsen wrote: 'it was the illusion of reality I wanted to produce. I wanted to evoke in the reader the impression that what he was reading really happened' (*The Oxford Ibsen*, vol. 4, p. 3).

33 Ibsen's use of visual symbols like the white shawl is discussed by Northam, *Ibsen's Dramatic Method*, p. 111, note 30.

34 The théâtre libre was founded by André Antoine in Paris in 1887. Among the other new theatres was Max Reinhardt's Kleines Theater in Berlin.

35 The ideas guiding Antoine were similar to those discussed by

Strindberg in his preface to *Miss Julie* in 1888. See: author's preface to *Miss Julie*, in: *The Plays*, vol. 1, M. Meyer (ed.), London, Secker & Warburg, 1975, p. 108. Strindberg's Intima Teatren opened in Stockholm in 1907.

36 Editor's introduction to *A Dream Play* in *The Plays*, vol. 1, p. 548, note 35. See also: author's note on *A Dream Play*, p. 553.

37 There are many dream plays before Strindberg; e.g., Shakespeare's *A Midsummer Night's Dream* and *The Winter's Tale*; and Calderón de la Barca's *Life is a Dream* – 'For on earth, everyone who lives, lives in a dream' – (London, Barron's Educational Series, 1958, p. 34); and Ibsen's *Peer Gynt*.

38 '*Verfremdungseffekt*' can be translated literally as 'alienation' or 'distancing' effect, although to do so leaves out something of what Brecht intended the term to convey. 'The theatre must amaze its public and achieves this by a technique for making the familiar strange,' he wrote: 'A short organum for the theatre', in: T. Cole (ed.), *Playwrights on Playwriting*, New York, Hill & Wang, 1960, p. 89. See also: K.E Kantor and L. Hoffman, 'Brechtian theater as a model for conjoint family therapy', *Family Process*, 1966, vol. 5, pp. 218–29; and M. Esslin, *Bertolt Brecht: A Choice of Evils*, London, Heinemann, 1959, especially ch. VI, 'The Brechtian theatre; its theory and practice'.

39 The term 'cybernetics' was introduced in 1947. The term 'systems' (or 'system') 'theory' came into general use a few years later. See: L. Bertalanffy, *General System Theory*, London, Allen Lane, The Penguin Press, 1968.

40 An example of a family myth is to be found in the account of Oswald given in Chapter 3. P. Watzlawick, J.H. Beavin and D.D. Jackson discuss the part played by family myths in *Pragmatics of Human Communication*, London, Faber & Faber, 1968, pp. 172–8.

41 For a discussion of behaviour in crisis, see: G. Caplan, *An Approach to Community Mental Health*, New York, Grune & Stratton, 1961.

42 *Times Literary Supplement*, 15 September 1961.

43 R.J. Lifton, *Thought Reform and the Psychology of Totalism*, London, Penguin Books, 1961.

5 REALITY AND ILLUSION

1 Several houses in Ibsen's plays are reminiscent of actual houses, the Werles' house being like that to be seen across the valley from Venstøp. There were houses like Hedda's near where Ibsen came to live in the 1890s.

2 Vika, the area inhabited by the *demi-monde*, was described in Christian Krogh's novel *Albertine*, published in 1886.

3 The author's preface to *Miss Julie* in: A. Strindberg, *The Plays*, vol. 1, Michael Meyer (trans.), London, Methuen, 1987, p. 95.

4 The author's note to *A Dream Play*, in: Strindberg: *The Plays*, vol. 2, Michael Mayer (trans.), London, Methuen, 1982, p. 175.

5 The Introduction by Mary Sandbach to A. Strindberg, *Inferno*, M. Sandbach (trans.), London, Penguin Books, 1979.
6 *Inferno*, p. 206, note 5. Other descriptions of *déjà vu* experiences in literature include: O. Zangwill, 'A case of paramnesia in Nathaniel Hawthorne', *Character and Personality*, 1945, vol. 13, pp. 246–60, the case being that recorded in *Our Old Home*. Nora Crook and Derek Guiton discuss in *Shelley's Venomed Melody*, Cambridge, Cambridge University Press, 1986, pp.56–7, Shelley's *déjà vu* experience of the mill while on a walk near Oxford.
7 This is an item in the definition of schizophrenic psychoses in *Glossary and Guide to the Classification of Mental Disorders in Accordance with the Ninth Revision of the International Classification of Diseases*, Geneva, World Health Organisation, 1978, p. 27.
8 Peter Watts, the translator of *Peer Gynt* in the Penguin Classics edition, makes this suggestion (p. 65). In Peter Stein's distinguished production in 1971, in which the eight stages of Peer's life were played by six different actors, Peer No. 3 lies down beside the unconscious Peer No. 2, and takes on the part as if in delirium.
9 The quotations are mostly from Peter Watts's translation, this on p. 94.
10 This advice is repeated in the fifth Act, p. 206 – 'Troll, to thyself be – enough', being a translation of 'Troll, vaer deg selv nok'.
11 Christopher Marlowe, *Dr Faustus*, R. Gill (ed.), London, Ernest Benn, 1978, l. 52–4.
12 'limbs, all torn asunder' (5.3.6–7) is reminiscent of the violent death of Pentheus at the hands of his mother – a point made by L.C. Knights, 'The strange case of Dr Faustus', in *Marlowe: Dr Faustus*, J. Jump (ed.), London, Macmillan, 1969 (Casebook series).
13 This theme is developed by H. Levin, *Christopher Marlowe: The Overreacher*, London, Faber & Faber, 1954. The frivolousness of Dr Faustus' escapades has been attributed, on slender grounds, to rewriting by other authors, but almost certainly reflects Marlowe's intentions – W.W. Greg, 'The damnation of Dr Faustus', *Marlowe: A Collection of Critical Essays*, C. Leech (ed.), Englewood Cliffs, NJ, Prentice-Hall, 1964.
14 Václav Havel, *Temptation*, London, Faber & Faber, 1988.
15 L.A. Fiedler, *The Stranger in Shakespeare*, St Albans, Paladin, 1974; and R. Schechner, 'The unexpected visitor in Ibsen's late plays', *Ibsen: A Collection of Critical essays*, R. Fjelde (ed.), Englewood Cliffs, NJ, Prentice-Hall, 1965.
16 Cited by J.W. McFarlane, *The Oxford Ibsen*, vol. 7, p. 467.
17 Anthony Storr, *Jung*, London, Fontana/Collins, 1973, p. 52. For a definition of 'animus', see: C.G. Jung, *Memories, Dreams, Reflections*, A. Jaffé (ed.), London, Fontana, 1983, p. 410 (Glossary).
18 Aeschylus, *The Oresteia: The Libation Bearers*, R. Fagles (trans.), London, Penguin Books, 1977, ll.1047–9.
19 Euripides, *Iphigenia in Tauris*, P. Vellacott (trans.), London, Penguin Books, 1974, p. 139.
20 T.S. Eliot, *The Family Reunion*, London, Faber & Faber, 1963, p. 57.

21 Euripides, *Hippolytus*, P. Vellacott (trans.), London, Penguin Books, 1974, p. 101.
22 Samuel Beckett, *Waiting for Godot*, London, Faber & Faber, 1965, p. 62. This passage has been discussed by M. Esslin, *The Theatre of the Absurd*, London, Penguin Books, 1968, p. 59; and A. Alvarez, *Beckett*, London, Fontana/Collins, 1973, p. 82.
23 *Inferno*, p. 151, note 5.
24 C.G. Jung, *The Integration of the Personality*, 1940, p. 107. See also Storr, *Jung*, p. 13, note 17.
25 Leonard Woolf, *Beginning Again*, London, Hogarth Press, 1964, p. 164. See also R. Poole, *The Unknown Virginia Woolf*, Cambridge University Press, 1978, ch. 13.
26 R. McHugh, (ed.), *Ah, Sweet Dancer: W.B. Yeats, Margot Ruddock, a Correspondence*, London, Gill & Macmillan, 1970, p. 95.
27 'Nøkken' and 'The White Horse' are depicted in well-known paintings by Theodor Kittelsen (1890).
28 *Blood Wedding* by Frederico Garcia Lorca in *Three Tragedies*, London, Penguin Books, p. 83. See also: Ian Gibson, *Frederico Garcia Lorca: A Life*, London, Faber & Faber, 1989, pp. 336–7.
29 Hallucination is imagery mistaken for perception of something outside the person.
30 R.D. Laing, *The Divided Self*, London, Penguin Books, 1959, p. 58.
31 B. Simon, *Mind and Madness in Ancient Greece*, London, Cornell University Press, 1978, ch. 4.
32 Harold Pinter, *Old Times*, London, Eyre Methuen, 1971.

6 FAMILY FEUDS

1 Euripides, *Medea*, in: *Medea and Other Plays*, P. Vellacott (trans.), London, Penguin Books, 1963, p. 32.
2 W.F. Bynum and M. Neve, 'Hamlet on the couch', *The Anatomy of Madness*, W.F. Bynum, R. Porter and M. Shepherd (eds), London, Tavistock, 1985, vol. 1, pp. 289–304.
3 Freud's views are discussed by W.F. Bynum and M. Neve, 'Hamlet on the couch', p. 298, note 2.
4 In Ingmar Bergman's 1986 production, Hamlet is presented as alienated from the political struggles in which Claudius and Fortinbras are engaged.
5 Heiner Müller's *Hamletmachine*, in *Hamletmachine and Other Texts for the Stage*, Carl Weber (ed. and trans.), New York, Performing Arts Journal Publications, 1984, tells a condensed story of Hamlet and Ophelia as if it is happening at a political crisis in a communist country in Europe after the Second World War.
6 P. Brook (trans.), *The Mahabharata*, a play by Jean-Claude Carrière, London, Methuen, 1985.
7 Four out of five murderers in contemporary Britain know the victim well. In about half cases the victim is a member of the family, and of these, half are children.

SCENES OF MADNESS

SCENES OF MADNESS

8 August Strindberg, *The Dance of Death*, Part 1, in *Plays Two*, M. Meyer (trans.), London, Methuen, 1982, p. 64.

9 Sophocles, *Antigone*, in: *The Theban Plays*, E.F. Watling (trans.), London, Penguin Books, 1982, p. 144, l.651.

10 Ernest Jones, 'A psychoanalytic study of Hamlet', *Essays in Applied Psycho-analysis*, London, International Psycho-analytical Press, 1923, p. 86.

11 Erich Fromm, 'The Oedipus complex and the Oedipus myth', in: R.N. Anshen (ed.), *The Family: its Function and Destiny*, New York, Harper, 1959.

12 Sophocles, *King Oedipus*, in *The Theban Plays*, note 9.

13 *Henry IV, Parts 1 and 2*, P.H. Davison (ed.), London, Penguin Books, 1968, 1977.

14 S. Freud, *The Interpretation of Dreams*, The Pelican Freud Library, vol. 4, London, Penguin Books, 1975, p. 362.

15 Freud lost his father in October 1896. About 8 months later he began to collect material for *The Interpretation of Dreams*, published in 1899. In the preface to the second edition he remarks that it was only after he had completed the book that he grasped that it was 'a portion of my own self-analysis, my reaction to my father's death – that is to say, the most poignant events in a man's life'. I have discussed this point in: 'The death of the artist's father: Henrik Ibsen', *British Journal of Medical Psychology*, 1973, vol.46, pp. 135–41.

16 G. Devereux, 'Why Oedipus killed Laius', *International Journal of Psycho-Analysis*, 1953, vol. 34, pp. 132–46. Critics have pointed out that Freud, abandoning his theory of parental seduction, exculpated parents, and attributed neurotic symptoms to the sexual fantasies of children.

17 E.g., A. Bernstein, 'Freud and Oedipus: a new look at the Oedipus complex in the light of Freud's life', *Psychoanalytic Review*, 1976, vol. 63, pp. 393–407.

18 The relationship between Oedipus and Laius is discussed by E.R. Dodds, 'On misunderstanding the *Oedipus Rex*', *Oxford Readings in Greek Tragedy*, E. Segal (ed.), Oxford, Oxford University Press, 1983, pp. 181, 184.

19 E.R. Dodds, 'Morals and politics in the *Oresteia*', *The Ancient Concept of Progress and Other Essays on Greek Literature and Belief*, Oxford, Clarendon Press, 1973.

20 *The Interpretation of Dreams*, pp. 366–8, note 14.

21 The references to *Hamlet* in Chekhov's plays and the similarities and differences in the relationships depicted are discussed by T.G. Winner, '*The Sea Gull* and *Hamlet*', *Chekhov: New Perspectives*, R. and N.D. Wellek (eds), Englewood Cliffs, NJ, Prentice-Hall, 1984.

22 *A Collier's Friday Night*, written in 1907–8, is one of a series of plays Lawrence wrote about family life in a mining community in Nottinghamshire.

23 Calderón, *Life is a Dream*, W.E. Colford (trans., New York, Barron's Educational Series, 1958, p.(20). See also: E.W. Hesse, '*La Vida es Sueno* and the labyrinth of illusion', *Approaches to the Theater of Calderón*, M.D. McGaha (ed.), Washington, DC, University Press of America, 1982.

192

24 The theme of the son's imprisonment by the father has been traced to oriental sources – 'The Introduction', to *Life is a Dream*, p. xii, note 23.

25 P.B. Shelley, *The Cenci*. In *Shelley: Poetical Works*, T. Hutchinson (ed.), Oxford, Oxford University Press, 1970.

26 Richard Holmes, *Shelley. The Pursuit*, London, Weidenfeld & Nicolson, 1974, p. 516.

27 N. Crook and D. Guiton, *Shelley's Venomed Melody*, Cambridge, Cambridge University Press, 1987.

28 *Shelley: Poetical Works*, p. 276, note 25.

29 C.G. Jung, 'On psychoanalysis', *Collected Papers on Analytic Psychology*, C.E. Long (ed.), London, Ballière, Tindall & Cox, 1917, pp. 228–9.

30 A version of the disastrous outcome of Orestes' courtship of Hermione is told in Racine's *Andromache*, E. Korn (trans.), London, Applause Theatre Book Publishers (The Old Vic Collection), 1988. See also: G. Steiner, *Antigones*, Oxford, Clarendon Press, 1984.

31 Eugene O'Neill, *Mourning Becomes Electra*, in: *Three Plays by Eugene O'Neill*, New York, Vintage Books, 1973. The play was first published in 1931.

32 'Schismatic' and 'skewed' are the terms used by T. Lidz, S. Fleck and A.R. Cornelison (*Schizophrenia and the Family*, New York, International Universities Press, 1965) to describe a pattern of relationships, like that in the play, and claimed to be typical of patients with schizophrenia.

33 Arthur Miller, *A View from the Bridge*, London, Penguin Books, 1955.

34 *Genesis* 39, 7–20. The virtuous Joseph rejected the amorous advances of Potiphar's wife. Saying, 'Lie with me', she caught him by his garment, which he left in her hand when he fled. She then told her husband that he had mocked her, and he was put into prison.

35 Raymond Williams, *Writing in Society*, London, Verso, 1984, pp. 22–30.

36 Euripides, *Hippolytus*, in *Three Plays*, P. Vellacott (trans.), London, Penguin Books, 1953.

37 Jean Racine, *Phaedra*, in *Four Greek Plays*, R.C. Knights (trans.), Cambridge, Cambridge University Press, 1982.

38 A.J. Boyle, *Seneca's Phaedra: Introduction, Text, Translation and Notes*, London, Francis Cairns, 1987. See also: *Seneca: Phaedra*, M. Coffey and R. Mayo (eds), Cambridge, Cambridge University Press, 1990, p. 25.

39 Introduction to *Phèdre*, in *Jean Racine: Five Plays*, K. Muir (trans.), London, Macgibbon & Kee, 1960, pp. 175–7.

40 Thomas Otway, *Tragedy of Don Carlos, Prince of Spain*, in: *The Works of Thomas Otway*, J.C. Ghosh (ed.), Oxford, Clarendon Press, 1932. Otway's play was written in 1676.

41 Friedrich von Schiller's *Don Carlos*, J. Kirkup (trans.), in: *The Classic Theatre*, E. Bentley (ed.), vol. 2, New York, Doubleday Anchor Books, 1959. Schiller's play was written in 1787.

42 *Desire under the Elms*, in *Three Plays by Eugene O'Neill*, note 31.

43 *Genesis* 4, 1–16.
44 Strindberg, *The Dance of Death*, Part. *1*, note 8.
45 F. Dürrenmatt, *Play Strindberg: Totentanz nach August Strindberg*, Zurich, Verlag der Arche, 1969.
46 David Hare, *The Secret Rapture*, London, Faber & Faber, 1988.

7 BREAKING FREE FROM THE PAST

1 Eugene O'Neill's dedication to his wife. He began writing *Long Day's Journey into Night* in the summer 1939. Many of the events it refers to occurred in 1912. His intention was that it should not be published until 25 years after his death. Nevertheless the first stage production was in 1956, three years after his death.
2 A. Gelb and B. Gelb, *O'Neill*, London, Jonathan Cape, 1962, p. 833.
3 From A. Alvarez, *Beckett*, London, Fontana/Collins, 1973, p. 100.
4 T.S. Eliot, *The Family Reunion*, London, Faber & Faber, 1939.
5 This theme has its counterpart in Eliot's feelings about having pushed his wife, not overboard, but into a mental nursing home under certificate. See: P. Ackroyd, *T.S. Eliot*, London, Hamish Hamilton, 1984; and M. Hastings, *Tom and Viv*, London, Penguin Books, 1985.
6 A. Chekhov, *Plays*, E. Fen (trans.), London, Penguin Books, 1954, p. 368. Trofimov, like Oswald, is 26, 27 years old.
7 B. Friel, *Fathers and Sons*, London, Faber & Faber, 1987.
8 H. Koht, *Life of Ibsen*, New York, Benjamin Blom, 1971, p. 331.
9 J. McFarlane, 'Apostasy in prose', *Scandinavica*, 1984, vol.23, pp. 101–18.
10 I discuss this topic in 'Death of the artist's father', *British Journal of Medical Psychology*, 1973, vol.46, pp. 135–41.
11 K.K.T. Wais, *Henrik Ibsen und das Problem der Vergangenen*, Stuttgart, W. Kohlhammer (Tübinger Germanistische Arbeiten), 1931.
12 Knut Hamsun, the novelist, then aged 32, had been sharply critical of the older generation at a public lecture attended by Ibsen. Hilde shares some of the characteristics of Hildur Anderson, a young woman with whom Ibsen had recently become friendly. Some aspects of Solness's wife Aline are reminiscent of Ibsen's wife Suzannah. See McFarlane's 'Commentary', *The Oxford Ibsen*, vol. 7, pp. 571, 573–5.
13 See D.R. Davis, 'A re-appraisal of Ibsen's *Ghosts*', *Family Process*, 1963, vol. 2, pp. 81–94; and D.B. Thomas, 'Patterns of interaction in Ibsen's *Ghosts*', *Ibsenaarbok*, Oslo, University Press, 1974, pp. 89–117.
14 The move was to Venstøp, the loft of which is the model for the Ekdal home in *The Wild Duck*.
15 Gunnar Brandell, *Freud: A Man of his Century*, I. White (trans.), Brighton, Sussex, Harvester Press, 1979, p. 19.
16 Sophocles, *The Theban Plays: King Oedipus*, E.F. Watling (trans.), London, Penguin Books, 1974, p. 59; p. 35.
17 S. Freud, *The Future of an Illusion*, The Pelican Freud Library, vol. 12.
18 Ibsen commented on the life-lie in his preliminary notes to *The Wild*

NOTES AND SOURCES

Duck: 'Liberty consists of giving the individual the right to liberate himself, each according to his personal needs' (cited by J. McFarlane, *The Oxford Ibsen*, vol. 6, p. 431).

19 *Ivanov* was written in 1887–89, a few years after *The Wild Duck* (1884).
20 These themes in *Rosmersholm* are discussed by D.R. Davis and D.B. Thomas, '*Rosmersholm*: existentialist tragedy or escapist fantasy?' *Contemporary Approaches to Ibsen*, vol. 4, Oslo, University Press, 1979, pp. 83–100.
21 A portrait on the wall is a common device for telling the audience that the events on the stage are influenced by the past; e.g., in the Wingfields' home in Tennessee Williams' *The Glass Menagerie*, a blown-up portrait of the dead father hangs on the living-room wall.
22 The second draft is in *The Oxford Ibsen*, vol. 5. See p. 399. Rebecca is replying to the housekeeper who has said: 'Every time one of the family died, then the white horse comes. In it comes after nightfall. Into the courtyard. Through the closed gate. Neighs loudly, kicks up its hind legs, gallops once round and then out again and away at top speed'. Ibsen had in mind the folk-belief in Eggedal that the white horse is a form taken by Nøkken, who is a personification of the demonic powers of the sea, from which he may be seen on occasions to emerge. Water, and especially the sea, represent mysterious forces within ourselves.
23 S. Freud, 'Some character-types met with in psychoanalytic work: those wrecked by success', *Art and Literature*, The Pelican Freud Library, vol. 14, pp. 299–316.
24 Brendel's words echo St Matthew's injunction (5.30): 'And if thy right hand offend thee, cut it off, and cast it from thee.'
25 See D.R. Davis, 'Interventions into family affairs', *British Journal of Medical Psychology*, 1968, vol. 41, pp. 71–9. Brandell (*Freud*, p. 47, note 15) repeats Ragnar Vogt's comment on the play as 'a first-rate example of a psychoanalytic cure'. See also E. Durbach, 'Ibsen's liberated heroines and the fear of freedom', *Contemporary Approaches to Ibsen*, vol. 5, Oslo, University Press, 1985, pp. 11–23.
26 See D.R. Davis and D.B. Thomas, 'Liberation and entrapment in *Little Eyolf*', *Contemporary Approaches to Ibsen*, vol. 5, Oslo, University Press, 1985, pp. 48–57.
27 In the German ending, Nora capitulates. See *The Oxford Ibsen*, vol. 5, pp. 287–8.
28 *The Oxford Ibsen*, vol. 7, p. 471.
29 W. James, *The Principles of Psychology*, London, Harvard University Press, 1981, vol. 2, pp. 1136–42, 1173–9. The similar idea that a person gradually defines himself by what he does is a theme in the plays of Jean-Paul Sartre, e.g., *Kean* (D. Brady, ed. Oxford, Oxford University Press, 1973).
30 The decisions taken in the plays of ancient Greece have been discussed by Hellenic scholars, with regard especially to the parts played by the freedom of the will and force, e.g., A. Lesky, 'Decision and responsibility in the tragedy of Aeschylus', *Oxford Readings in Greek Tragedy*, E. Segal (ed.), Oxford, Oxford University Press, 1983.

8 RECOVERIES

1 K. Jaspers, *General Psychopathology*, Manchester, Manchester University Press, 1963, p. 839.
2 B. Simon, *Mind and Madness in Ancient Greece: The Classical Roots of Modern Psychiatry*, London, Cornell University Press, 1978, pp. 76–7.
3 Another account of Orestes' recovery is given by Euripides in *Iphigenia in Tauris*, P. Vellacott (trans.), London, Penguin Books, 1974, pp. 160–1.
4 For comment on the Duke's 'function' see R.A. Foakes's 'Introduction' to the Arden Edition of *The Comedy of Errors*, London, Methuen, 1962, p. xlviii.
5 A. Strindberg, *Inferno*, M. Sandbach (trans.), London, Penguin Books, 1979.
6 P. Watzlawick, J.H. Beavin and D.D. Jackson, *Pragmatics of Human Communication*, London, Faber & Faber, 1968.
7 G.B. Shaw, *The Quintessence of Ibsen*, London, Constable & Co, 1926, pp. 192, 205.
8 This section recapitulates my paper, 'The therapist as mediator: lessons from plays', *Family Therapy*, 1979, vol. 1, pp. 65–73.
9 *Prometheus Unbound* was first published in 1820. See: *Shelley: Poetical Works*, T. Hutchinson (ed.), Oxford University Press, 1970. For discussion, see: N. Crook and D. Guiton, *Shelley's Venomed Melody*, Cambridge, Cambridge University Press, 1986, ch. 11.
10 This section recapitulates my paper, 'Interventions into family affairs', *British Journal of Medical Psychology*, 1968, vol. 41, pp. 73–9.
11 E.g., E.Z. Friedenberg, *Laing*, Fontana/Collins, 1973; and S. Walrond-Skinner, *Family Therapy*, London, Routledge & Kegan Paul, 1976.
12 T.S. Eliot, *The Cocktail Party*, London, Faber & Faber, 1940.
13 E. Albee, *A Delicate Balance*, London, Penguin Books, 1966.
14 The effect of the destruction of a family myth is discussed by P. Watzlawick, J.H. Beavin and D.D. Jackson, *Pragmatics of Human Communication*, London, Faber & Faber, 1968, with reference to *Who's Afraid of Virginia Woolf?* and *Little Eyolf* especially.
15 J.B. Priestley's *An Inspector Calls* was first produced in 1946.
16 Edvard Munch includes the father in a lithograph of Oswald and his mother he made for Max Reinhardt's 1906 production of *Ghosts* in Berlin, and notably in a charcoal drawing.
17 Eric Rohmer's *Le Trio en Mi Bemol* ('Trio in E flat') is an example of a play about three people, with a cast of two actors, a man and a woman, formerly lovers, trying to restore their relationship, and an absentee, who is a recent lover of the woman.
18 The first production of Eugene O'Neill's *The Hairy Ape* was in 1922.
19 H. Pinter, *A Slight Ache*, London, Eyre Methuen, 1961.
20 P. Shaffer, *Equus*, in *Three Plays*, London, Penguin Books, 1962.
21 An outcome like that predicted for Alan is sought by the Hamlet character in Heiner Müller's *Hamletmachine*, who wants to be

'a machine. Arms for grabbing, legs for walking, no pain, no thought.'
22 A review of the psychotherapeutic issues in the play has been provided by G.A. Plunka, *Peter Shaffer: Roles, Rites and Rituals in the Theater*, London, Associated Universities Press, 1988. A harsh critic is the psychoanalyst Sanford Gifford, 'Pop psychoanalysis, kitsch and the "as if" theater: further notes on Peter Shaffer's *Equus'*, *International Journal of Psychoanalytic Psychotherapy*, 1976, vol. 5, pp. 46–71.
23 This is how Freud once described the purpose of psychoanalysis.
24 The restoration of ordinariness as an objective in therapy is discussed by Elaine Showalter, *The Female Malady*, Virago, 1985, pp. 192–4, with reference also to Virginia Woolf's *Mrs Dalloway*.
25 The term 'Othello syndrome' gained currency as a result of the review by M.D. Enoch, W. Trethowan and J.C. Barker, *Some Uncommon Psychiatric Syndromes*, Bristol, Wright, 1967. The jealousy tends to be regarded as delusional.
26 The term 'triangulation' was introduced to describe the invoking of a third person to make a triangle in order to stabilise a precarious relationship by M. Bowen, 'Family therapy after twenty years', S. Arieti (ed.), *American Handbook of Psychiatry*, 1975, vol. 5, pp. 367–92.
27 E. Albee, *Who's Afraid of Virginia Woolf?*, London, Penguin Books, 1962.
28 J. Osborne, *Look Back in Anger*, London, Faber & Faber, 1957.
29 An example of a ménage-à-trois is to be found in the poet Shelley's second marriage. He eloped with Mary Godwin in 1814, the couple being accompanied by Claire Clairmont, who had grown up with Mary in the Godwin household. Claire spent much of the remaining eight years of Shelley's life as a part of the ménage. See P. Foot, *Red Shelley*, London, Bookmarks, 1984, p. 140.
30 E.g., G. Brown and T. Harris, *Social Aspects of Depression*, London, Tavistock Publications, 1978.
31 These points made about Horatio by G.F. Bradby in *The Problem of Hamlet* are cited by J. Dover Wilson in *What Happens in Hamlet*, Cambridge, Cambridge University Press, 1959, pp. 232–3.
32 E. Welsford, *The Fool: His Social and Literary History*, London, Faber & Faber, 1935; and S. Billington, *A Social History of the Fool*, Brighton, Sussex, Harvester Press, 1984.
33 Michael Gambon as King Lear and Anthony Sher as the Fool interacted as if the Fool were the king's other self in Adrian Noble's 1982 production at Stratford-upon-Avon.
34 J. Racine, *Andromache*, Eric Korn (trans.), London, Applause Theatre Books, 1988.

9 CONCLUSIONS

1 Quoted by T. Szasz, *Karl Kraus and the Soul Doctors*, London, Routledge & Kegan Paul, 1977, p. 108.

2 Euripides, *The Bacchae*, G.S. Kirk (trans.), Englewood Cliffs, NJ, Prentice-Hall, 1970.
3 Karl Jaspers, *General Psychopathology*, J. Hoenig and M.W. Hamilton (trans.), Manchester, Manchester University Press, 1963.
4 A. Strindberg, 'Author's preface to *Miss Julie'*, *The Plays*, vol. 1, M. Meyer (ed.), London, Secker & Warburg, 1975, p. 93.
5 For a discussion of interpretative explanations, see: N.M. Cheshire, *The Nature of Psychodynamic Interpretation*, London, John Wiley, 1975.
6 Miller makes this comment through a character in *The Archbishops's Ceiling*, London, Methuen, 1984, p. 10.
7 Macbeth speaks of 'sleep that knits up the ravelled sleave of care' and 'the balm of hurt minds' (2.2.37,39).
8 Both Ibsen in *Ghosts* (1881) and Hauptmann in *Before Sunrise* describe the effects on the son's constitution of the father's dissolute life and drinking to excess.
9 M. Sinden, *Gerhart Hauptmann: The Prose Plays*, New York, Russell & Russell, 1957.
10 E. O'Neill, *Three Plays*, New York, Vintage Books, 1973.
11 Thomas Middleton and William Rowley, *The Changeling*, P. Thomson (ed.), London, Ernest Benn, 1964.
12 In *Essay Concerning Human Understanding*, written in 1690 – cited by K. Doerner, *Madmen and the Bourgeoisie*, Oxford, Blackwell, 1981, p. 31.
13 J.C. Prichard, *A Treatise on Insanity*, London, Marchant, 1833.
14 Cited by V. Skultans (ed.), *Madness and Morals: Ideas on Insanity in the Nineteenth Century*, London, Routledge & Kegan Paul, 1975, p. 174.
15 This list is a heavily edited version of a definition formulated in the course of discussions on the revision of the Mental Health Act. See: *A Review of The Mental Health Act 1959*, Department of Health and Social Security, London, HMSO, 1976.
16 Constance in *King John* expresses similar sentiments, cited on pp. 42–4.
17 E.g., J. Daalder, 'Folly and madness in *The Changeling'*, *Essays in Criticism*, 1988, vol. 38, pp. 1–21.
18 Una Ellis-Fermor, *The Jacobean Drama*, 5th edn., London, Methuen, 1965, p. 147.
19 That a change for the worse is an essential element in illness or disease has often been argued, e.g., by J.C. Bucknill, 'Deterioration of behaviour', in V. Skultans (ed.), *Madness and Morals*, pp. 84–5, note 13.
20 L. Pirandello, *Henry IV*, J. Mitchell (trans.), London, Methuen, 1985, e.g., p. 33.
21 J.D. Wilson, *What Happens in Hamlet*, Cambridge, Cambridge University Press, 1959, pp. 222–3.
22 T. Szasz, *Karl Krauss and the Soul Doctors*, p. 127, note 1.
23 A person may be detained under the Mental Health Act if he is deemed to suffer from mental illness of a nature or degree to warrant detention for assessment if to do so is in the interest of his own health or safety or with a view to the protection of other persons.
24 Sophocles, *Antigone*, in: *The Theban Plays*, E.F. Watling (trans.), London, Penguin Books, 1947.

NAME INDEX

SUBJECT INDEX

Laura and the Captain 56–8,
Leontes and Hermione 46–7,
Ellida and Dr Wangel 134–5,
141, 148; sisters – Ella and
Gunhild 116, Isobel and Marion
118
relationships: vertical 98, 108–15;
fathers and daughters – Beatrice
106, Cordelia 44–6, 109–10,
Desdemona 18, 110, Ophelia 40,
110; fathers and sons – Arkady
and Yevgeny 123–4, King
Oedipus 5–6, 101, Prince Hal
100, Prince Segismundo 105–6;
mothers and daughters –
Electra 28, 107, Lavinia 108–9;
mothers and sons – Hamlet 34–9,
103, Orestes 28–30, 143–5,
Orin 108–9, Oswald 50–4, 126–7,
Treplev 105; step-fathers and
step-daughters – Catherine
110–1; step-mothers and step-
sons – Don Carlos 113–14,
Phaedra, Phèdre 111–13
Renaissance 94

sanity defined 176
schizophrenia 4, 7, 20, 52, 154

science 2, 15–17
sleep 165
strangers 79, 87–8, 133, 134
sub-text 62–3, 91
suicide 70; Ajax 31; Beata 132;
Constance 43–4; Don Carlos
114; Hedda Gabler 70; Ivanov
55–6; Jocasta 102–3; Lady
Macbeth 42; Ophelia 40–1; Orin
108; Phaedra, Phèdre 113;
Portia 41; Rosmer and Rebecca
134
syphilis 52–4, 106, 147
systems theory 7, 73–6

theatre of the absurd 63, 71–2,
91
theatres, little 71, 80
therapists, therapy 23, 27, 32, 142,
151–2, 160, 176–7
tragic characters 3, 10, 24
triangulation 156–7
trolls 27, 83, 85, 126
twins 32, 67–8

vicious circle 121, 172

witches 75, 87, 93, 172